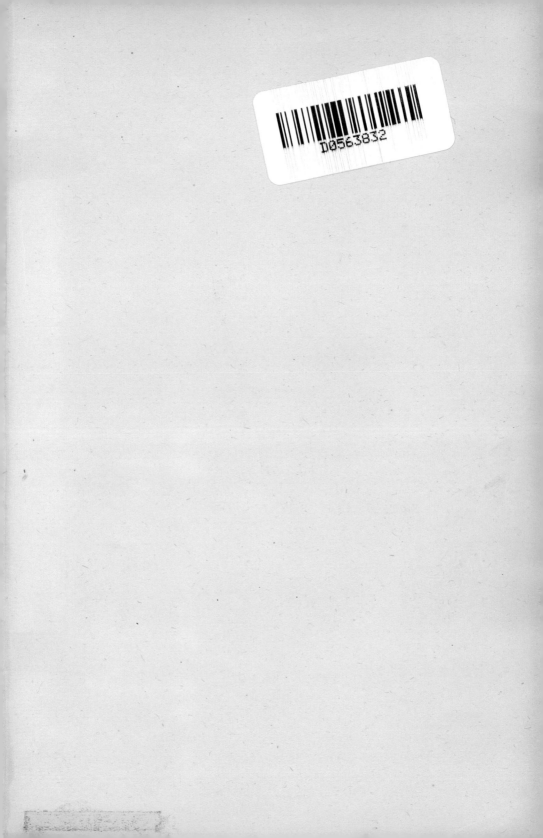

FREEDMEN IN THE
EARLY ROMAN EMPIRE

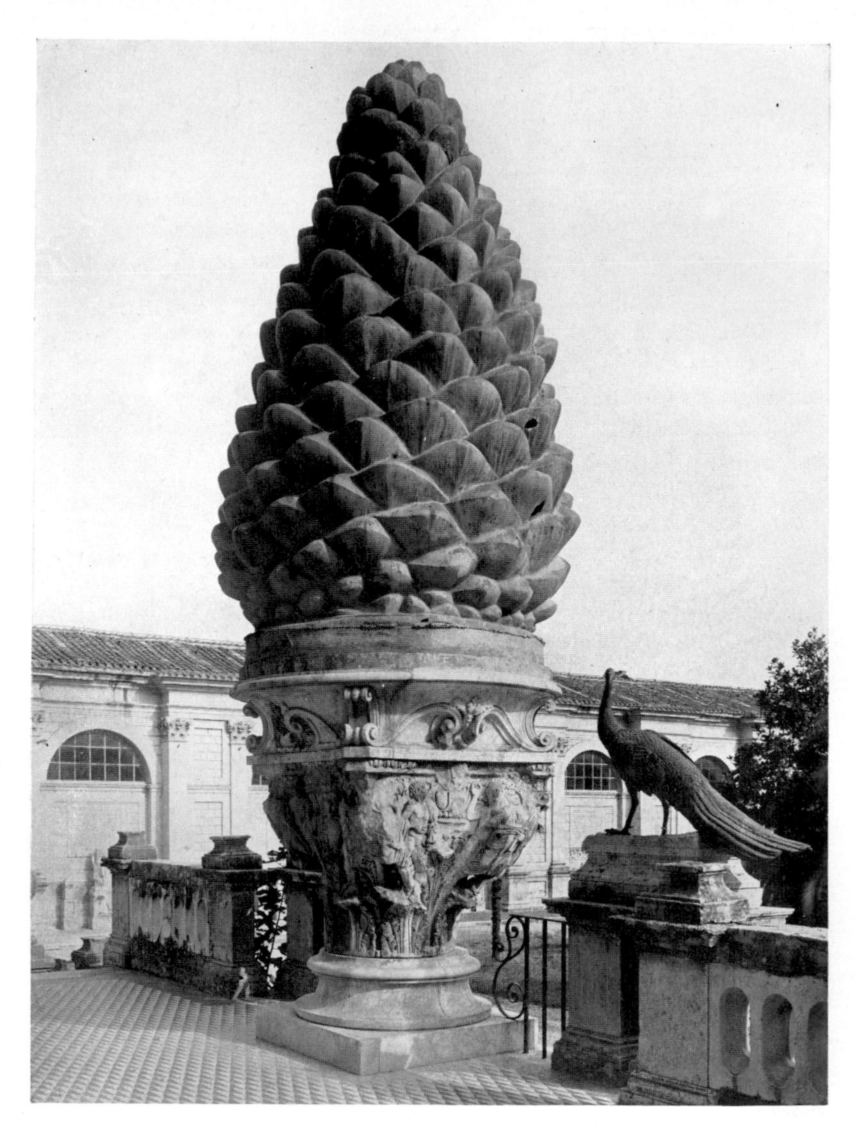

I. COLOSSAL FIR-CONE OF BRONZE

BY A FREEDMAN ARTIST

Perforated with holes, it served as a fountain. Its inscription states 'P. Cincius P. l. Salvius fecit'. Now in one of the gardens of the Vatican, Rome

FREEDMEN IN THE EARLY ROMAN EMPIRE

BY A. M. DUFF, M.A., B.LITT.
Sometime Scholar of Oriel College,
Oxford; Assistant Lecturer in Greek,
University of Aberdeen

OXFORD
AT THE CLARENDON PRESS
1928

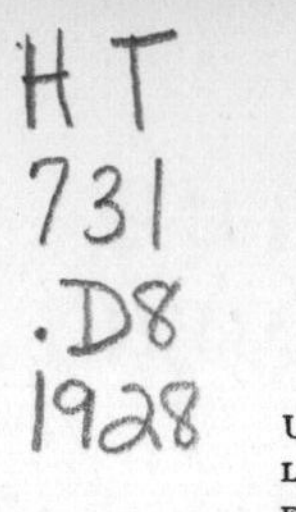

OXFORD
UNIVERSITY PRESS
LONDON : AMEN HOUSE, E.C. 4
EDINBURGH GLASGOW LEIPZIG
COPENHAGEN NEW YORK TORONTO
MELBOURNE CAPETOWN BOMBAY
CALCUTTA MADRAS SHANGHAI
HUMPHREY MILFORD
PUBLISHER TO THE
UNIVERSITY

Printed in Great Britain

PREFACE

THIS work is a revised and amplified edition of a thesis submitted to Oxford University in July 1925 for the degree of Bachelor of Letters. A great part of the material was gathered during a stay of seven months in Rome, where the British, French, and American Schools generously accorded me the use of their libraries. During the last three years I have enjoyed special privileges as a borrower from several University libraries in this country and as a consultant of the library of the Society of Antiquaries in Newcastle-upon-Tyne.

In writing on 'Freedmen under the Early Roman Empire', I have followed a course of study which has not been overrun, but which, nevertheless, is fertile in its interest. The freedman was ubiquitous in the Rome of the first two centuries; as imperial official or as servant of his patron, as successful man of business or as humble shopkeeper, he was a constant figure in society. Therefore a study of the freedman necessarily reveals a great part of what is to be known about life in the Roman Empire, so that the subject is no petty or unimportant one. And yet, in a way, it is a fresh subject. Freedmen have been treated from single standpoints in legal, political, social, and economic histories; but a comprehensive discussion of their many-sided activity and influence has been looked for in vain. This is the gap I have aspired to fill.

At the same time it may be claimed that, though the theme involves the marshalling of much familiar matter, certain portions consist of what is new or at least not generally known. The causes of manumission and the governmental policy towards freedmen (to take two examples) have seldom been discussed in the past, and a large amount of the epigraphical material used here has rarely been laid under contribution before.

One or two explanations as to methods of citation are necessary. I refer to ancient authors, where possible, in the Oxford Classical Texts, and, failing these, in the Teubner series. In citing Cassius Dio I have thought it convenient to avoid Boissevain's division of Books LXI–LXXX and to adhere to the old arrangement. The references to Dionysius of Halicarnassus are to his *Ῥωμαϊκὴ Ἀρχαιολογία*.

My obligations are many and various. I owe my enthusiasm for ancient history primarily to the inspiration of my former tutor, Mr. M. N. Tod, Fellow of Oriel College, Oxford. In especial I have pleasure in recording the generous interest which Mr. H. M. Last, Fellow of St. John's College, Oxford, has taken in my book from the time that he was one of my examiners for the B.Litt. degree. His guidance and the information with which he supplied me obviated many an error and made a great contribution towards widening the range of this treatise. His kindness extended also to a complete reading of the proofs.

For many valuable suggestions I am indebted to Dr. T. Ashby, late Director of the British School at Rome, my supervisor while I was a postgraduate student, and to Mr. G. H. Stevenson, Fellow of University College, Oxford, who along with Mr. Last examined my dissertation. My father, Professor J. Wight Duff, of Armstrong College, Newcastle-upon-Tyne, has read through my book once and in parts twice, correcting inaccuracies and making serviceable criticisms, and my mother very kindly copied the original manuscript for the typist. In the checking of references in notes and index I am very grateful for the help of Miss Margaret Wood, Assistant Lecturer in Greek in Aberdeen University.

My sincere thanks are due to the Delegates of the Clarendon Press for the honour they have done me in publishing my book; and to the Craven Committee and the Provost and Fellows of Oriel College for generous assistance towards the costs of publication. Messrs. Methuen were good enough to grant me permission to quote a portion of G. B. Gardiner's translation of Cicero, *De Officiis*. My book was in the press before the appearance of Mr. R. H. Barrow's *Slavery in the Roman Empire*, which otherwise I should have been happy to consult.

A. M. D.

June, 1928.

CONTENTS

I. THE SLAVE MARKET

Republican wars — piracy and debt — wars of the Empire — predominance of Eastern names among servile inscriptions — slave-breeding in provinces and in Italy — Greek names belonging to Western slaves — character and fate of Western slaves — freedom granted to some — character of Oriental slaves — Egyptians — Syrians — Jews — Greeks 1

II. MANUMISSION

Why freedmen were less prominent in Greece than in Rome — causes of manumission among the Romans — The *peculium* — aristocratic vanity — respect for the slave's intellectual abilities — for his rights as a human being — benevolence and gratitude — *congiaria* — methods of emancipation — informal manumission — its popularity — *manumissio vindicta* — *censu* — *testamento* — the *fideicommissum* — tax on manumission — situation in the time of Augustus — his reforms — particular limits to testamentary manumission — general restrictions on manumission — other means of obtaining liberty apart from manumission 12

III. LEGAL RELATIONS BETWEEN PATRON AND FREEDMAN

Origin of the *obsequium* and *officium* — principles which followed from the *obsequium* — nature of the *officium* — punishment of ungrateful freedmen — the *tutela* — patron's share in the succession — the *operae* — means of exemption from them — limits to the patron's power — obligations of the patron towards the freedman — conception of patron and freedman as father and son 36

IV. SOCIAL STATUS OF FREEDMEN

The term *libertini* — a freedman's name — dress — family rights — intermarriage between the orders — criminal law — respect of rank by the government — positions closed to freedmen — taunts which they had to endure — inequality at the dinner-table — prejudice not so marked among the lower classes in the towns of Italy and in the provinces — *libertini* ranked higher than ordinary provincials 50

V. GRADES OF FREEDMEN

VI. FREEDMEN IN PRIVATE LIFE

VII. FREEDMEN IN PUBLIC LIFE

VIII. IMPERIAL FREEDMEN

APPENDICES

LIST OF ILLUSTRATIONS

I

THE SLAVE-MARKET

Republican wars — piracy and debt — wars of the Empire — predominance of Eastern names among servile inscriptions — slave-breeding in provinces and in Italy — Greek names belonging to Western slaves — character and fate of Western slaves — freedom granted to some — character of Oriental slaves — Egyptians — Syrians — Jews — Greeks.

IT was in Rome and especially in imperial Rome that the problem of slaves freed by private manumission assumed its greatest proportions. With respect to this, no other state of the ancient or modern world can be named in comparison. In Greece slave-owners never manumitted with so lavish a hand, and in modern America freedmen did not present a serious problem until the public wholesale emancipation after the Civil War.

With the freedmen of the early Roman Empire the present thesis deals. It is proposed to show how they came to be freed, to define their legal status and their relations with their patrons or former owners, and to trace the part they played in public life and the influence they exercised on social and economic history.

Before treating of the freedmen themselves, or even of the means by which they obtained their liberty, something must be said of the sources whence Rome procured her slaves. As the origin of the slave is, of course, the origin of the freedman, the question of the slave-supply is of vital importance in determining the character of the freedman class.

During the Republic the servile population in Rome must have been perpetually on the increase, but it was in the last two centuries before our era that its growth was swiftest. These centuries were the age of Rome's Mediterranean expansion. They saw Gaul, Spain, Africa and practically the whole of the civilized East reduced under her yoke; they saw the captured inhabitants of these vast regions poured into Italy in wholesale numbers to do the menial work of house or farm. In Epirus, for instance, at the end of one campaign 150,000 were captured and brought to Italy as slaves.[1] Similarly in Asia Minor, Sulla, Lucullus and Pompey must have thrown thousands of Eastern prisoners into the slave-market: even Cicero's petty war in the fastnesses of Cilicia yielded some slaves.[2] After the reduction of the Aduatuci, Caesar claims to have sold 53,000 Gauls;[3] while in the course of Octavian's advance in Dalmatia in 35 and 34 B. C. numbers of Illyrian captives must have been enslaved by the conqueror. Moreover war, though the principal, was not the only source. Pirates plied an active trade in Eastern Mediterranean waters, until Pompey suppressed them in 67 B. C. Republican extortion[4] in the provinces often brought about cases of debt, and insolvency would end in the enslavement of the debtor.

Under the Empire, however, these sources of the slave-supply tend to diminish, if not to disappear altogether. The collection of tribute was more closely controlled by the imperial authorities, and, with the consequent diminution of extortion, enslavement for debt must have become less frequent; illicit kidnapping, if carried on at all within the bounds of the Empire, was a negligible factor, and beyond the frontier it can only have yielded negroes or Scythians or other barbarians. Furthermore the wars of the imperial period were not waged on nearly so great a scale as those of the preceding centuries, and therefore cannot have been so productive in captives. The final subjugation of Spain, the campaigns in Germany, the revolts in Gaul and Dalmatia, the rebellion of Tacfarinas in Africa, the insurrections in Judaea, and the intermittent struggle for Armenia doubtless swelled the market to some

[1] Livy, xlv. 34.

[2] *Ad Att.* V. xx. 5.

[3] *B. G.* ii. 33.

[4] Cf. *Ad Att.* V. xxi. 10–13; VI. ii. 7–9, where the Roman usurer attempts to charge the people of Cyprian Salamis 48 per cent. interest. Cicero, an unusually good governor, fears to do more for the Salaminians than leave the settlement over to his presumably unjust successor.

extent; and the conquest of Britain and Dacia probably made larger contributions. But, apart from the fact that the numbers of captives in general were much less than in the age of Republican conquest, it must be noted too that there was no chance in any of these military campaigns, except in the Jewish revolts, of reaping a harvest of slaves from the Hellenistic and civilized East. And yet epigraphy suggests that, directly or indirectly, the Orient continued in the imperial age to be the main source of slaves. A study of the inscriptions relating to slaves and freedmen in Rome shows that 70 per cent. of that class bore Greek names. This is Professor Tenney Frank's conclusion,[1] and an examination of five hundred[2] names of imperial freedmen gives 353 Greek and 147 Latin, statistics which substantially support his statement. In Latium, according to Professor Frank, the proportion was 64 per cent., in South Italy 53 per cent., and in Cisalpine Gaul 46 per cent.

So, despite the comparative rarity of Eastern wars, Greek-named slaves predominate to a surprising extent. If war was not their source, whence did they come? The only reasonable hypothesis is that they were descended from slaves of the Republican age, and that among that class the birth-rate was higher than is generally supposed. In the Eastern provinces perhaps slaves were reared for the dealer's profit to an extent which has not yet been realized among historians. But doubtless in Italy, too, slaves were expected to marry and produce offspring. For the second century B. C. perhaps this statement is not true. Masters of the Catonian kind would believe it more economical to buy new slaves than to allow time to be wasted in the procreation of slave children. But later authors tell a different tale. From Varro,[3] who can speak for the last generations of the Republic, and from Columella, an authority for part of the first century of the Empire, we know that slaves in the *familia rustica* were

[1] See his article in the *American Historical Review*, 1916, p. 689 ff.
[2] *C. I. L.* vi. 8403 ff.
[3] Varro, *R. R.* II. i. 26.

not only allowed, but encouraged, to propagate.[1] Indeed Columella tells us that rewards of leisure and even liberty were given to the more productive of the female slaves. In the *familia urbana* conditions were easier, and therefore we should expect here more liberty still in the matter of marriages and births.

Professor Frank,[2] in search of evidence on this point, has examined various inscriptions of the city of Rome. Counting the cases in which the birth of children or the fact of marriage can be inferred he has investigated 3,000 inscriptions in miscellaneous servile *columbaria*, 1,000 in the *columbaria* for servants of aristocratic households, 460 on the memorial stones of imperial slaves and freedmen, and 14,000 among those of the general population of Rome.[3] The results are given below; for convenience's sake the numbers are increased or reduced to the ratio of 1,000.

	Number of inscriptions per 1000.			
	recording offspring.	*recording marriage.*	*probably recording marriage.*[4]	*Total.*
Miscellaneous *columbaria*	154	111	73	338
Columbaria of the Livii, Drusi, Marcelli and Volusii	151	99	152	402
Familia Augusta	290	220	78	588
General population of Rome	280	184	39	503

It is true that the *columbaria* show the lowest proportion, but it must be remembered that the epitaphs of the third and fourth classes were engraved on ample stone, where detail on detail could be recorded. In the *columbaria* the inscriptions are confined to the space afforded by tablet or urn, and, being therefore of the briefest character possible, may have failed to mention a *contubernium*

[1] Colum. I. viii. 19. Cf. Petr. *Sat.* 53. Trimalchio reads a report of events on his Cumaean estate. In the report is mentioned the birth of seventy slave-children.

[2] See his article in the *American Historical Review*, 1916, p. 689 ff.

[3] *C. I. L.* vi. 4881–7880, 3926 ff. and 7281 ff., 8639 ff., 10424 ff.

[4] Here we have the names of a man and a woman whose relation is not specified, but is probably that of husband and wife, e. g. no. 4478.

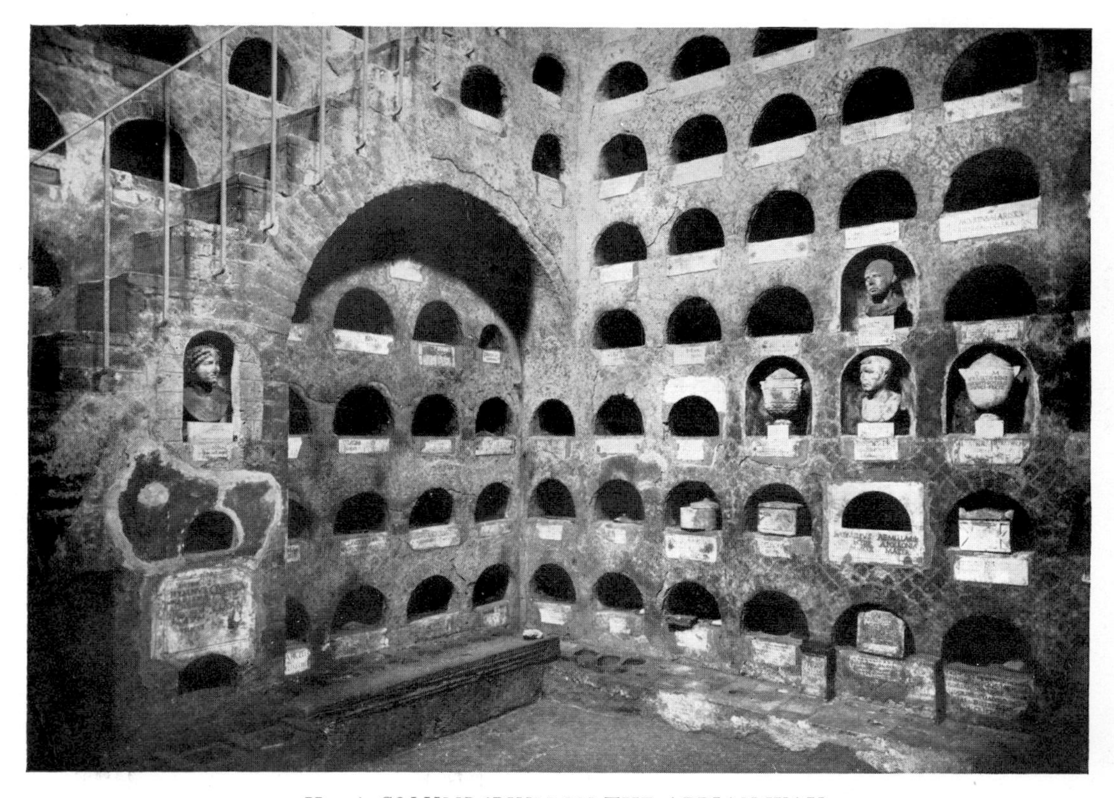

II. A *COLUMBARIUM* ON THE APPIAN WAY

Vigna Codini, Rome

in many cases where it took place. It is not surprising that these two classes point to the lowest birth-rate. Nevertheless it is probable that the ratios fall only in proportion to the brevity and inadequacy of the memorial. Considering the small space in which these humble menials had to record what was worth recording about their deceased comrades, one cannot but suppose that slaves and freedmen reproduced in as large numbers as the free-born population.

Naturally the breeding of slaves did not increase under the Empire to such an extent as to be an efficient substitute for the wholesale captures in Republican wars. It failed to fill the gap which the *pax Romana* left in the slave-supply, and a shortage began to make itself felt. Yet, less abundant as it was, it must have been responsible for the majority of the servile population under the Principate.

Slave-breeding, then, took the place of war as a source of the slave-supply. Some further considerations will explain the prominence of Greek names in servile inscriptions. In the first place the Greek name is not an infallible sign of Greek birth. Quite one-third of the Emperor's Germanic guardsmen bore Greek names.[1] Moreover among the inscriptions which record explicitly a slave's nationality many show Spaniards or Gauls whose names are Hellenic.[2] So it is certain that some Greek names represent Westerners. Slave-merchants, being generally Greek, probably used their own language to name their slaves whatever their nationality, and the purchasing masters must often have allowed the name thus given to remain. A slave might even be called after the dealer himself. Thus, we hear from Varro, a slave was called Artemas after Artemidorus the merchant from whom he was bought.[3] Other masters might give a Greek name through

[1] *C. I. L.* vi. 4337–45 and 8802–10; cf. Dessau, *Ins. Lat. Sel.* 1717 ff.

[2] From Spain: *Phoebus*, *Eros*, *Philocyrius*, *Carpime*; from Gaul: *Syntropus*, *Phoebe*; from Dalmatia: *Pempte*; from Sardinia: *Charito*; from Africa: *Helpis*. Cf. Bang, *Die Herkunft der römischen Sklaven*, *Röm. Mitth.* xxv. (1910), p. 223.

[3] Varro, *De Ling. Lat.* viii. 21.

an interest in Greek literature. Moreover certain names were appropriate to particular occupations. Asclepiades was thus a favourite name with doctors. Actors assumed names of celebrated predecessors, as Pylades or Paris, or else names appropriate to the stage like Apolaustus or Thymele.[1]

In the second place inscriptions are not representative of the slave population as a whole. Epitaphs of freedmen concern those who were once domestic slaves rather than those who had worked on the farm; for the former were in closer contact with their master and had therefore better chances of manumission. Slaves who rose to the honour of an inscription were those who performed some office in the house and not those who laboured in the fields. Consequently the proportions cited above apply more particularly to the *familia urbana* and cannot be accepted as true of the *familia rustica*. Epigraphy knows little of the vast hordes of Western captives who glutted the market during the Republic and to a lesser degree under the Empire. Their fate was determined by a national character which militated against them from the outset. In Juvenal's famous account of the patron's dinner to his clients, the 'Gaetulian groom' or the 'dusky Moor' is obviously not so high in his lord's favour as the 'flower of Asia'.[2] For the Oriental is reserved the more gentle employment which brings him into close contact with his master. The 'dusky Moor' performs the more menial work, and on this occasion has the thankless task of attending a client who has nothing wherewith to reward him. The Western nations were all too highspirited to bend to anything but brute force; nor in the main had they the particular qualities which might promote slaves in their masters' service and ultimately win for them the cap of liberty. Sardinians were always unruly—hence they were continually on sale, as the proverb *Sardi venales* bears

[1] Cf. for this paragraph Mary L. Gordon, *The Nationality of Slaves under the Early Roman Empire*, *J. R. S.*, xiv (1924), p. 38 ff.

[2] Juv. v. 52 ff.: 'cursor Gaetulus', 'nigri Mauri,' 'flos Asiae.'

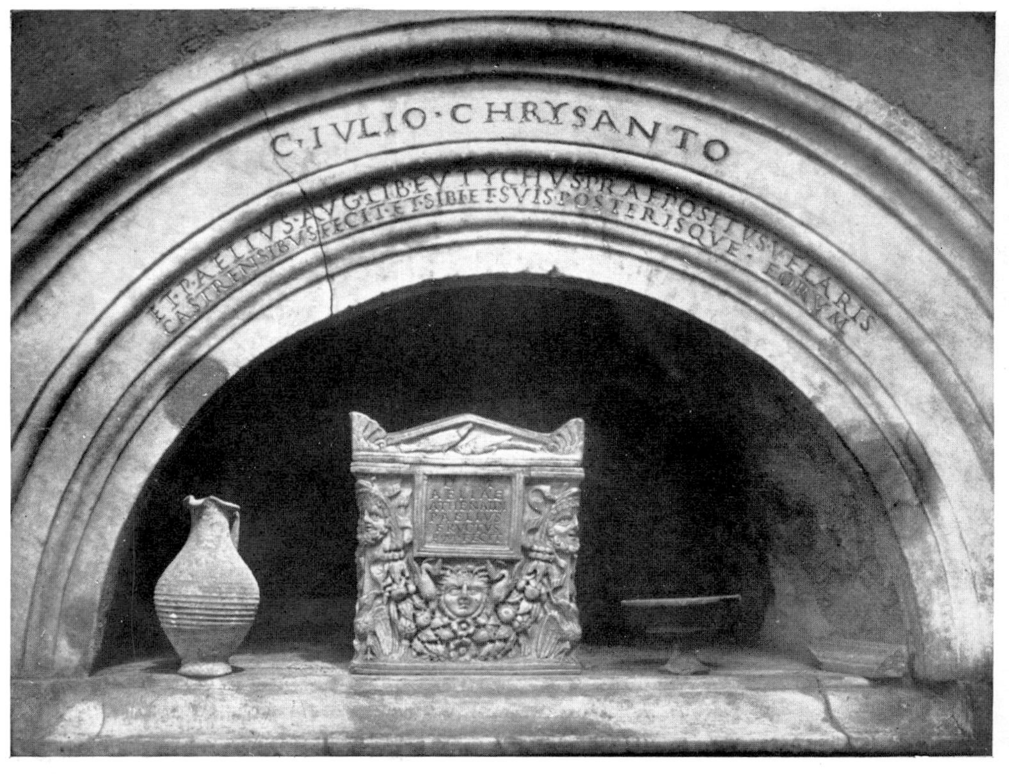

III. PART OF A *COLUMBARIUM*
Vigna Codini, Rome

out. Their Iberian kinsmen in Spain had shown by their long resistance to the Roman arms how they would chafe against servitude. The children of the Cimbrian and Teutonic captives that Marius took at Aquae Sextiae and on the Raudine Plain formed the backbone of Spartacus' rebellion.[1] They of course were extirpated in that hopeless conflict, and descendants of theirs must have been few. As for the Gauls, perhaps their pride had expired with Vercingetorix, but as far as intelligence went they could not compete with the versatile Easterner. Indeed, even if members of these Western peoples showed that they could submit to discipline and were prepared to earn their liberty by good service, they were constantly beaten in the race by the superior genius of the Greek and the Asiatic.

What then happened to the war-captives of the West? Some were wiped out in the revolt of Spartacus, and no doubt the servile armies of the earlier Sicilian wars had drawn their recruits largely from the proud Spaniards and untamed Sardinians. But the West generally, though inferior to the East in culture and intellect, was its superior in strength and physique. Consequently its children, unsuited to domestic positions where intelligence was a recommendation, were often packed off for unskilled work in field and mine, where opportunities of reproduction were less than in the home, and where such children as were born would continue in the same employment as their parents. Here the prospects of liberty, or even of becoming known to posterity through an inscription, were slight in the extreme; and so in a great measure they disappear from our ken.

Nevertheless we must not exaggerate the disparity between the Eastern and Western minds. Great as it was in the last two centuries before Christ, the gulf became more and more narrow under the Empire. Apart from the fact that, as seen above, some Greek names represent Western slaves, the number of Latin names among freedmen, though in South Italy less than that of Greek names,

[1] Caes. *B. G.* i. 40.

and in Rome and Latium considerably less, is by no means negligible. And it cannot be supposed that all or nearly all of these Latin names were borne by Greeks. Greek slaves of course must sometimes have been given Latin names, especially those who did not come from the Orient but were born of Greek slaves in Italy; and it will be seen hereafter that freedmen sometimes substituted a Latin name for that awkward evidence of servitude, the Greek *cognomen*. Yet these two categories cannot make up the full proportion of Latin-named slaves and freedmen which inscriptions reveal, namely, thirty per cent. in Rome, thirty-six per cent. in Latium, forty-seven per cent. in South Italy, and fifty-four per cent. in Cisalpine Gaul. Many of these Latin names, in the case both of slaves and freedmen, must represent men from the Western provinces. Spaniards and Gauls and other Westerners, despite a rebellious nature and a barbarian clumsiness, must often have settled down to servitude, won their masters' favour and obtained liberty and enfranchisement. Under the civilizing effect of the Roman Empire, the character of the Spaniard was so far tamed that he received Latin rights from Vespasian,[1] while the Gauls of Claudius' time had made such progress that they could be called by Tacitus 'rich and unwarlike'.[2] And if the Western inhabitants of the Empire could adapt themselves to the *pax Romana* and could advance in Roman culture and civilization, surely slaves from these parts, if once given a fair chance in an Italian household, would sometimes learn the arts of peace, rise to responsible positions and attain to a well-deserved manumission. It is such slaves and freedmen who are represented by many of the Latin names among that class; Roman masters finding their barbarian names difficult to pronounce would give them a Latin and more palatable appellation.

Before we leave the question of the slave-supply, some words must be said of the character of the Oriental who

[1] Pliny, *Nat. Hist.* iii. 30. [2] Tac. *Ann.* xi. 18: 'dites et imbelles.'

became so ubiquitous in Rome. The conquests of Alexander had carried Greek manners and civilization over Asia Minor, Syria and Egypt, and had bequeathed to them the heritage of Greece's golden age. Consequently, the citizen of these regions, which became known as the Hellenistic world, was usually an intelligent and cultured man. But long ages of despotism had rendered Hellenistic peoples patient and servile, and through their immemorial trading activity they had acquired an aptitude for business unsurpassed by any race of their day. Many ancient authors afford evidence as to the character of these nations. To begin with Egypt, the author of the *Bellum Alexandrinum* can call the Alexandrians 'most shrewd and astute',[1] and these qualities were often accompanied by craft and deceit. 'To play the Egyptian' was a synonym for underhand dealing.[2] Inland, the Egyptian was ignorant, quarrelsome and fanatical. Juvenal's fifteenth satire is the story of a feud between two Egyptian towns which arises from religious fanaticism. Tacitus' account of the province is well known. 'It does not know the meaning of constitutional government, and it is thrown into discord by superstition and lack of restraint.'[3]

The Syrians as a race were credited by Herodian with sharp wits, a quality which he said they shared with the rest of the East.[4] They had pleasing gifts of drollery and satire,[5] their speech was graceful,[6] and as dancers and flute-players their talents were of no mean rank.[7] But they

[1] 'Ingeniosissimi atque acutissimi,' *Bell. Alex.* iii.

[2] Suidas, *s. v.* *Αἰγυπτιάζειν*.

[3] Tac. *Hist.* i. 11: 'superstitione ac lascivia discordem, insciam legum, ignaram magistratuum'.

[4] Herodian, III. xi. 8.

[5] Herodian, II. x. 7: *ἐπὶ τὸ χαριέντως καὶ μετὰ παιδιᾶς ἀποσκῶψαι ἐπιτήδειοι Σύροι.*

[6] Eunapius, *Vitae Soph.*, on Libanius.

[7] The *ambubaiae* of Hor. *Sat.* I. ii. 1 were Syrians. Cf. Juv. iii. 62–5:

'Iam pridem Syrus in Tiberim defluxit Orontes
Et linguam et mores et cum tibicine chordas
Obliquas nec non gentilia tympana secum
Vexit.'

acquired a notoriety for their fickleness[1] and villainy. Indeed Cassius Dio speaks of the 'rascality of the Syrians'[2] as if it were a speciality of theirs.

The general servility of the East, however, was not a characteristic of the Jews, who swelled the slave-market after the fall of Jerusalem. They had imbibed something of Greek culture and education, and in the days of the Empire were doubtless to a large extent possessed of that shrewdness in business which has always been theirs in medieval and modern times. But these talents, which alone would have made them good slaves and enabled them to rise in their masters' grace and to receive the reward of manumission, were somewhat discounted by the pride and obstinacy begotten by their theocratic ambitions. They had a religious fanaticism like that which inspired, as said above, a large portion of the Egyptian race. This was a quality which could never help slaves towards gaining their liberty; on the contrary it might be the cause of their being sent to the mine or the farm as unsuitable in the home. Indeed, in Tiberius' reign, some 4,000 Jews and Egyptians, mostly freedmen, were deported to Sardinia for the undesirable character of the religious or quasi-religious practices they adopted in Rome.[3]

As regards the Greek, either of Europe or Asia, his versatility is well known through Juvenal's third satire:

> Masseur, diviner, painter, rhetorician,
> Professor, necromancer or physician,
> Or tight-rope dancer or geometrician.[4]

The hungry Greekling is at home in every trade. He will jump to the sky, if you bid him. In a previous passage,

[1] Herodian, II. vii. 9: *φύσει κοῦφον τὸ Σύρων ἔθνος.*

[2] Dio, lxxvii. 10: *τὸ πανοῦργον τῶν Σύρων.*

[3] Tac. *Ann.* ii. 85. Cf. Heidel, 'Why were the Jews banished from Italy?' *American Journal of Philology*, 1920.

[4] Juv. iii. 76–7:

> 'Grammaticus, rhetor, geometres, pictor, aliptes,
> Augur, schoenobates, medicus, magus.'

the satirist has attributed to the Greek 'quick wits, damned insolence and ready speech'.[1] He could divine at once his own interest, and by his varied gifts would come out superior from every conflict. As doctors or artists, as copyists or secretaries, as tragic or comic actors, it was inevitable that Greek slaves in large numbers should earn the gratitude of their masters, and through manumission become citizens of what was now cosmopolitan Rome.

Such then are the races which supplied the freedmen of Rome. Many Gauls and Spaniards and other Westerners contending in valiant but uneven struggle against more astute Orientals, and many more Egyptians and Syrians with keen wits and a culture of a sort derived from Greece, claim our attention; but most prominent of all are the Greeks, whether of Asia or of Europe, endowed with musical and histrionic gifts, possessed of business ability, pre-eminent in art and science, and heirs to the tradition of a literature, a philosophy and a civilization which rank among the most sublime that the world has known.

[1] Juv. iii. 73:

'Ingenium velox, audacia perdita, sermo
Promptus.'

II
MANUMISSION

Why freedmen were less prominent in Greece than in Rome — causes of manumission among the Romans — the *peculium* — aristocratic vanity — respect for the slave's intellectual abilities — for his rights as a human being — benevolence and gratitude — *congiaria* — methods of emancipation — informal manumission — its popularity — *manumissio vindicta* — *censu* — *testamento* — the *fideicommissum* — tax on manumission — situation in the time of Augustus — his reforms — particular limits to testamentary manumission — general restrictions on manumission — other means of obtaining liberty apart from manumission.

IN the foregoing chapter an account was given of the origin and character of Rome's slave population. We have now to discuss why masters freed their slaves and what means they employed in so doing. Manumission in Rome became such a common feature in every-day life [1] that special causes have been thought necessary to explain its frequency. The problem often occurs to the mind, Why did the Romans, a people far less humane than the Greeks, yet show greater liberality in the freeing of their slaves?

One or two suggestions in answer may be made before we deal with Roman manumission in detail. In the first place, the number of freedmen in Greece and especially in Athens is often greatly minimized. There is a tendency to treat the whole metic population of Athens as free-born immigrants from foreign lands and their descendants. But freedmen were ranked as μέτοικοι, and there is no doubt that a very considerable proportion of these resident aliens were ex-slaves or their children.

[1] Cicero treats the general expectation of slaves that sometime in their life they would be freed as a well-founded one, *Pro Rab. perd. reo*, 15. Indeed in *Phil.* viii. 32 he implies that honest and industrious captives could win their liberty after six years of slavery. But it is unlikely that he is thinking of conditions outside the *familia urbana*, while in naming six years as a term of servitude he is influenced by the metaphorical 'captivity' of the Republic, which had lasted six years.

In the second place, the proportion of slaves was less in Greece. Before Alexander, Greek states never waged wars of conquest on such a scale as those which supplied the slave-market of Republican Rome. Athens could derive few slaves from her conflicts. The campaigns of Cimon were probably the most fertile in captives; in the Persian Wars of 480 and 479 the barbarian foe fell fighting rather than suffer himself to be taken prisoner. In the later Hellenic struggles it is true that the women and children of captured cities were sometimes sold into slavery; but the cities in question were usually of no great size, and the growth of the convention that Greek prisoners should be held to ransom rather than enslaved must have prevented any Greek general foreshadowing the conduct of Aemilius Paullus in Epirus or of Caesar in Gaul.

Moreover, the slaves whom warfare or kidnapping did supply to the Athenian market were not of a character adapted to the attainment of freedom. An inscription [1] of the time of Alcibiades places on record a typical household of slaves. There are five Thracians, three Carians, two Illyrians, two Syrians, a Colchian, a Melitenian from Cappadocia and a Lydian. The only slaves whose prices rise above the barbarian standard are the two Syrians (probably Phoenicians) and one of the Thracians. This individual household may speak for the general slave population in Greece; the most part were barbarians from the wilds of Thrace or Caria, from Illyrian highlands or Scythian steppes; they would be assigned the unskilled labour in factories and mines; they would not have that docility, charm or intelligence which would render them capable of winning their freedom. Others, to be sure, but not in great numbers while the Persian Empire was still intact, were from more civilized parts, such as Lydia and Syria; and slaves from these regions were on a much higher intellectual level than the barbarians of the North. Aristotle in discussing foreign peoples credits the Northerner with courage, unaccompanied by intelligence.

[1] Hicks and Hill, *Greek Historical Inscriptions*, 72, frag. 4, § 3.

On the other hand, the Asiatic is said to possess intelligence without courage. Compared with the Greek, the presumed possessor of both qualities, the philosopher holds these races to be naturally fitted for slavery.[1] The few Easterners therefore succeeded where the many Northerners failed. Unsuited to work which required strong physique, they would be capable of holding responsible positions in their masters' household and of appreciating the fact that good service was the road to liberty. Indeed it was recognized among the Greeks, in the case of domestic servants and of skilled workmen, that efficient service was best secured by holding out liberty to them as the final reward.[2]

Yet the occasions on which slaves were likely to earn the gratitude and even the respect of their masters were never so numerous in Greece as in Rome. No doubt slaves were employed in responsible offices, and might be set up in business themselves by their masters; Pasion the rich banker of Demosthenes' day,[3] if he did not owe his manumission to the gratitude of his master, doubtless bought it with savings made through the business in which he had been set up, or which he carried on for his master. But, whereas in Rome Orientals dominated trade and business primarily because they had superior ability, in Greece, on the other hand, slaves and freedmen did not enjoy the same monopoly of responsible posts in the commercial and industrial world. The Greek master surpassed his slave in education and capacity; he had his own mental resources; he was not thrown back on those of a clever slave. Consequently in Greece it was the exception rather than the rule to let the slave be the financial agent; freeborn Greeks tended to fill those posts which in Rome fell to Oriental slaves and gave them superb opportunities

[1] Arist. *Pol.* 1285 a, III. xiv. 6; 1327 b, IV (VII). vii. 2 and 3.

[2] Xenophon, *Econ.* v. 16; Arist. *Pol.* 1330 a, IV (VII). x. 14; *Econ.* I. v. 6.

[3] He was the freedman of Archestratus, Demosthenes, xxxvi. 43, 45, 48.

both of ingratiating themselves with their masters and of earning or embezzling enough money to buy their liberty.

Nor were the same prospects within the domestic sphere open to the slave in Greece. The Greeks never had those vast urban households of four or five hundred slaves [1] in which very many servants would come into personal contact with their master and have a fair chance of manumission. Nicias' thousands of slaves did not attend upon him, but were hired out to work in silver mines, where they could not meet their master and inspire his benevolence by conscientious attention. Furthermore the same artificial conventions did not apply in Greece as they did in Rome. Senators during the imperial age could not go about the city without a large following of clients, and if they had not a sufficient number of free-born clients the only course was to free some of their slaves and in this way provide a number to satisfy their vanity. But in Greece to parade greatness was not necessary—it might even be dangerous. In Greek lands, therefore, slaves were not freed simply and expressly to become the free clients of their former masters.

These considerations help to explain why manumission never reached very high proportions in Greece. Slaves were less numerous than in Rome, and did not, as they often did in Italy, surpass their masters in culture or talent. Neither in industry nor in domestic service had they the same opportunities of making money or of winning their masters' favour; and lastly, a social convention which in Rome led to wholesale manumission was non-existent in Greece.

We must now examine in detail the causes which led Roman masters to free so many of their slaves. In the first place manumission was often the result of a mere commercial transaction by which the slave bought his liberty. Masters frequently found it the wisest plan to allow their slaves to acquire property in the form of small savings,

[1] A *praefectus urbis* of Nero's time had 400 slaves: cf. Tac. *Ann.* xiv. 43.

although such property was the legal possession of the masters. This indulgence generally ensured good behaviour on the part of the slaves, who always worked well if they could entertain a hope of buying their liberty. As a rule, the master respected the earnings of his slave and kept his hands off them, though instances are suggested where the *peculium*, as this servile property was called, excited the master's avarice.[1]

How intensely slaves yearned for their liberty is shown by the desperate efforts they made to increase their *peculium*. Their allowance of corn and oil was never very liberal, but many of them contrived to save some small portion, and to sell it for profit. Seneca draws a lurid picture of the rigid economies of the slave, how he 'cheated his stomach' in order to increase the food he had for sale.[2] But the *peculium* could grow by less miserly methods. It was recognized that servants might sell the remains of a banquet for their own profit,[3] and porters in aristocratic houses could reap a handsome profit from gratuities given by those who wished speedy access to his lordship.[4] Further, slaves might easily resort to theft and ultimately present their masters with their own property in return for their liberty.[5] Of course the *peculium* was not confined to Roman times. In ancient Greece slaves were allowed to acquire property of their own, but, as we have seen, the number of domestic slaves, all of whom had varying opportunities of making money, was far greater under the late Roman Republic and the Empire than in the palmiest days of Athenian power. Moreover, in Rome,

[1] Ter. *Phormio*, 43 ff.:

> 'quod ille unciatim vix de demenso suo
> suom defraudans genium conpersit miser,
> id illa univorsum abripiet, haud existimans
> quanto labore partum.'

[2] Sen. *Ep.* lxxx. 4: 'ventre fraudato.'

[3] Apul. *Met.* x. 14.

[4] Juv. iii. 189.

[5] Dishonesty among slaves was well known, cf. Dion. Hal. iv. 24. It was a common *motif* in Plautine comedy.

the last century before Christ witnessed a great development in the extent of the *peculium*. Senators definitely prevented themselves by law from engaging in commerce, and a social stigma fell on merchants generally. Consequently wealthy citizens would put slaves into business, and according to the terms of the bargain both parties would profit. The Digest is full of instances where responsible financial positions are filled by slaves. A slave might carry on a bank or be a partner in a firm.[1] Sometimes the slave would be lent capital by his master, who received the annual interest, while the commercial profits went to the slave.[2] At other times the profits fell to the master, and the slave-agent obtained his remuneration either in presents or regular wages.[3] It is obvious that able slaves, given these opportunities, could soon increase their *peculium* out of all recognition; a slave might build a small temple out of his ample savings or co-operate with freedmen in constructing *Lares Augusti* for a large town like Neapolis;[4] so, in the Digest we find the *peculium* actually including slaves, land, inheritances, mortgages, obligations and so forth.[5]

The price a slave might have to pay for his freedom was naturally subject to variation. If the manumission was purely a commercial affair and the goodwill of the master contributed nothing, then the full value of the slave would have to be paid. Sometimes even more might be demanded by niggardly masters. But assuming that generally the slave paid the price he would fetch in the market, we may bring forward as evidence Horace's implication

[1] *Digest*, II. xiii. 4, § 3; XVII. ii. 63, § 2.

[2] An action arising out of this sort of agreement was called an *Actio Tributoria*, *Dig.* XIV. iv.

[3] An action arising out of this sort of agreement was called an *Actio Institutoria*, *Dig.* XIV. iii.

[4] *I. L. S.* 3581: 'Faustus Versenni P. ser. Priapum et templum d. s. peculi. f. c.'; and 3611: 'C. Caesare Aug. f. L. Paullo cos. Lares Augustos Q. Numisius Q. l. Legio, L. Safinius L. l. Hilarus, Sodalis C. Modi Cimbri ser., Aeschinus Octavi M. ser. magistr. de suo f. c.'

[5] *Dig.* XV. i. 7, § 4–5; XV. i. 57.

that 500 drachmae (£20) was the price of an ordinary servant.[1] In Egypt in 77 A.D. an eight-year-old slave girl fetched 640 drachmae (£25).[2] In 129, 1,200 drachmae were paid for a female slave aged twenty-five.[3] In the *Satyricon* of Petronius one of Trimalchio's fellow-freedmen says he bought his liberty for 1,000 denarii (£40), and he would be a valuable slave, for, after manumission, his ability won him the Augustal sevirate.[4] Pliny the Elder records some exceptional fancy prices paid for or by slaves. Under the Republic a grammarian cost 700,000 sesterces (£7,000) and the actor Roscius 500,000 (£5,000). Nero's *dispensator* who had managed the finance of the Armenian War was manumitted for 13,000,000 (£130,000), while a eunuch belonging to Sejanus was apparently worth the gigantic sum of 50,000,000 sesterces (£500,000).[5]

Manumission, however, was not always purchased, either with these almost incredible sums or with the more ordinary 500 to 1,000 drachmae or denarii. It was often a free gift made by the master to the slave. As was remarked above, the Roman aristocracy felt constrained by convention to have a large *clientèle* among the free but poorer citizens, and to manumit a few slaves was an easy way of swelling their retinue. Moreover, this was not merely a concession to an irksome convention; it pleased the patron's vanity to have a throng of clients paying the official morning call (*salutatio*), joining his procession to the city and applauding his legal speeches or his literary recitations. Pride showed itself in another way. Many a master on the point of death would console himself with the thought of a pretentious funeral and would free a

[1] Hor. *Sat.* II. vii. 43: 'quingentis empto drachmis.'

[2] Grenfell and Hunt, *Ox. Pap.* ii. 263.

[3] *Ib.* i. 95. It must be borne in mind that money now has probably only a fifth of its purchasing power under the early Empire.

[4] Petr. *Sat.* 57.

[5] Plin. *N.H.* vii. 128–9. Further evidence for more average prices in the second century will be found in Bruns, *Fontes Iuris Romani Antiqui*, 1909, nos. 130–2, and in Girard, *Textes de droit romain*, 1923, pp. 849–52. The prices vary from 200 to 600 drachmae or denarii.

number of slaves by his will, in order that his body might be followed to its last resting-place by a crowd of grateful freedmen.

Vanity however was not the only motive. Disinterested altruism played an important part even in the life of the Romans who have been almost proverbially credited with hard hearts. Frequently a master felt it a matter of common justice that a slave should be freed. In Rome the slave was so often a man of education, so entirely remote from the *φύσει δοῦλος* of Aristotle, that the blunt Roman master must have felt the incongruity of his possessing slaves who were intellectually his superiors. In their foreign policy the Romans showed a phil-hellenism which sometimes went beyond the bounds of prudence; how much more would a Roman noble, coming into personal contact with a Greek worthy of the name, be inspired with sentiments of admiration and goodwill?

In the first and still more the second century A. D. the teaching of the Stoics proved itself another potent factor. The philosophy of the Stoa permeated the ranks of Roman high society and instilled into their minds the doctrine of universal brotherhood. Where master and slave were conceived as brothers, frequent manumission could not help being the result, and, as will be seen later, Stoicism was not without its influence on slavery legislation.

Furthermore, apart from doctrines of human brotherhood, from sentiments of phil-hellenism, and from consideration for the slave's intellectual standard, simple gratitude or benevolence might impel a generous master to bestow freedom on a faithful servant. Nurses and teachers were often recompensed in this way.[1] Vanity cannot be assigned as the only motive for those numerous manumissions which characterized a wealthy Roman's will. There was a particular interest taken in slaves who were born in the house. Such *vernae*, as they were called,

[1] 'Liberta et nutrix,' e. g. *C. I. L.* iii. 4260. For teachers, cf. Sueton. *Gramm. Ill.*, *passim*, and *Dig.* XL. ii. 13.

won their freedom in large numbers,[1] while the bond of affection that could subsist between master and slave is well exemplified in that exquisite epigram of Martial where a dying *amanuensis* is freed in order that he may go to the other world a free man.[2]

The bestowal of freedom was often accompanied by a sum of money, by promotion in the master's service, or even by a proposal of marriage. Martial[3] mentions a gift of as much as 10,000,000 sesterces (£100,000), while not infrequently a slave was freed in order to become a *procurator*[4]—an official who combined the supervision of the household slaves with the work of a legal representative. Both male and female slaves (especially the latter) were frequently liberated for the express object of marriage,[5] since unions between the bond and the free were not legally recognized.[6]

One other feature of Roman society which led to a few manumissions deserves to be mentioned. Victorious generals in Republican times and emperors after the establishment of the Principate were in the habit of giving periodical *congiaria* or largesses to the citizens of Rome. A short time before each *congiarium* a slight but discernible increase in the number of manumissions probably took place. The poorer citizens of Rome speculated on the *congiarium* and freed as many of their slaves as possible—no doubt with plenty of stipulations—in order that their

[1] 'Verna libertus,' e.g. *I. L. S.* 6163, *C. I. L.* xiv. 943, 1427, 1520.

[2] Mart. i. 101, esp. l. 5 ff.:

> 'Ne tamen ad Stygias famulus descenderet umbras,
> Ureret implicitum cum scelerata lues,
> Cavimus, et domini ius omne remisimus aegro:
> Munere dignus erat convaluisse meo.
> Sensit deficiens sua praemia meque patronum
> Dixit ad infernas liber iturus aquas.'

[3] *Ib.* v. 70.

[4] *Dig.* XL. ii. 13; Gaius, i. 19. 'Libertus et procurator,' e.g. *I. L. S.* 1137, 1200, 3018, 3530, 7387–8, 8379, 9173.

[5] *Dig.* XL. ii. 19. For female slaves alone cf. Gaius, i. 19.

[6] Ulp. v. 5.

own shares might be multiplied. Suetonius relates how Augustus defeated these machinations and excluded recently liberated slaves from his bounty.[1]

These then were the historical causes that led to the manumissions which were of such frequent occurrence at Rome. The legal methods by which the slave obtained his liberty are generally divided into two main classes, formal and informal manumission (*manumissio iusta* and *manumissio minus iusta*). It will be convenient to discuss the latter first.

Informal manumission could be accomplished in three ways. The master might write a letter to his slave granting him his freedom in the terms of the letter; or he might make his slave sit down at table with him, thereby marking his rise to liberty; or lastly, among a few friends acting as witnesses, the master might declare his bondsman free. Of these three forms (*per epistulam*, *per mensam* and *inter amicos*) the last was the most frequent. Indeed, legal texts speak of the *manumissio inter amicos* as covering the whole field of informal manumission.[2] Of course the *manumissio per mensam* must always have been *inter amicos*, since a number of fellow-diners would certainly be present at table to act as witnesses.

Curiously enough, although one of the conveniences of informal manumission was its lack of legal form and ceremony, the only Latin deed of manumission which we possess is that of one performed *inter amicos* in Egypt in the third century.[3] It is written on both sides of a diptych wooden tablet and is divided into three parts; first the deed itself written out twice in Latin cursive, followed by the signatures of the parties to the contract and concluded by those of the witnesses, all in Greek cursive. I quote

[1] Suet. *Aug.* 42. Cf. Dion. Hal. iv. 24, where citizens are said to have even freed their slaves in order to secure shares in the corn-bounties.

[2] e. g. Gaius, i. 41, 44; *Fragmentum Dositheanum* (contained in Girard, *Textes de droit romain*, 5th edition, 1923, p. 505), § 4.

[3] Seymour De Ricci, *A Latin Deed of a Manumission of a Slave*; reprinted from *Proceedings of the Society of Biblical Archaeology*, May–June, 1904. Contained also in Girard, *op. cit.*, p. 854.

Mr. De Ricci's translation of the deed and the signatures of the contractors:

'Marcus Aurelius Ammonion son of Lupergus son of Serapion . . . from Hermupolis Maior the Ancient and Magnificent, has set free between friends his female house-born slave, Helene, about 34 years old, and has bidden her to be free and has received for her freedom from Aurelius Ales son of Inarous, from the village of Tisichis in the Hermupolite nome, two thousand two hundred Augustal drachmae[1], which Ales son of Inarous has himself made a present of to Helene the above-named freedwoman. Done at Hermupolis Maior the Ancient and Magnificent; the seventh day before the Kalends of August, Gratus and Seleucus being consuls,[2] the fourth year of the Emperor Caesar, Marcus Aurelius Antoninus, the Pious, the Happy, the first day of the month of Mesore.

'I, Markos Aurelios Ammonion son of Lupergos son of Serapion, I have set free between friends my house-born female slave Helene, about thirty-four years old, and have received for her freedom two thousand two hundred Augustal drachmae from Aurelios Ales son of Inarous, as written above.

'I, Aurelios Ales son of Inarous, have paid two thousand two hundred silver drachmae and will make no claim on Helene the above-named freedwoman. I, Aurelios Ammonios son of Hermeinos, have written for him, as he knoweth not letters.'

Such was the simple deed of an informal manumission. This mode of freeing slaves was exceedingly popular throughout Roman history. It could be performed in the master's house, no reference had to be made to official authorities, and superfluous ceremony was avoided. Under the Republic, *manumissio minus iusta* had not been deemed to confer legal freedom on the slave. Technically the step was revocable and the freedman could be called back into slavery at any time, although in actual fact the praetors usually protected liberty from being thus wantonly revoked.[3] There was the additional attraction of

[1] About £88. But as coinage had been several times debased since the early Empire the difference between the purchasing value of money then and now would not be so great as is suggested on p. 18, note 3.

[2] 221 A.D.

[3] *Fragm. Dosith.* § 5: 'hi autem, qui domini voluntate in libertate erant, manebant servi, et si manumissores ausi erant in servitutem denuo

avoiding expense. The five per cent. tax on the value of liberated slaves was probably not chargeable in the case of informal manumission until it was legally recognized under the early Empire.[1]

However, despite the popularity of this easy method of freeing one's slaves, formal manumission always retained its importance. One of three different forms might here also be employed—Manumission by the Rod, by the Census, or by Will.[2] The first of these ceremonies was performed usually before the praetor; but other state officials are mentioned as competent by the jurists. *A fortiori* consuls and pro-consuls could officiate;[3] while the same privilege was extended to Caesar's legates and to the prefect of Egypt.[4] To one of these magistrates went the master and the slave. The ceremony then was a fiction of a law-suit concerning property. In such an action each party took in his hands a rod, the symbol of property, and, touching the disputed article, declared it was his. For the implement in use there were two terms, *vindicta* (rod or staff) and *festuca* (straw or stalk).[5] The latter had once been the sign of landed property, but later it came to be identified with the rod, the symbol of property in general.

Accordingly in this simulated law-suit the rod was used. The slave, having no legal rights, was represented by the magistrate's *lictor* or some other person, who was called the *assertor libertatis*. This man, taking up a rod, touched the slave and declared that he was free. The master, of course, made no defence, and the praetor pronounced judgement in favour of the *assertor*. The master then turned the slave round and gave him a slap [6] (*alapa*),

eos per vim redigere, interveniebat praetor et non patiebatur manumissum servire.'

[1] For this tax, the *vicesima libertatis*, cf. *infra* in this chapter, pp. 28–30.

[2] *Vindicta*, *Censu*, *Testamento*.

[3] Ulp. i. 7.

[4] Dig. XL. ii. 7 and 21.

[5] Gaius, iv. 16.

[6] Schol. *ad* Pers. v. 78: 'Quia quotiens manumittebant, eos alapa percussos circumagebant et liberos confirmabant.'

and henceforth he was a free man. As regards the *alapa*, its precise significance is shrouded in mystery; it was probably analogous to the accolade of medieval chivalry; indeed Du Cange says the accolade is derived from the slap of manumission;[1] but unfortunately no certain explanation of the accolade has yet been given. Consequently we must resort to conjecture for a theory of the *alapa*. It may have been administered originally to avoid the evil eye and to impress the newly freed slave that a severe nemesis awaited any assumption of undue pride in his new status, or it may resemble the *tactio aurium* [2] used to stimulate the memory, especially the memory of a witness whom a litigant wished to secure.[3] If that be so, the purpose of the slap would be to impress upon the slave's mind the true importance of this, the most momentous event of his life. What appears the most likely hypothesis is that the blow symbolized the last affront the master could inflict, and called attention to the freedman's future immunity from all insults to which servitude had exposed him.[4]

During the Republic another form of manumission was available, the *manumissio censu*. This was only possible while censors were in office; at the quinquennial registration the favoured slaves by order of their masters caused the censors to place their names on the roll of Roman citizens.[5] But with the abolition of the censorship this form of manumission became extinct. We hear of no examples during the Empire, even when various emperors gave the censorship a brief spell of renewed life. *Manumissio censu* is mentioned in certain passages of the jurists,[6] but they are probably recording what was on the statute-

[1] *Alapa militaris*—'mos, ni fallor, derivatus a manumissionibus.'

[2] This is the theory of Mr. R. G. Nisbet (*J.R.S.* Vol. VIII), who discusses both the question of the *alapa* and that of the accolade.

[3] Hor. *Sat.* I. ix. 76–7.

[4] Gibbon (*Decline and Fall*, ch. 58) gives a similar explanation of the accolade: 'An emblem of the last affront which it was lawful for him to endure.'

[5] Ulp. i. 8.

[6] Gaius, i. 17, 44, 138, 140; *Fragm. Dosith.* 17.

IV. MANUMISSION *VINDICTA*

Bas-relief fragment, Mariemont, Belgium. A lictor is touching the kneeling slave with the *vindicta*. A slave already freed (on the left) is shaking hands with a fourth person, probably his master. Perhaps in some parts the *alapa* was softened down into a mere handshake. Both slaves wear the *pilleus*

book and ignoring the fact that there were no longer any circumstances in which it could arise. Ulpian refers to this method of emancipation as if it were antiquated,[1] and if it had been anything but a dead letter we should have expected it to be mentioned in texts where the other forms appear.[2]

The third method of formal manumission was that by will. *Manumissio testamento* was at all times the most popular form. All expenses and formalities fell on the heirs, as its effects naturally did not take place till after the testator's death; and it has been indicated how vanity and benevolence both played an important part in rendering this form popular. Persons freed by testament were called *orcini*; they belonged, as it were, to Orcus, the realm of the dead. To make the manumission valid, the slave had to be the property of the testator when the will was made as well as when the master died. If the emancipatory provision was not in the will or in a codicil confirmed by the testator, the claim to liberty was not valid. The manumission must be directed by an order. Some word meaning command or an imperative mood had to be employed. *Liber esto Stichus*, or *iubeo Stichum esse liberum* were valid, but *volo Stichum esse liberum* had no legal weight. Either the name of the slave or a correct description of him was sufficient for purposes of demonstration.[3] The slave was often freed and made heir or partial heir at one and the same time, for instance, *Stichus liber et heres esto*; but the institution of the slave as heir without any mention of liberty was invalid. If there was another heir mentioned, the slave went with the whole estate to him; if there was no other heir, he was forfeit to the Emperor.

Conditions were often made. Sometimes the effects of manumission were not to take place till so long had elapsed or till such and such a person had died. Or perhaps liberty

[1] Ulp. i. 8: 'Censu manumittebantur olim.'

[2] e. g. *Fragm. Dos.* 13.

[3] Gaius, ii. 239; Paul, IV. xiv. 1.

might depend on the slave's rendering his accounts and on their being satisfactory, or the slave might have to pay a certain sum either to the heir or to another party.[1]

Finally there remains fideicommissary manumission. In form it is *manumissio vindicta*, but in fact it is far more a *manumissio testamento*. As in manumission by will, the slave freed really owed his liberty to an act of his dead master, though legally it was the heir to his master's estate who became his patron. A dying master often asked his heir to free a certain slave who came to the said heir by the will. Without absolutely directing in the will that the slave should be free, the master might express a wish that he should receive his liberty. All the invalid formulae of testamentary manumission such as *Stichum volo esse liberum* are really *fideicommissa* given to the heir. For a long time there was no legal obligation to obey a *fideicommissum*. Throughout the Republican period and the whole of the first century A. D. the duty was no more than moral: the heir might consult his conscience or his interest as he chose. But in the second century the humanitarian programme of the imperial government was in full swing. Under the influence of the Stoic philosophy, which was now in the ascendant, a large number of *senatusconsulta* and imperial *constitutiones* were issued with reference to fideicommissary manumission, and every one of these favoured the acquisition of liberty. The following are the most important provisions. In 103 A. D. the *Senatusconsultum Rubrianum* authorized magistrates in Italy to perform the act of manumission if the heir refused to be present at the ceremony; at the same time the slave became a *libertus orcinus*, and the heir forfeited the rights of patronage by his failure to obey the *fideicommissum*.[2]

[1] *Dig*. XL. iv. *passim*.

[2] *Dig*. XL. v. 26, § 7: 'Subventum libertatibus est senatusconsulto quod factum est temporibus divi Traiani Rubrio Gallo et Caelio Hispone consulibus in haec verba: Si hi a quibus libertatem praestari oportet, evocati a praetore adesse noluissent, si causa cognita praetor pronuntiasset, libertatem his deberi eodem iure statum servari ac si directo manumissi

The *Senatusconsultum Articuleianum* (123 A. D.) extended the same order to the rest of the Empire; and the governor of the province where the death occurred was authorized to act in cases in which the praetor acted in Rome, even if the heir was not under his jurisdiction.[1] About the same time, the *Senatusconsultum Dasumianum* provided for the case in which the heir's failure to appear was not mere evasion, but could be covered by a reasonable excuse; in such circumstances the manumission took place in the heir's absence, but the slave did not become *orcinus* and the heir retained his patronal rights.[2] In 127 the *Senatusconsultum Iuncianum* ordered the praetor to execute the *fideicommissum* even if it referred to a slave not included in the legacy and not belonging to the testator at the time of his death.[3] According to the letter of the law, the testator could thus assure liberty to any slave he wished, whether belonging to himself, the heir or a third party; in order to fulfil the *fideicommissum*, the heir might thus be compelled not only to free a slave left him in the legacy, but also to manumit a slave of his own or buy another man's slave and liberate him. Naturally he could refuse the legacy if he found the cost too heavy, but if he accepted any portion of it he must undertake the responsibilities as well as the privileges. Undoubtedly, however, the law of 127 primarily contemplated cases where the slave belonged to the heir,[4] and probably there were very

essent.' Ordinarily the term *orcinus* was only applied to a person manumitted *testamento verbis directis*, not to one freed *ex fideicommisso* (sometimes called *manumissus testamento verbis precativis*).

[1] *Dig.* XL. v. 51, § 7.

[2] *Dig.* XL. v. 36; 51, § 4.

[3] *Dig.* XL. v. 28, § 4: 'Si quis servum non hereditarium rogatus manumittere latitet, factum est senatusconsultum Aemilio Iunco et Iulio Severo consulibus in haec verba: Placere, si quis ex his qui fideicommissam libertatem ex quacunque causa deberent servo qui mortis tempore eius, qui rogavit, non fuerit, isque adesse negabitur, praetor cognoscat, et, si in ea causa esse videbitur, ut si praesens esset manumittere cogi deberet, id ita esse pronuntiet: cumque ita pronuntiasset, idem iuris erit, quod esset, si ita, ut ex fideicommisso manumitti debuisset, manumissus esset.' Cf. XL. v. 51, §§ 8–9.

[4] The words 'sed proprium' (*Dig.* XL. v. 51, § 8) suggest this.

few occasions on which the slave of a third party obtained liberty *ex fideicommisso*.[1]

In the reign of Antoninus Pius the progress in favour of liberty continued unabated. Various difficulties and ambiguities were swept away. If one of the heirs was mentally deficient, his consent to the manumission, when likely to involve delay, was declared unnecessary.[2] If a female slave bore a child between the death of her master and the execution of the *fideicommissum*, the child was pronounced free-born.[3] In the end, Marcus practically declared in a rescript that no consideration whatever could hinder the *fideicommissum* taking its due course.[4]

With these avenues of manumission open and with so many factors in Roman society always making for emancipation, the streets of Rome in the last century before Christ began to be crowded with citizens who had but recently issued from servitude. With the growth of luxury in Rome the personal needs of the wealthy became more manifold, and employment was thereby found for all the countless captives that were poured into the market from foreign lands. As the influx of these human chattels appeared to continue unabated, masters never feared that the frequency of manumission might in time leave them faced with a scarcity of slaves. Consequently, full rein was given to emancipation, and the only check upon it was the five per cent. tax on the value of liberated slaves. It has been a matter of some controversy which party paid the tax, the slave or the master. Some authority can be found for each view, but the apparently conflicting texts

[1] Yet the case of a *servus alienus* is expressly covered by *Dig*. XL. v. 47, § 1. On the complications arising from such a case, see Buckland, *Roman Law of Slavery*, Cambridge, 1908, pp. 530–2. If the owner of a *servus alienus* refused to sell him at a reasonable price, the fulfilment of the *fideicommissum* was not obligatory, and the slave remained in servitude. Ulp. ii. 11.

[2] *Dig*. XL. v. 30, § 7.

[3] *Dig*. XL. v. 26, §§ 2 and 5.

[4] *Dig*. XL. v. 30, § 16: 'Divus etiam Marcus rescripsit, fideicommissas libertates neque aetate neque condicione neque mora non praestantium, tardiusve reddentium corrumpi aut in deteriorem statum perduci.'

can be reconciled by assuming that the financial responsibility was assigned according to the conditions of manumission. If the emancipation was due to the initiative of the slave, if, in other words, the slave bought his liberty, then the burden of the tax fell on him. If, on the contrary, the slave had his liberty thrust upon him, if the master, whether from egoistic or altruistic motives, presented his slave with his freedom, then it was from the master that the tax was due.[1]

Yet this tax failed altogether to arrest the tide of manumission. Even in the 148 years between 357 and 209 B. C. the revenue derived from the liberation of slaves had amounted to 4,000 pounds of gold,[2] which represents approximately £1,776,000. That is to say, £1,200 came in annually from the emancipation of slaves, and, assuming that £20 was an average price and therefore that £1 was an average tax, we may conclude that before and during the Punic Wars each year saw 1,200 manumissions. This may seem a small number at first, but it must be borne in mind that the tax was probably levied only on Roman citizens, and that, during the times to which our statistics apply, the franchise had not been extended far outside Rome. Moreover the great wars of conquest had not yet begun to pour crowds of captives into the market.

A way of evading the tax was soon discovered. It has been said that slaves were often freed informally. Sometimes this was to avoid an irksome ceremony of manumission, but more frequently to escape the payment of the tax.[3] Consequently in the late Republic a large number of Orientals, actually free but legally still in servitude, mingled without restraint in Roman society and contributed to the foreign aspect of the population. But

[1] Examples where the slave pays the *vicesima* may be found in Petr. *Sat.* 58, and Arrian, *Discourses of Epictetus*, IV. i. 33. For an example in which the master pays it, cf. Arrian, *op. cit.* II. i. 26.

[2] Livy, VII. xvi. 7; XXVII. x. 11–12.

[3] It is here assumed that under the Republic informal manumissions were not taxed, though actual evidence on the subject is not forthcoming.

the number of regular manumissions was always large, especially those by will, where the heirs and not the manumissor suffered the economic loss. The tax, therefore, if imposed for purposes of revenue, must be considered a great financial success. If, however, its object was to discourage manumission and preserve the native Roman character of society, then it must be pronounced a dismal failure. Whether by paying or evading the tax, Romans continued to free their slaves at an alarming rate, and, by so doing, filled society with a mass of foreigners whose presence transformed Rome into a cosmopolitan city. Evidence is plentiful regarding this feature of the city under the Caesars. Lucan speaks of Rome as 'filled with the dregs of the world',[1] and Juvenal declares he cannot endure a Greek city and laments the fact that the Syrian Orontes so long ago poured his waters into the Tiber.[2] Earlier than these writers, Dionysius of Halicarnassus[3] noticed how slaves who had committed heinous crimes mixed in no small numbers with the free population.

It was to resist this tendency that Augustus placed restrictions on manumission. A genuine conservative statesman, he viewed with alarm the changing character of the Roman proletariat and the Eastern aspect of the population. When he saw cunning slaves gaining undeserved ascendancy over their masters, and imprudent owners lightly and thoughtlessly lavishing enfranchisement on low-born Orientals; when he reflected on the chaos and crime of the revolutionary period in which slaves had so often been enlisted in a rebel army; then he decided that this scum of the earth must be prevented from corrupting the time-honoured Italian character, and that, if Rome could not avoid importing Orientals to minister to citizens' needs and desires, the free-born masses must at all costs be preserved from their contagious taint. Realizing then that the future of Roman civilization was at

[1] Lucan, vii. 405: 'mundi faece repletam'. Cf. Sen. *Ad Helviam*, vi. 2: 'maxima pars istius turbae patria caret'.

[2] Juv. iii. 58 ff.

[3] Dion. Hal. iv. 24.

stake, and that its peril was in great measure due to the new blood that now permeated the plebeian ranks, Augustus in 2 B. C. opened a campaign against the emancipation of slaves.[1] Testamentary manumission was the first to be attacked.

This had been the most mischievous of all the several forms. Dionysius of Halicarnassus tells us that dying masters had been known to free every one of their slaves, many of whom were of desperate character, simply in order that they might all grace their funerals with caps of liberty on their heads.[2] It was the form of manumission that cost least trouble and expense to the actual giver of liberty, and it is on the point of death that one feels particularly desirous of perpetuating one's memory by munificent actions. Moreover, many a master who was genuinely grateful for the good work of his slaves perhaps had postponed the recompense until the last minute, when he would hurriedly insert an emancipating clause into his will. It was to check these over-lavish manumissions that the *Lex Fufia Caninia* of 2 B.C. was devised. By this act a kind of sliding scale was arranged to regulate the maximum number of slaves that might be freed by will.[3] If the total number of slaves a master owned was between two and ten, one-half might be left their liberty. Of a household consisting of between ten and thirty one-third, and of one containing thirty to a hundred only one-fourth, were allowed to be set free. Finally, if the number was between one hundred and five hundred, one-fifth was the limit; and in no case could a testament freeing more than a hundred slaves be admitted. Of

[1] In a sense Augustus had already opened a campaign against the emancipation of slaves. By the *Lex Iunia* he had probably discouraged manumission. Cf. Chap. V, and Appendix I. But his direct attack on manumission begins in 2 B. C.

[2] Dionys. Hal. iv. 24: *ἔγωγ᾽ οὖν ἐπίσταμαί τινας ἅπασι τοῖς δούλοις συγκεχωρηκότας εἶναι ἐλευθέροις μετὰ τὰς ἑαυτῶν τελευτάς, ἵνα χρηστοὶ καλῶνται νεκροὶ καὶ πολλοὶ ταῖς κλίναις αὐτῶν ἐκκομιζομέναις παρακολουθῶσι τοὺς πίλους ἔχοντες ἐπὶ ταῖς κεφαλαῖς.*

[3] Gaius, i. 42–6; Paul, IV. xiv. 4; Ulp. i. 24; Just. *Inst.* i. 7.

course, a man was always allowed to consider himself as possessing less slaves than he really did. For instance, a man with ten slaves could free five, but, according to the above rules, one with twelve could only free four. This anomaly, the jurists are careful to say, did not exist. The owner of twelve could consider himself an owner of ten, and therefore free five slaves. That is to say, one could never be prevented from manumitting up to the highest number allowed to the class immediately below. These restrictions probably applied also to fideicommissary manumission; otherwise they would have lost more than half their force in the first century, and after the *fideicommissum* had been made legally binding in 103 A. D. they would have been entirely useless.[1]

These were the restrictions laid on testamentary manumission. In 4 A. D. the legislation of the *Lex Fufia Caninia* was reinforced by an attack on manumission in general. By the *Lex Aelia Sentia* Augustus annulled all manumissions made by debtors to defraud their creditors.[2] If a man in debt deliberately sacrificed his rights over his slave to diminish his property and to become insolvent, then, in the interests of the creditors, the manumission was declared null and void. If, however, a master, dying insolvent, by testament freed a slave and made him his only heir, then the manumission was upheld.[3] A more important clause of this *lex* limited the power of young masters to free their slaves. Clever Orientals, whose characters were sometimes of the criminal order, often gained such ascendancy over imprudent and weak-minded masters that they easily acquired their liberty though they were entirely unworthy of it. Augustus felt he could not insult the prudence of adult Romans by generally restricting the rights of manumission, but he did not hesitate to prevent young boys of immature judgement recklessly

[1] No text actually says these restrictions applied to *fideicommissa*, but Paul's example, IV. xiv. 1, is only applicable to *fideicommissa*.

[2] Gaius, i. 37, 47; *Dig.* XL. ix. 27, *pr.*; Ulp. i. 15; Just. *Inst.* I. vi. *pr.*

[3] Ulp. i. 14.

throwing liberty and citizenship among their slaves. Consequently he forbade all masters under twenty to manumit, unless the cause was approved by a special council which in Rome consisted of five senators and five knights.[1] But the nature and extent of the causes which the council might approve show Augustus to have been both broad-minded and generous. The interest of the slave is as much considered as that of Roman society. No hindrance is offered to the master who wishes to reward good service. The general definition of the just causes that might be approved was as follows: 'Causes that spring not from luxury but from benevolence'; and the council was to use its authority in favour 'not of the love of pleasure but of well-founded affection'.[2] Thus gratitude for notable services in the past or for conscientious attention as nurse or teacher or in other like capacity constituted a just cause.[3] If the slave had been left to the master with a *fideicommissum* asking him to free him, the council would authorize compliance with the dead man's request.[4] A slave might be freed if his master wished to make him his *procurator*, or again no objections would be made if a master, even under twenty years of age, fell in love with his girl-slave and wished to free her in order to marry her.[5] On the other hand, it was not considered a just cause for manumission if a mistress wished to free a male slave for the purpose of marriage, unless both mistress and slave had once been fellow-slaves, and he had been left to her with the express object that they should marry.[6] Finally a master might free any blood-relation.[7] It may be asked how these circumstances could come about. The answer is that the clause applies to freedmen wishing to redeem parents or brothers or sisters who were still in servitude. Their only course was

[1] Gaius, i. 38, 39, 40; Ulp. i. 13; Just. *Inst.* I. vi. 4–6. In the provinces the council consisted of twenty Roman citizens.

[2] 'Non ex luxuria sed ex affectu descendentes' and again 'non deliciis sed iustis affectionibus,' *Dig.* XL. ii. 16.

[3] *Dig.* XL. ii. 9 and 13; Gaius, i. 19, 39; Just. *Inst.* I. vi. 5.

[4] *Dig.* XL. ii. 15, *pr.*

[5] Gaius, i. 19; *Dig.* XL. ii. 13.

[6] *Dig.* XL. ii. 14, § 1.

[7] Gaius, i. 19.

to buy such relatives and free them. But it would have been an intolerable anomaly if a man had been legally the slave of his son or his daughter even though he had been bought for the purpose of manumission. Consequently this also was regarded as a just cause.

It will be seen from this that Augustus had no idea of opposing the just claims of a faithful servant to liberty or the commendable ambitions of a newly freed slave to share his good fortune with his relatives. What Augustus had in mind was to prevent a vain impulsive youth from freeing unlimited numbers of his slaves simply to swell his *clientèle* or for similar purposes of ostentation.

There were one or two other limits to manumission. Until the time of Hadrian, municipal corporations of provincial towns[1] were not allowed to manumit their slaves, while the burial and mutual help societies (*collegia*[2]) did not obtain the right until the reign of M. Aurelius. Masters condemned or on trial, apparently under any of Sulla's criminal laws, were not allowed to free slaves, and deported exiles were under the same disability.[3]

Other measures were taken by Augustus to check the process of Orientalization. Indirectly they affected manumission; but in their direct action they were restrictions not on manumission but on the attainment of the franchise. Two fresh classes were created into which slaves manumitted in certain circumstances were placed. These two classes will be treated in a later chapter.

It only remains to indicate very briefly two means other than manumission by which a slave could obtain his liberty. In the reign of Claudius an edict was published granting liberty to slaves whom their masters had abandoned when ill,[4] and later Vespasian issued an edict by

[1] *Cod. Iust.* VII. ix. 3. [2] *Dig.* XL. iii. 1.

[3] *Dig.* XL. i. 8, § 2; XLVIII. xxii. 2. Though the rescripts concerning these regulations belong to the time of Antoninus Pius, praetorian jurisdiction probably had hitherto withheld its sanction at least from formal manumission in these circumstances.

[4] *Dig.* XL. viii. 2; slaves thus freed became *Latini Iuniani*. Justinian

which in certain circumstances freedom was bestowed on a slave prostituted by her master.[1] The number of slaves who obtained their liberty through these enactments can never have been at all considerable, but the spirit which the laws show returns a strong negative to the sweeping denunciations often levelled against the Roman law of slavery. Roman law in imperial times did not treat slaves as mere soulless chattels, and did not deny them all the elementary rights of a human being. In the second century A. D. the amelioration of servile conditions was so marked as to become a historical common-place, but, even before that period, some account was taken of the interest and rights of the slave. We have seen how Augustus took care that his restrictions should not prevent loyal service receiving its reward or family affection among slaves realizing its legitimate aspirations. And here in these two edicts of the first century it is explicitly recognized that the slave had a claim on his master for the relief of physical suffering, and that even in servitude the sacred rights of a woman's body could not be violated with impunity.

directed that a slave abandoned when sick by his master should be a *civis Romanus* and that the master should forfeit the patronal rights. *Cod. Iust.* VII. vi. 1, § 3.

[1] *Dig.* XXXVII. xiv. 7, *pr.* In selling a female slave a master was allowed to contract with the buyer that she should not be prostituted. If despite this contract the new owner prostituted the slave, then, by Vespasian's edict, she was to go free.

III

LEGAL RELATIONS BETWEEN PATRON AND FREEDMAN

Origin of the *obsequium* and *officium* — principles which followed from the *obsequium* — nature of the *officium* — punishment of ungrateful freedmen — the *tutela* — patron's share in the succession — the *operae* — means of exemption from them — limits to the patron's power — obligations of the patron towards the freedman — conception of patron and freedman as father and son.

WHEN the newly-freed slave entered into society, he still laboured under many disadvantages which sprang from his servile origin. On the one hand, though in normal conditions[1] a fully fledged Roman citizen, he was by no means in a position of equality with such of Rome's population as vaunted themselves free-born. On the other hand, though the *alapa* of manumission may have symbolized the last affront which could be inflicted, yet the authority of the master was still a living reality. While this authority was not considered to be exactly that of a master over a slave, it was a power which could be enforced, and one which it was generally unwise to attempt to evade.

The relation of patron to freedman approximated to that of father to son. Indeed the Digest places the two relations in close juxtaposition. 'By freedman or son the person of patron or father should always be honoured and held sacred.'[2] This filial respect which the freedman was expected to pay towards his patron is summed up in those somewhat vague terms *obsequium et officium*. The actual duties included in these words are never formulated. Everyone in Rome knew what they signified, but not everyone could express in words what he meant by them. Their origin must be sought in the early days of Roman

[1] Cf. *infra* on the classes of freedmen, Chap. V.

[2] *Dig.* XXXVII. xv. 9: 'Liberto et filio semper honesta et sancta persona patris ac patroni videri debet.'

history, when the number of slaves and freedmen was small and when the slave was not a product of Greek civilization, but some Italian captive whose intelligence and talents did not surpass those of his master. When such a servant obtained his liberty, he would in all likelihood be still dependent on his master for food and shelter. The only work he could do for his living would in most cases be agricultural or domestic, and, as he had not sufficient capital to buy land, he must perforce remain in his master's house. Here the habit of obedience, begotten from years of slavery, would naturally exercise a strong influence over the rest of his life. In later times, what was originally a custom arising from circumstances gradually erected itself into a tradition binding on all freedmen, whatever their means of livelihood. Throughout the Republic the *obsequium* and *officium* had no judicial sanction, but merely constituted a custom which every freedman was expected to follow. In the first century B.C., however, when a more independent class of freedmen came into being, ambitious parvenus, if they found their patrons barring their way to greatness, were not to be deterred by a convention sprung from a bygone age. In those times of revolution cases of disloyalty must have been frequent, and the old quasi-feudal idea of the patron as father of his freedmen must at times have been sorely strained. Consequently, when the advent of Augustus heralded an attempted reform of manners, the relations between patron and freedman received their due portion of the legislator's attention, and in the *Lex Aelia Sentia* of 4 A.D. a punishment was fixed for ungrateful freedmen.

Obsequium had more a negative than a positive connotation, and, to explain what it meant, the easiest way is to mention a few prohibitions that logically followed from it. In the first place, it was generally considered a violation of the *obsequium* to bring a civil lawsuit against one's patron. Just as a son was not supposed to act in a desirable manner if he summoned his father into court, so it was thought an infringement of the patron's rights if his freedman brought an action against him. Special permission therefore had to be obtained from the praetor before a freedman could sue his patron or even the parents or children of his patron.[1] Severe penalties were imposed on the freedman if he transgressed this regulation. The patron was allowed to sue his freedman for instituting a process from which he was debarred by the praetor's edict and heavy damages might be awarded him.[2] Nor was the praetor's permission easily obtained. Consulting the dignity of a patron rather than the justice due to a freedman, he often refused the right of citation. The freedman was regularly forbidden to serve on his patron an *interdictum unde vi*, or praetorian pronouncement against a defendant for wrongfully seizing a plaintiff's land.[3] In the time of the Empire this disability cannot have been of great import, for in such cases the ordinary procedure by *actio*, differing very slightly from that by *interdictum*, was always open to the freedman, subject of course to the praetor's preliminary permission. But there were other disabilities. Freedmen were not allowed to bring against their patrons any action for fraud;[4] complaints for injury were only admitted in the most serious cases; and no doubt there was a considerable proportion of individual cases[5] in other categories that the praetor stopped at the outset.

Similarly, in criminal procedure, the right of the freedman to accuse his patron was strictly limited. The only criminal action that could be brought by a freedman

[1] 'Praetor ait "Parentem patronum patronam liberos parentes patroni patronaeve in ius sine permissu meo ne quis vocet".' *Dig.* II. iv. 4, § 1.

[2] Gaius, iv. 46. 10,000 sesterces (£100) is cited as the award in Gaius' example.

[3] *Dig.* XXXVII. xv. 2 and 7, § 2.

[4] *Ibid.*

[5] 'Nec enim ferre praetor debet heri servum hodie liberum conquerentem quod dominus ei convicium dixerit, vel quod leviter pulsaverit vel emendaverit, sed si flagris si verberibus si vulneravit non mediocriter, aequissimum erit praetorem ei subvenire.' *Dig.* XLVII. x. 7, § 2; cf. XXXVII. xv. 2 and 7, § 2; XLVII. x. 11, § 7.

against his patron was that for *maiestas*.[1] Some emperors were so anxious to suppress conspiracy at its inception that they did not hesitate to relax their conservative respect for the *obsequium*. When it was a case of peril to his throne or the violation of the *obsequium*, many an emperor preferred that the *obsequium* should suffer. Accordingly the information of Milichus against his patron at the time of Piso's conspiracy was accepted.[2] But in all other cases attempts to accuse a patron were severely punished. Claudius himself, whose reign has been called the *Saturnalia* of the freedmen,[3] was a stern corrector of those who presumed to plot against their patrons.[4]

Freedmen were thus forbidden to initiate criminal suits against their patrons. Evidence however might be borne by the ex-slave against his former master. But even here the peculiar family-like relations between patron and freedman might stand in the way of legal justice, and not merely to the protection of the patron but even to that of the freedman. From a willing witness evidence might be taken, but no compulsion could be used to make either the freedman give information against his patron or the patron against his freedman.[5] The two were supposed to form one family whose unity it was sacrilegious to dissolve by force; but this laudable ideal was probably subject in reality to the exception of prosecutions for *maiestas*.

One or two other laws appear to be applications of the *obsequium*. If the patron takes his freedman in the act of adultery with his wife, he may slay him on the spot.[6] On the other hand, the freedman is not allowed to slay his patron when the latter is the offender. Measures also are taken to prevent unfaithfulness on the part of a

[1] *Dig.* XLVIII. iv. 7, § 2; *Cod. Theod.* IX. vi. 1 (376 A. D.).

[2] Tac. *Ann.* xv. 54, 55.

[3] L. Friedländer-G. Wissowa, *Darstellungen aus der Sittengeschichte Roms*, 9th–10th ed., Leipzig, 1919–21, vol. i, p. 41; *Roman Life and Manners* (Eng. trans. of an earlier ed.), vol. i, p. 39.

[4] Dio, lx. 13.

[5] *Lex Iulia de publicis iudiciis* (reign of Augustus); *Dig.* XXII. v. 4.

[6] *Lex Iulia de adulteriis*, 18 B. C.; *Dig.* XLVIII. v. 25, *pr.*

freedwoman who has become the wife of her patron. If she deserts him, she is not allowed to marry another person without his consent.[1]

From these laws, the logical corollaries of the *obsequium*, some idea of that principle may be formed. It was more a negative than a positive right; by it were meant a number of vague prohibitions; in virtue of the *obsequium* the patron was immune from anything that might detract from his dignity as patron.

The positive rights corresponding to the *obsequium* were embodied in the term *officium*. The duties included under this head are again hard to define. It is difficult to draw a hard and fast line and say 'Here the rights of the patron end'. Miscellaneous small services were the legitimate demands of the patron. He could, if he so wished, invest his freedman with the care and protection of his children.[2] He could make him their guardian, their teacher, their companion. It was perhaps part of the *officium* that the freedman should perform the duties of a client, or accept the domestic position of *dispensator* or *procurator* according to the patron's desire. Doubtless, too, it was recognized by tradition that part of the freedman's *officium* was to support his patron if fallen in need—a tradition that had to be reinforced by legal sanctions in the time of the Antonines.[3]

The frequency with which ungrateful freedmen and the measures taken against them appear in the pages of historians and jurists seems to betoken a retrogression in the relations between patron and freedman. The normal state of affairs, however, is never fully represented in jurists or in ancient historians. Even if every freedman in Rome had shown exemplary conduct towards his patron, such a unique circumstance would certainly not have been a thing to interest the jurists, and it is doubtful whether it would have won as much recognition among the

[1] *Lex Iulia de maritandis ordinibus*, 4 A. D.; *Dig.* XXXVIII. xi. 1, § 1.

[2] *Dig.* XXVII. i. 14; *Cod. Iust.* V. lxii. 5.

[3] *Dig.* XXV. iii. 5, § 18–26; iii. 9.

historians as did an emperor's severe correction of a few remiss freedmen. The main object of Tacitus and Suetonius was to record prominent events, changes and scandals; and it is only to explain these that the permanent social and economic background appears through their writings. We must not, therefore, take the repeated punishment of ungrateful freedmen as at all typical of their relations with their patrons.

Nevertheless, there must always have been a number of crafty Orientals who, on occasions, saw an advantage in plotting against the man who had given them their freedom; while others, more proud and high-spirited, might so hotly resent some slight ill-treatment at their patron's hand, in which he had somewhat strained his authoritative rights, that they would return blow with blow or abuse with abuse. Claudius ordered freedmen who neglected the *obsequium* and *officium* to be relegated to slavery;[1] and certainly the question of ungrateful freedmen assumed such a serious aspect in Nero's reign that it occasioned a debate in the Senate.[2] Some wished to make manumission a revocable step, at least in the case of those who injured their patron in any way. But, as probably the patron was to be the judge whether the conduct of his freedman amounted to a breach of *obsequium et officium*, the motion was regarded as an attack on the whole class of freedmen. The final decision, therefore, was that individual cases were to be examined, and probably in the event of a sufficiently grave offence the freedman was to be re-enslaved; but no infringement of freedmen's rights in general was allowed.

Tacitus is unfortunately brief in recounting a debate of great importance in the history of freedmen, and, what is worse, he only gives the arguments as each side advanced them. We are not even given the exact motion. According to Tacitus, one side moves that patrons should be allowed to re-enslave ungrateful freedmen, and the other does not

[1] Suet. *Claud.* 25: 'ingratos et de quibus patroni quererentur revocavit in servitutem.'

[2] Tac. *Ann.* xiii. 26–7.

meet this point, but argues that an attack on the whole class is not justifiable. Obviously some important fact has been omitted. The proposers of the motion must have brought forward some clause which endangered the rights of all freedmen, and which threatened to make the innocent many suffer for the guilty few. It has been supposed above that this clause was one which left the rights and wrongs of the case to the patron's discretion, thus virtually putting every freedman at his patron's mercy. Similarly the result of the debate is veiled in obscurity. We are told that individual cases were to be investigated;[1] but whether we are right in supposing, as we have above, that extreme offences were punished with the loss of liberty, Tacitus gives no hint. Anyhow, whatever course was adopted, it was not sufficient to prevent a few cases arising in later times. Hadrian sent offenders against the rights of a patron to labour in the imperial quarries,[2] and in the time of the Antonines the *non obsequens*, the freedman who violated the *obsequium*, was condemned to be beaten with rods.[3] On some occasions the ungrateful freedman was dismissed with an admonition for the first offence, but in the case of subsequent offences a period of exile was the punishment for insult or abusive language.[4] When, however, the freedman raised his hand against his patron, or played the informer, or in any way conspired against him, the punishment, probably even for a first offence, was one of the most severe under the Roman Empire—forced labour in the mines.

It will be seen from this that the practice of handing over ungrateful freedmen to their patrons as slaves, followed in individual cases by Claudius[5] and probably by Nero after the senatorial debate, was discontinued in the second century, and that the state undertook the punish-

[1] 'privatim expenderent causam libertorum quoties a patronis arguerentur,' Tac. *Ann.* xiii. 27.

[2] Dositheus, *Divi Hadriani sententiae et epistulae*, 3: 'in lautumias.'

[3] *Dig.* I. xvi. 9, § 3: 'fustium castigatio.'

[4] *Dig.* XXXVII. xiv. 1.

[5] Suet. *Claud.* 25.

ment. Probably the former system was found unsuitable. The patron vented his spite on the freedman by excessively cruel treatment, and the re-enslaved freedman gave very poor service now that all chance of liberty was gone for ever. The former conduct was morally bad, and the latter economically disadvantageous to the patron. Accordingly, while some safeguard was necessary for the maintenance of the *obsequium* and the *officium*, the punishment was at any rate taken out of the hands of the patron.

If the *obsequium* and the *officium* express the duties which the freedman owed to his patron, the protection which a patron was understood to give to his freedman went by the name of *tutela*. All freedmen under twenty years of age and all freedwomen of whatever age were under the *tutela* of their patrons. This meant that the patron was supposed to protect their interests, give them legal advice, and guide them in the administration of any property they might hold. Technically he was allowed, if he so wished, to prevent any alienation of their landed property,[1] though it is hardly likely that this right was exercised in the imperial period.

The responsibility of the *tutela* was converted into a privilege by the fact that it conferred on the *tutor* a certain share in the control of the succession;[2] even the heirs of freedmen who in virtue of their sex and age had been free from the *tutela* nevertheless had in certain cases to admit the patron to a share in the legacy. Under the Republic in the legacies of freedmen the heirs could bar the patron's claim to half the estate, only if they were the actual descendants of the deceased. After the *Lex Papia Poppaea* (9 A.D.), if the estate was worth 100,000 sesterces (£1,000), the freedman had to have three actual descendants or else the patron shared equally with the one or two descendants who were left; and, if the heirs were not actual descendants, then the patron exercised his right to

[1] Gaius, i. 192.

[2] Gaius, iii. 39–53; Ulp. xxix. The account here given of the patron's share in the succession does not apply to *Latini Iuniani* (*q.v.*, pp. 78–9).

one-half as under the Republic. In a freedwoman's legacy, the patron or his male descendant exercised the full *tutela* before the establishment of the Principate. The whole estate was his unless he specially authorized the freedwoman to bequeath it to other heirs. The *Lex Papia Poppaea*, however, exempted freedwomen with four children from the *tutela*; and Claudius is said to have allowed freedwomen who invested their capital in the corn trade and in the feeding of Rome to be deemed to have four children. Consequently the rights of patrons over freedwomen in these categories were excluded.

The rights of a freedman or freedwoman over the succession to his or her estate always tended to increase when he had three and she four children, when the patron was a woman, or when the patron only left female descendants, but the details are so much a matter of antiquarian interest that the subject will not be further pursued here. The whole matter is clearly and concisely summarized in Abdy and Walker, *Gaius and Ulpian*, 3rd edition, Appendix M.

Such were the claims which patrons had on their freedmen. The very status of libertinity involved its holder in the duties of *obsequium* and *officium*, and, as we have seen, in many cases exposed his legacy to the control or partial control of the patron. In addition the patron might, if he found it convenient to his interests, contract with his freedman that the latter should perform certain services, which went by the name of *operae*. At manumission an oath would be imposed on the slave to give so many days' work in his patron's household or factory; the duty of performing these *operae* followed from the contract and not from the mere status of being a freedman. In other words, if the master did not exact the oath before freeing his slave, he could not claim systematic service such as the *operae* meant, but could only demand what those ill-defined terms *obsequium* and *officium* implied.

The *operae* were of two sorts, *officiales* and *fabriles*. The former were chiefly domestic, while the latter consisted in skilled labour, such as that of a physician, artist or architect, or in manufacture of all kinds. For instance, one duty that a freedman doctor had to fulfil was to attend the friends of his patron.[1] The *operae fabriles*, besides being of greater economic value than the *officiales*, had the further advantage from the patron's point of view that they passed to his heir,[2] though of course the freedman's obligation died with him and was not imposed upon his heir. The *operae officiales*, on the other hand, probably exceeded by very little the privileges which the *officium* conferred on the patron; the oath exacted at manumission was not much more than the definition and confirmation of the duties implied by the *officium*. Accordingly, when the master to whom the ex-slave owed his freedom died, it seemed incongruous to maintain a connexion whose basis, properly speaking, had passed away. The right of demanding these *operae*, therefore, was not inherited. But the *operae fabriles* were of a more commercial character. If a flourishing firm at the death of its director suddenly lost its right to the labour of perhaps a hundred men, its business would be to a great extent dislocated. The liability to the *operae fabriles* was, for this reason, made to continue to the death of the freedman except in certain conditions which will be indicated later.

The *operae* were a serious burden on freedmen who wished to rise in society and carry on business on their own responsibility. Even while they were engaged in labour for their patron, it appears they were sometimes called upon to supply their own food,[3] though, if the master did not actually furnish it, he had at least to allow them sufficient time each day to earn their food by some other work.[4] It is probable, therefore, that most patrons would find it the most convenient and economical plan to supply the food themselves.

1 *Dig.* XXXVIII. i. 27.

2 *Dig.* XXXVIII. i. 6.

3 *Dig.* XXXVIII. i. 18; (*contra*) 33.

4 *Dig.* XXXVIII. i. 19, 22, § 2, 50, §1.

As the *operae* could be hired to a third party, freedmen might at any moment be told to serve a different master.[1] Indeed, in the second century so irksome did some find their obligations that they compounded in advance with a payment of money.[2] There must have been a limit to the amount the patron could demand as compensation for the *operae*, because, as the jurists often expressly state, it was illegal to impose the promise of a large sum of money simply in order to make one's freedman one's debtor for life.[3]

There were other means by which freedmen could become immune from the *operae*. A provision in the *Lex Iulia de maritandis ordinibus* (4 A. D.), probably confirmed by the *Lex Papia Poppaea* (9 A. D.), liberated from the *operae* a freedman who was the father of two free children,[4] and the master was not allowed to prevent him from marrying.[5] In the time of Claudius, when he accorded the privileges of four children to freedwomen who engaged in the corn trade,[6] it is reasonable to suppose that freedmen also in the trade obtained the immunity which was granted to their sex for two children. Nevertheless women secured release from the *operae* much more easily than men did. A woman of fifty years of age was not expected to give further service.[7] A freedwoman who married her patron was *ipso facto* exempt, and indeed if she married another person she was in this case also released, provided the marriage was not against the patron's wishes.[8] It seems to have been understood that, in view of her domestic responsibilities, the mistress of a household could not with reason be called upon to perform other work.

These burdens laid upon the newly freed slave were to

1 *Cod. Iust.* VI. iii. 4.
2 *Cod. Iust.* VI. iii. 1.
3 *Dig.* XXXVIII. i. 32; ii. 1, *pr.*; XLIV. v. 1, § 5.
4 *Dig.* XXXVIII. i. 37, *pr.*
5 *Lex Iulia de maritandis ordinibus*, 4 A. D.; *Dig.* XXXVII. xiv. 6, § 4.
6 Suet. *Cl.* 19; cf. *supra*, p. 44.
7 *Dig.* XXXVIII. i. 35.
8 *Dig.* XXXVIII. i. 48, *pr.*

some extent balanced by limits to the power of the patron and by claims that the freedman had upon him. The freedman had full rights over his property during his life. After twenty years of age he was not under the *tutela* of his patron and so could sell land or spend money as he wished. Some patrons devised a way of circumventing this right which belonged to the freedman. At manumission they might compel the freedman to promise to pay a large sum of money, well knowing that the money never could be paid. The patron's object was to encumber the freedman's liberty with a load of debt,[1] and as his perpetual creditor to possess a moral right to the control of his property. Such promises in the time of the Empire were never allowed to be binding.[2]

In the matter of marriage also, freedmen were safe from the interference of their patrons. At a time when the decline in the population was a vital question as it was in the reign of Augustus, an oath of celibacy was naturally not allowed to be exacted.[3] A patron with his eyes upon the succession to a freedman's property might well have cause to oppose the latter's marriage, but legally his opposition was of no avail. With a freedwoman, however, it is slightly different. She was under the *tutela* of her patron, and a *tutor* might reasonably expect to have some say in the matter. A patron could not force his freedwoman to marry him,[4] but she was at least discouraged from marrying without his consent; for, if she did so, her marriage did not release her from the *operae*.[5] But legally she was certainly free to marry whom she would. This appears from the passages in the Digest[6] where it is stated that, if a freedwoman has married her patron and deserted him, she is not allowed to marry another without his consent;

[1] 'onerandae libertatis causa', *Dig.* XXXVIII. i. 32; XLIV. v. 1, § 5.

[2] *Dig.* XXXVII. xiv. 15.

[3] *Dig.* XXXVII. xiv. 6, § 4; XL. ix. 31.

[4] *Dig.* XXIII. ii. 28–9.

[5] *Dig.* XXXVIII. i. 48, *pr.*

[6] *Lex Iulia de maritandis ordinibus* and *Lex Papia Poppaea*, *Dig.* XXXVIII. xi. 1, § 1; XXIII. ii. 45; XXIV. ii. 11.

if the freedwoman was in general not allowed to marry without her patron's approval, it would not be explicitly stated that in particular her desertion of one who was both her patron and her husband disqualified her from this right.

The freedman could not be accused by his patron of any crime where the punishment was death or exile,[1] and we have seen that, generally speaking, no evidence could be borne unwillingly by the patron against his freedman or *vice versa*.[2] To this law, as indeed to all others, the crime of *maiestas* was a probable exception. Roman law aimed at binding patron and freedman together in what was almost a family bond, but, where the paramount interests of the state were directly concerned, then the bond had to be loosed.

Such were the liberties that the freedman possessed. The hand of the patron was capable of grasping a great deal, but these rights at least were free from it. Further, the freedman or his family had two positive claims upon the patron in return for the many services the latter might exact. According to Modestinus,[3] by the *Lex Aelia Sentia*, the patron, on pain of losing the right to the *operae* and the succession, had to furnish food for his freedman; but, in view of the facts that the freedman was expected to support his patron if the latter fell upon evil days, and that even while performing the *operae* for his patron he might be left to supply his own food, the statement of Modestinus has to be qualified. Two solutions are possible. Perhaps the patron had to supply at manumission some capital, land[4] or permanent employment which could be deemed a means of livelihood for any industrious freedman. Another possibility is that the patron was compelled to

[1] *Dig.* XXXVII. xiv. 10. If the patron transgressed this rule he could not obtain the *bonorum possessio contra tabulas*; i. e. he forfeited his share in the succession to the freedman's estate.

[2] *Dig.* XXII. v. 4.

[3] *Dig.* XXXVIII. ii. 33.

[4] Marquardt, *Privatleben*, ed. of 1886, p. 177, says that the patron probably gave a small plot of land to a freedman in his service.

supply food only if his freedman was in actual want. He had to prevent a freedman of his from dying of starvation, just as the freedman had to support his patron if he had fallen into need; at the same time, no countenance was given to a freedman who wished to be a permanent parasite on his master.

One other obligation was laid on the patron, but it must have been on comparatively rare occasions that he was called upon to fulfil it. If a freedman was the victim of murder or manslaughter, it was the duty of the patron to bring the offender to justice, on pain of losing his share in the succession.[1] If the family of the dead freedman chose to retain his property, a master who had not taken all possible steps to avenge the death was refused by the praetor the right of *bonorum possessio*, which it was the custom to grant to any person whose rightful share in an estate was being withheld.

In these two privileges which were conferred on the freedman we see yet further examples of that idea, still holding the field in the time of the Empire, by which the master of the household not only is the father of his own children, but also is regarded as a fatherly protector of his freedmen. Just as insults and injuries were thought more heinous offences if they were committed against one who was, so to speak, a legal father, so also the patron had to avenge the death of his freedman as if he were his next of kin; just as judicial proceedings between the one and the other were regularly discouraged as damaging the unity of what essentially was considered a family, so, in the case of poverty and indigence, patron had to succour freedman and freedman patron. The two, like father and son, had to stand or fall together.

[1] *Dig.* XXXVIII. ii. 37, § 1.

IV

SOCIAL STATUS OF FREEDMEN

The term *libertini* — a freedman's name — dress — family rights — intermarriage between the orders — criminal law — respect of rank by the government — positions closed to freedmen — taunts which they had to endure — inequality at the dinner table — prejudice not so marked among the lower classes, in the towns of Italy and in the provinces— *libertini* ranked higher than ordinary provincials.

THE newly freed slave had additional difficulties to face on entering free Roman society. Not only was he hampered by obligations to his former master, but in comparison with the free-born he found himself on a distinctly lower social plane, and he laboured under many disabilities which were the heritage of his servile days. Nothing, not the most unselfish patriotism, not the most enlightened public spirit, not the possession of new-won wealth, not even the friendship and confidence of an emperor, could wipe out the original stain of slavery. While a freedman was a *libertus* in relation to his patron, he and his fellows formed a definitely marked-off class called *libertini* in relation to the *ingenui* or free-born.

It may be well to point out here that the old view by which the term *libertini* was held to apply to the sons of freedmen has been completely exploded as far as the imperial age is concerned. Gaius' dogmatic statement[1] '*Ingenui* are those who have been born free; *libertini*, those who have been freed from lawful slavery' is sufficient warrant for the second century A. D. His view is shared by Marcian, Ulpian, Modestinus, and lastly Justinian.[2] Moreover, not only do the jurists imply that some *libertini* have passed through slavery, but they declare the children of freedmen *ingenui*. Tryphoninus takes a case of a female slave who had been freed by testament; here the liberty is only to take effect when she has borne three

[1] Gaius, i. 11: 'Ingenui sunt qui liberi nati sunt, libertini qui ex iusta servitute manumissi sunt'.

[2] *Dig.* XL. xi. 2; I. vii. 46; XL. xi. 5, § 1; Just. *Inst.* i. 5.

children. The slave bears one child first, and then her family is increased by triplets. Tryphoninus asks not which child is 'libertine' but which is 'ingenuous', a question which he answers in favour of the last born.[1]

We may, however, go further back than the period of the Antonines: Seneca, Tacitus and Suetonius all understand by *libertinus* a man who has been freed.[2] Varro says most *libertini* if freed by a municipality take their gentile names from their respective towns,[3] and passages from Cicero and Plautus support our view of the *libertinus*.[4] Even in Livy, who has often been supposed to use *libertini* for the sons of freedmen, some texts have been found in which the term must mean actual ex-slaves.[5]

On the other hand, in the early Republic there is no doubt that *libertinus* signified not the freedman himself but his son. Suetonius gives valuable information when he says Claudius was unaware that in the times of Appius Caecus and for some time after not the persons who were freed but their free-born children were called *libertini*.[6] Some by manipulating the text[7] have made it appear that in the fourth century before Christ the class of *libertini* covered both the freedmen themselves and their sons, whereas the text, as we have it, asserts that only the children of freedmen were so called. But that question does not concern us here. Whether the sons of freedmen in those early times were the only class that bore the name *libertini* or whether they shared the epithet with their parents, it is certain that later in Republican history they lost the degrading appellation, and it was applied solely to those who had actually passed through slavery.

Accordingly the Roman freedman is not only the

[1] *Dig*. I. v. 15.

[2] Seneca, *De Vita Beata*, 24; *De Benef*. iii. 28; Tac. *Ann*. xii. 53; Suet. *Aug*. 25.

[3] Varro, *De Ling. Lat*. viii. 82, 83.

[4] Cicero, *In Verr*. II. i. 47; Plaut. *Mil. Glor*. 961–2.

[5] Livy, xxxix. 9–13; xlv. 15.

[6] 'Ignarus temporibus Appi et deinceps aliquandiu libertinos dictos non ipsos qui manu emitterentur sed ingenuos ex his procreatos.' Suet. *Cl*. 24.

[7] i. e., by changing *non ipsos* into *non solum ipsos*.

libertus of his patron; he is also a *libertinus* as opposed to an *ingenuus*. He is a member of a class of men and women who, in virtue of having once been slaves, are for ever branded with the stigma of their former condition.

What then were the particular manifestations of this general distinction between the free-born and the freed? In the first place, it showed itself in every individual freedman's name. The freedman never recorded the name of his tribe on inscriptions; that was a privilege belonging to the free-born. After being freed, the slave would generally take the *praenomen* and the *nomen* of his patron, while he would retain his servile name as his *cognomen*. Thus Tiro, the slave of Marcus Tullius Cicero, on attaining his liberty became *Marcus Tullius Tiro*. But whereas free-born citizens recorded their fathers' names on inscriptions, as for instance *M. Tullius M. f. Cicero*, the freedman could not analogously inscribe his father's name. All he could do was to use the name of his patron, his legal father, while at the same time he had to record the fact that he was his freedman and not his son. Thus Tiro's official title was *Marcus Tullius Marci libertus Tiro* or, in the usual abbreviated form, *M. Tullius M. l. Tiro*. But, as women had no *praenomen*, a convention had to be devised for the name of a freedman whose patron was a woman. Unless the mistress was a member of the imperial household, not her name but only her sex was recorded on the inscriptions of her freedmen. Sometimes the words *mulieris libertus* or *mul. l.*, 'freedman of a woman', are found;[1] but more often another method was devised. *Gaius*, probably the commonest Latin *praenomen*, was turned into the feminine, and the name *Gaia*, thus formed, was the regular epigraphic representation of a woman. When abbreviated the words *Gaiae libertus* would read *C. l.*, which is indistinguishable from the contraction for *Gaii libertus*. The *C.* is therefore reversed to reveal the feminine gender, and the epitaphs of those who owe their freedom to a woman are generally of the type *Sex. Fonteius Ɔ. l. Trophimus*.[2]

[1] *Mul. lib.*, *C. I. L.* ii. 2138.

[2] *I. L. S.* 3308.

A freedwoman, like an ingenuous woman, had two names. She took the gentile name of her patron and her own slave name, and, like the male ex-slave, had inscribed on her epitaph the fact that she was the freedwoman of so and so.[1]

To these general rules there are a number of exceptions. Firstly, a freedman sometimes bore four names. Often this second *cognomen* ended in *-anus*, and perpetuated the memory of a master who had sold him to the man from whom he subsequently received his freedom, or recorded the fact that he had served another slave as his substitute or *vicarius*. Thus *T. Flavius Aug. lib. Phoebus Othonianus*[2] had belonged to Otho, but with the rest of Otho's property he had passed into the hands of Vespasian by whom he had been manumitted. Similarly *Agrypnus Caesaris Aug. Maecenatianus*[3] was a slave of Augustus to whom he had probably been left by Maecenas. If he had obtained his liberty, he would have been called *C. Iulius Aug. lib. Agrypnus Maecenatianus*.

Quite often influential slaves in important houses owned other slaves as part of their *peculium*. These under-slaves were called *vicarii*, as they performed some of the duties assigned to their owners. More often than not they would be relinquished by their servile masters, when the latter were freed, as part of the price of liberty, and if they subsequently attained their freedom they would preserve not only the names of their patrons but also those of the slaves whom they had previously served. Thus *Ti. Claudius Epictetus*[4] was once a *vicarius* of Nero's mistress Acte. Later he became part of Nero's estate and was called *Epictetus Acteanus*. Finally, on being freed by Nero, he assumed his imperial master's *praenomen* and *nomen*. So also *Myrtilus Caesaris Diogenianus*[5] was a slave in the

[1] e. g., *Aurelia C. l. Nais*, *I. L. S.* 7500.

[2] *C. I. L.* xiv. 2060; cf. vi. 99: *Gemellus Aug. l. Poppaeanus.*

[3] *C. I. L.* vi. 4032.

[4] *C. I. L.* vi. 15027; cf. *I. L. S.* 3896: *Carpus Aug. lib. Pallantianus.*

[5] *C. I. L.* vi. 3942; cf. *Diognetus Ti. Aug. ser. Alypianus* and *Flavius Aug. lib. Myrtilus Ianuarianus*, *I. L. S.* 1821, 7349.

imperial household who had acted as *vicarius* to Diogenes, another of Caesar's slaves.

Freedmen who rose in the world sometimes adopted a fourth name. Actors, if they received a complimentary name from the Emperor or the public, would keep it as an advertisement;[1] or those who entered some dignified profession would despise the humility of their common servile names and add one more suitable to their respectability. Such was the case of the physician, P. Decimius Eros.[2] Eros was the commonest Greek name among slaves and freedmen, and the vanity of Decimius revolted against it. He did not succeed in suppressing altogether his slave name, but he added the fine-sounding Roman *cognomen* of Merula to his name.

A second exception is that freedmen are found bearing names other than those of their patrons. *P. Annaeus Q. l. Epicadus, Sex. Marius L. l., Sex. Raecius M. l. Alexander*[3] may be cited as examples. Apart from the fact that the regular custom must have varied at times owing to the caprice of master or slave,[4] it may be suggested that when a slave had been freed by two or more masters he might take the *praenomen* of one and the *nomen* of another, and that in fideicommissary manumission, though taking one of his names from the heir who legally freed him, he might take another from his late master in grateful memory of the man to whose suggestion he owed his freedom.

One or two other irregularities are sometimes found. The patron might be designated by his *cognomen* instead of by his *praenomen*. Invariably imperial freedmen call

[1] e. g., *L. Aurelius Apolaustus Memfius*, where *Apolaustus* ('Delightful') is the name given him for his histrionic talents, *I. L. S.* 5190. On the other hand it may be that Memfius called himself *Apolaustus* in memory of another celebrated actor of the same name who flourished during the reign of Trajan, *I. L. S.* 5184.

[2] *I. L. S.* 5369 = 7812.

[3] *I. L. S.* 7166; *C. I. L.* iii. 1784; xiv. 3790.

[4] e. g., when Atticus freed Dionysius, he called him *M. Pomponius Dionysius*, *Marcus* after Cicero and *Pomponius* after himself. *Ad Att.* IV. xv. 1. Similarly Atticus calls another freedman *T. Caecilius Eutychides*, the gentilician name being derived from his uncle. IV. xv. 1.

themselves *Augusti* (not *Gaii*, *Tiberii*, *Titi*, &c.) *liberti*. This custom extended into aristocratic families. *T. Statilius Tauri l. Antiochus*, *L. Iunius Silani l. Paris*, *M. Aemilius Lepidi l. Clymenus* are only three of many examples.[1] Even the lower classes sometimes liked to adopt the practice. A. Septicius Alexander calls himself *Salvii libertus* and Q. Publicius Ingenuus *Felicis libertus*.[2] Further, there were occasions on which the freedman did not inscribe his full name. Now he appears without his *praenomen*, now he lacks a *cognomen*, now though not a slave he only bears his *cognomen*. Often these omissions would simply be due to neglect or caprice, but sometimes, when a name had to be scratched on to an urn, a lamp or a pipe, one or even two of the freedman's names had to be sacrificed for lack of space.

The above is a brief account of the regulations concerning the names of a freedman.[3] It will be seen that he suffered in relation to the ingenuous citizen in three ways. He was not allowed to record the name of his tribe. Secondly, while a free-born citizen proudly put on record his father's name and signified the relation he bore to him, the freedman suffered perforce the humiliation of inscribing the name of his patron and revealing the fact that he had once been his slave. No wonder many freedmen found it convenient to omit those ignominious letters *M. l.*, *C. l.*, *T. l.*, &c. on their tombstones.[4] Thirdly, the most tell-tale evidence of a man's servile extraction was the *cognomen*, which in most cases was identical with his servile appellation. The customs in accordance with which the freedman recorded his status and omitted his tribe in

[1] *I. L. S.* 7622, 4973; *C. I. L.* vi. 11056.

[2] *I. L. S.* 7617, 6683; cf. 1837: *Papia Erotis l.*

[3] For a full account of the matter, see Lemonnier, *Condition privée des affranchis*, pp. 167–81 and 304–18, from which a large part of this section is drawn.

[4] Inscriptions show that this was frequently done. In many cases a name includes neither the designation *f.* (*filius*) nor *l.* (*libertus*), but the mention of *patronus*, *conservus*, *collibertus*, or *contubernalis* reveals the man's true status: e. g. *C. I. L.* vi. 10689; x. 1549, 1996, 6037.

formally naming himself bear testimony now to the rigid caste division that separated the free-born and the freed, yet they did not seriously affect the individual freedman during his lifetime; for they could only take effect in legal documents and in inscriptions. But the *cognomen* was the name by which he was known in society. He could not make a livelihood without revealing his *cognomen*. This was usually the name he had borne as a slave, and in Rome seven out of every ten slaves had Greek names; while the number of Greek-named freedmen and descendants of freedmen exceeded several times that of *peregrini* from the East.[1] Accordingly the first thing that a Greek name suggested was servile origin or extraction. Moreover, even those freedmen who bore Latin names were not invested with really ingenuous *cognomina*. *Gracchus*, *Marcellus*, *Celer*, *Cinna*, *Flaccus*, were never, or at any rate very rarely, the names of slaves. Slaves, on being freed, passed into society, if not with Greek *cognomina*, at least with names that suggested or even betrayed a servile origin. *Successus*, *Dama*, *Apparatus*, *Primitivus*, *Primigenius*, *Optatus*, *Felix*, *Fortunatus*, *Amatus*, were shunned not only by aristocratic Romans but also by poorer citizens of the native Latin stock. They were thought peculiarly fitting to slaves; indeed some are perhaps nothing more than Latin equivalents for names borne by Greek slaves. *Optatus*, *Felix*, *Fortunatus* and *Amatus*, for instance, may simply be manipulations of *Erastos*, *Eudaemon*, *Eutyches* and *Philetos*. Thus oppressed with the burden of a servile name, it was hard for a freedman to pass as a man of ingenuous Roman birth. How he still felt the incubus of a past slavery, how his spirit revolted against the slur to which his origin exposed him, is shown by his efforts to start afresh in life with a new name. As long as intimate relations continued with his patron, it would probably be difficult to rid himself of the name which he had borne in servitude; but, if his patron were dead, or if he were separated by several miles from him, it is quite conceivable that a freedman

[1] Cf. p. 112 n.

could pose as an ingenuous citizen. One of Suetonius' famous grammarians, Pasicles, succeeded in assuming the name of Pansa which had belonged to a consul of 43 B.C.[1] Similarly one of Martial's epigrams is directed against a freedman who, objecting to his name of Cinnamus, assumes that of Cinna, which ought to indicate blue blood in every one of his veins.[2]

However skilfully they attempted disguise, freedmen must have been many times detected, as Cinnamus was by Martial. Yet if they failed to break down the social barrier in their own generation, they often took good care that no ignominious name should hinder their children's chances of success. Very many freedmen parents bearing Greek names themselves gave their children Latin names. An examination of the inscriptions where the names of both father and son appear yields interesting conclusions. The son of Aristaeus becomes Silvanus; Philodoxus is the father of Proculus; Eutyches calls his son Maximus.[3] Indeed after counting all the instances where parent and child are mentioned, Professor Frank[4] has found that fathers with Greek names were remarkably prone to give Latin names to their children and that in one generation the percentage of Greek *cognomina* sinks from 64 to 38. The actual statistics are as follows:

	Greek Cognomen.		*Latin Cognomen.*	
Father	859		488	
	Greek	*Latin*	*Greek*	*Latin*
Son	460	399	53	435

Some of the fifty-three cases where a Latin reverts to a Greek name in the second generation are explained by the fact that either the mother's name is Greek or the

[1] Suet. *Gramm.* 18.

[2] Mart. vi. 17: 'Cinnam, Cinname, te iubes vocari.
non est hic, rogo, Cinna, barbarismus?
tu si Furius ante dictus esses,
Fur ista ratione dicereris.'

[3] *C. I. L.* ii. 496; xiv. 407, 3359.

[4] *Op. cit.*

son's gentile name differs from that of the father who is probably a step-father.

These figures show that, though the freedman's efforts to gain equality generally failed of their object in his own case, they were remarkably successful in that of his children. *Silvanus*, *Proculus* and *Maximus* are not names which at once cast suspicion on their bearer; they belong rather to men of Roman stock such as those who entered the cohorts of the praetorian guard. Freedmen often chose their children's names well, and, in banishing the Greek *cognomen* from the family tree, took good care that the Latin substitute did not also betray servile extraction.

This prejudice against Greek and servile names reveals how freedmen felt that they were despised as ex-slaves, how they realized that equality was not obtained by manumission alone, and how bitterly they resented the slur cast upon them by free-born citizens, who might themselves be sprung from libertine ancestors at no very distant period in the past. The inequality shows itself further in the matter of dress. It is true that they were allowed to wear the *toga*, but they were distinguished from the rest of society by a close-fitting cap called the *pilleus* which all *libertini* were supposed to wear.[1] It is not known on what occasions it had to be worn; it is hardly probable that freedmen wore it regularly. We know from Dionysius of Halicarnassus[2] that they wore it at their patron's funeral, and this suggests that it was part of a ceremonial dress. Freedmen would therefore appear in the *pilleus*, it is likely, at those processions in which they attended their patron as his clients.

In early times there was another distinction in the matter of dress. It was the custom in Rome to dress children under sixteen years of age in the *toga praetexta* or the gown with coloured border which curule magistrates and senators wore. This privilege was at first denied to *libertini*, but probably the regulation was so consistently dis-

[1] Liv. xlv. 44, *sub fin.*; Polyb. XXX. xvi. 3; Appian, *Bell. Mithr.* 2.
[2] iv. 24.

regarded that in the time of the Empire no distinction was observed.[1]

The inequalities with regard to family rights which subsisted till the second century A.D. arose not so much from a prejudice against freedmen, as they were the logical outcome of the ancient law of slavery. The slave had no personal rights, and therefore the marriages he might contract with fellow-slaves were ranked as nothing more than cohabitation. In Latin a special term, *contubernium*, was applied to slave marriages. The master might recognize these or not as he pleased; legal compulsion in the matter there was none. Of course, a son born to a freedman after he had been freed was his own and was under the *patria potestas*. But until the second century the family formed by a slave during servitude was not under his *patria potestas*, even when all the members of the family had won their liberty. If freed by their master, they were under his patronage; if bought by their father and freed by him, they were not his family but his freedmen.

Yet apparently a certain amount of recognition was always accorded even to slave marriages. No objection seems to have been made to the use in inscriptions of terms like *coniunx*, *uxor*, *filius*, *filia*, where the marriage is no more than a *contubernium*.[2] Relations such as father and daughter, son and mother, uncle and sister's daughter, even if they are the result of a *contubernium*, are nevertheless a bar against marriage;[3] and, as seen above, connexions formed in slavery are valid causes of manumission which a master under twenty can plead before the Council.[4]

The recognition of the *contubernium* in certain cases could not but extend into other spheres. Papinian and jurists of the early third century recognized the same regulations in a freedman's family as in any other. The same respect for the head of the family was enjoined, whether

[1] Macrob. *Saturn.* I. vi. 12 and 13.

[2] Lemonnier, *op. cit.*, p. 189. See inscriptions in *columbaria* for examples: *C. I. L.* vi. 3926–8397.

[3] *Dig.* XXIII. ii. 8; ii. 14, § 2; Just. *Inst.* I. x. 10.

[4] G. i. 19.

the family was ingenuous or libertine. If the whole family was freed by a master, naturally they were all under his patronage, though at the same time it was recognized, at least from the Antonine age, that they were legally a family, and that a son born in slavery was no less the freedman's legitimate child than one born after manumission.[1] Much easier was legal recognition when there was only one authority, and when the privileges of patron and father were vested in the same person, as was the case when a slave after being freed redeemed his wife and children from servitude. By early Roman law they were merely the freedmen of him who had first obtained his liberty, for he it was who bought them as slaves from their former masters and then freed them. But in this case the same man was patron and father, and the legalizing of his paternal as well as patronal rights was not burdened by the difficulty of conflicting authorities.

That the redemption of his family from slavery was the first object of many a newly freed slave we cannot doubt. In some inscriptions we find the words *filio et liberto*, *patri et patrono*, *frater et libertus* and *dominae et sorori*, which can only mean that some one after being freed has devoted his or her energies and resources to the rescue of a relative from servitude.[2]

With regard to intermarriage[3] between *ingenui* and *libertini* Roman law seems remarkably generous, considering that Orientalization of the population was one of the problems which Augustus made most strenuous efforts to solve. Throughout the Republic there had existed a prejudice, amounting almost to prohibition, against intermarriage between the two classes;[4] but when

[1] Even Trebatius Testa, a jurist of Cicero's time, appears to have recognized this; but Labeo, who lived during the reign of Augustus, made a distinction between a son born in slavery and one born after manumission. Javolenus of the time of Antoninus Pius and all subsequent jurists recognized children in both categories as legitimate. *Dig.* XXVIII. viii. 11.

[2] e. g., *C. I. L.* xiv. 3360; iii. 2371; v. 4389; *I. L. S.* 8388.

[3] Special regulations existed in Egypt. See Appendix V.

[4] Livy, xxxix. 19. A senatorial decision is necessary to allow the freedwoman Hispala Fecennia to marry a free-born citizen.

Augustus came to the fore and commenced his campaign against the influx of foreign blood into free society it occasions some surprise to note that he recognized as legitimate all marriages between *ingenui* and *libertini*, provided the free-born party was not a member of a senatorial family.[1] It needs no explanation why Augustus, in his anxiety to preserve intact the aristocratic order, introduced this exception; but why did he allow intermarriage at all? Probably the decline in the Roman stock had reached such a point that reforming legislators were glad enough if pure-blooded Romans would marry at all. Besides, according to Cassius Dio,[2] among the higher classes, for instance the knights, the number of males was greatly in excess of that of females. To remove this obstacle to frequent marriage he says that Augustus allowed unions between freedwomen and free-born males except in senatorial families. There is no doubt that he also authorized marriages between *libertini* and *ingenuae*,[3] although these latter did not receive equal encouragement. The Council of Manumission always allowed the master's plea that he was freeing his female slave in order to marry her; a mistress, however, was only permitted to plead this cause in certain specific circumstances.[4]

Marriage was of considerable frequency between *ingenui* and *libertinae*, and in especial between patrons and freedwomen.[5] But in the inverse sense, between female patrons and freedmen, intermarriage, as we have seen, did not receive the same countenance from official quarters. In the nature of things it was regarded with disfavour,

[1] *Dig.* XXIII. ii. 44; *Cod. Iust.* V. iv. 28, *pr.* [2] Dio, liv. 16.

[3] *Dig.* XXIII. ii. 16, *pr.* 'Oratione divi Marci cavetur ut si senatoris filia libertino nupsisset, nec nuptiae essent; quam et senatusconsultum secutum est.' *Senatoris filia* would not be specifically inserted if marriage with *libertini* was refused to all free-born women. Marriage between *patrona* and *libertus* was not forbidden till the reign of Septimius Severus, *Cod. Iust.* V. iv. 3.

[4] See *supra*, ch. II, on the Council for Manumission, pp. 33–4.

[5] e. g., *I. L. S.* 7063, 'liberta et coniunx'; 1519, 2049, 8219, 'patronus et coniunx'; 1552, 7413, 7488, 'patronus idem coniunx'.

since it set in opposition the rights of the patron and those of the husband. Finally Septimius Severus forbade such unions altogether.[1] Though some examples have been found in inscriptions,[2] they were never of such frequent occurrence as the corresponding unions between patrons and freedwomen.

Among the aristocracy there always lingered the prejudice inherited from Republican days against marriages with the freedman class. True, legal marriage between the two orders was common, but the less lawful bond of concubinage was recognized as the type *par excellence* of such unions.[3] Few things could better illustrate the sentiments of contempt and hostility that existed among the upper classes against those who had passed through slavery. Roman law realized that libertine marriages were necessary if the numbers of citizens were to be maintained; and it acquiesced in the necessary course. But it acquiesced with a very bad grace. While urging a citizen to produce children for the state, and pointing out that freedwomen were there to supplement the dearth of ingenuous women, it bade him remember his own status and begged to remind him that, though a freedwoman might be necessary, concubinage would accomplish the desired results without compromising his dignity.

In the case of senatorial families the law was more pressing. It did not gently restrain, it sternly forbade. Up to the time of Marcus Aurelius the marriage once contracted was allowed, though the whole family of the offender lost its senatorial status. In the time of Marcus Aurelius even this penalty was not considered severe enough and the marriage was declared null and void.[4] But concubinage between the senatorial and libertine classes was always allowed,[5] and even emperors were not above stooping to concubinage with their freedwomen.

[1] *Cod. Iust.* V. iv. 3.

[2] e. g., *C. I. L.* xiv. 881; *I. L. S.* 8259.

[3] *Dig.* XXV. vii. 1, *pr.* 'Quippe cum honestius sit patrono libertam concubinam quam matremfamilias habere.'

[4] *Dig.* XXIII. i. 16; ii. 16, *pr.*

[5] *Dig.* XXIV. i. 3, § 1.

V. TOMBSTONE OF REGINA, FREEDWOMAN AND WIFE OF BARATES

Public Library, South Shields. Erected by Barates of Palmyra in memory of his British freedwoman and wife, who is represented holding needlework in her left hand and opening a box with her right; a workbasket is at her left side. The Palmyrene characters below the Latin have been rendered: 'Regina, freedwoman of Barates, alas!' Cf. *Archaeologia Aeliana*, new (2nd) series, x. 239 ff.

Vespasian and Caenis, and Antoninus Pius and some unknown woman, were united in this relation which, though illegitimate, was not considered dishonourable.[1] In exceptional cases, however, even marriage might be permitted by a special dispensation of the Emperor. Felix, the freedman procurator of Judaea, married Drusilla granddaughter of Antony and Cleopatra, and thus became connected with the imperial family.[2] Later Agaclytus, freedman of Verus, was allowed by his patron to marry the wife of Libo, a senator and cousin to the Emperors.[3]

A further distinction between the free-born and the freed appears in respect of criminal law. One of the fundamental rights of a Roman citizen was his exemption from torture. Freedmen were denied this privilege. They could be tortured at the investigation of crimes of which they were suspected, but, with the probable exception of impeachments for *maiestas*, they never had to bear witness under torture if their patron was on trial.[4] On the other hand, this barbarous mode of inquisition was stringently employed if their patron had been assassinated. The *Senatusconsultum Silanianum* (10 A.D.) made it obligatory in the case of slaves, and in 57 A.D. a *Senatusconsultum Claudianum* ruled that those whose freedom was provided for in the will of the murdered master were to be deemed slaves and not freedmen.[5] These regulations were extended by Trajan. Even slaves who already had been freed, whether formally or informally, were to be questioned under torture in the case of a murdered master, but probably only if they were living under his roof at the time of the murder.[6]

The further question arises whether the freedmen of a murdered patron were to be put to death. It is well known that when a slave killed his master all slaves of

[1] Dio, L. xvi. 14; Suet. *Vesp.* 3; *Hist. Aug.*, *Anton. Pius*, 8.
[2] Tac. *Hist.* v. 9; Josephus, *Ant. Iud.* vii. 1.
[3] *Hist. Aug.*, *Verus*, 9.
[4] *Dig.* XLVIII. xviii. 1, § 9; *Cod. Iust.* IX. xli. 6.
[5] *Dig.* XXIX. v. 3, § 16.
[6] *Dig.* XXIX. v. 10, § 1; v. 11.

the household were liable to the death penalty; after a debate in the Senate this law was actually put into effect in Nero's reign despite the protests of a more enlightened populace.[1] But were freedmen included in the penalty? In the case which is cited above, no doubt the slaves who were to receive their liberty in their master's will underwent the extreme rigour of the law in accordance with the *Senatusconsultum Claudianum*. Their fate was one of the hardest that man has ever been called upon to suffer. At the moment when they were on the threshold of freedom, the moment to which all their hopes and ambitions had aspired, not only liberty but life itself was snatched away from them. But the freedmen of the house, who were quite as likely as the slaves to be accomplices in the crime, were not exposed to this penalty unless their guilt was proved. It was indeed proposed in the Senate that they should be banished, but Nero refused his sanction to the motion, which was accordingly dropped.

Jurists and politicians, however, still continued to be puzzled by the question what was the proper fate of freedmen in domestic service if their master were murdered. It seemed unreasonable to put all the slaves to death, if at the same time every freedman was to go free. In Trajan's reign, as we have seen, it was directed that freedmen living under the roof of the murdered man should be tortured for information, and perhaps at the same time injunctions were issued which made them liable to punishment and decided its nature. About the same period occurred the case of Afranius Dexter who was found dead, a victim either to murder or to suicide. Pliny[2] mentions a debate in the Senate on the question of his freedmen. Some were for acquittal, others for banishment to an island, and the rest for the punishment of death. Which cause ultimately triumphed is not told. Pliny's correspondent knew the result of the trial, and like knowledge is assumed for the subsequent reader of his letters. All that is revealed to us is that the motion for the death penalty did not win the

[1] Tac. *Ann.* xiv. 42–5. [2] *Ep.* viii. 14.

day. Those in favour of acquittal greatly outnumbered each of the other parties, but we are not informed what was decided when those in favour of death voted with the advocates of exile.

There are two judicial or quasi-judicial incidents in the first century which show in clear colours the general prejudice of government and society against freedmen. In Tiberius' reign the celebrators of Jewish and Egyptian rites made themselves objectionable in Rome and the Senate decided on strong measures.[1] The free-born among the offenders were threatened with exile from Italy if they persisted in their undesirable practices; freedmen, however, were not given this chance; they were exiled at once, and were not even allowed to choose their place of banishment. Sardinian brigandage had for some time been a thorn in the flesh of the imperial authorities. The offending freedmen, about 4000 in number, were formed into a brigade for the unpleasant task of suppressing the robbers. If they should perish at the hands of their enemies or succumb to the notorious Sardinian climate, the government comforted itself with the reflection that it could well afford to lose them.[2]

The year of the four emperors supplies another incident typifying the hostility which freedmen had to encounter. When Otho succeeded to his ill-omened throne, he at once took vengeance on those favourites of Galba whose crimes had excited the public wrath. Of these, two were outstanding, Laco, the equestrian prefect of the praetorian guard, and Icelus, the confidential freedman of the late emperor. Each of these richly deserved death, but, while the new emperor feared to execute a Roman knight publicly, he felt he would make a good impression if an

[1] Tac. *Ann.* ii. 85; Jos. *Ant. Iud.* XVIII. iii. 4–5. Jewish proselytizers were especially successful with women, whom sometimes they persuaded to become temple prostitutes. It was this conduct on the part of some who professed Judaism that led to the comprehensive punishment in Tiberius' reign. Cf. Heidel, *A. J. P.*, 1920, p. 38 ff.

[2] 'Vile damnum,' Tac. *Ann.* ii. 85.

insolent freedman suffered the extreme penalty before all eyes. Accordingly Laco's ostensible punishment was exile, though in fact a soldier was sent after him to dispatch him secretly. But 'Being a freedman', says Tacitus, 'Icelus Marcianus was executed in public.'[1]

Besides these inequalities, an ambitious freedman found a number of disabilities barring his rise in public life. If he wished to enter the army, he found the best paid and most honourable regiment, the praetorian guard, closed to him. The legions and the urban cohorts also were reserved for free birth.[2] If his aspiration was to serve a time-honoured Roman deity, here too he would be told that a Roman priesthood did not recruit its members from ex-slaves. Let him be an attendant on the priest or serve one of his own strange deities imported from the East. Even in the towns of Italy and the provinces he was barred, except in Julius Caesar's colonies,[3] from entering the local Senate; so persistently did his past cling to him. *A fortiori* he was excluded from the senatorial and equestrian nobility at Rome. Even the sons of freedmen were declared inadmissible to knighthood by a *senatusconsultum* in 23 A.D.,[4]

[1] Tac. *Hist.* i. 46: 'In Marcianum Icelum ut in libertum palam animadversum.'

[2] On critical occasions freedmen might be enrolled in the army. According to Appian, *B. C.* I. xlix. 2, the Social War produced the first instance. Some imperial *auxilia* were recruited from freedmen.

[3] Julius Caesar seems to have had more sympathy with the aspirations of freedmen than either Augustus or Tiberius. Freedmen formed the nucleus of his colony at Corinth (Strabo, VIII. vi. 23), and no doubt in other cases bulked large among his colonists. Where the freedman predominated it was impossible to cut him off from municipal office. In two Caesarian colonies therefore we find freedmen *duoviri*, in another we find a freedman aedile (*I. L. S.* 5320; 1945), and the *Lex Coloniae Genetivae Iuliae*, the charter of Caesar's colony at Urso in Spain, declares (§ 105) that libertinity is no bar to the decurionate. Probably this was the rule in all colonies of the Dictator Caesar. (See *Ephem. Epig.* ii., p. 132, and Mommsen's note there; also *I. L. S.* 6087 and E. G. Hardy, 'Three Spanish Charters', p. 49.)

[4] Plin. *N. H.* xxxiii. 32. This decree of Tiberius' reign was of no effect as far as the gold ring was concerned, but probably it prevented the grant of the *equus publicus* to men of libertine parentage. See appendix II.

although previously, under Augustus, Vedius Pollio, a son of freed parents, had attained to equestrian rank.[1] Some relaxation of this rule came from that incorrigible friend of freedmen, the Emperor Claudius. He allowed freedmen's sons to be adopted by knights and to make their way into the Senate.[2] Naturally such indulgence produced a reaction. Nero reverted to the old system,[3] and it was only the grandsons of freedmen that finally emerged into full equality with the free-born. There are, however, one or two individual exceptions. Under the Republic, P. Furius, the son of a freedman, became tribune of the *plebs*; prominent in the Marian party, he was the inexorable opponent of Metellus Numidicus' recall.[4] C. Thoranius, tribune in 25 B.C., was the son of a freedman and was not ashamed to give his father a tribune's seat beside himself in the theatre.[5] Another freedman's son became praetor about the end of the first century A.D., but, unlike Thoranius, so far forgot his servile origin as to make his haughty cruelty intolerable to his own slaves, by whom he was eventually murdered.[6] In 174 A.D. Pertinax, whose father was a *libertinus*, reached the consulship in virtue of his military achievements and excited the utmost horror in society; men quoted the line of Euripides: 'Such things are wrought by war's foolhardy course'.[7] Their invectives against the times were probably stronger when the same man became Emperor nearly twenty years after.

Apart from legal disabilities, the freedman had to contend against various unwritten prejudices, and many a time some self-made man, proud of his rise from nothingness to what he thought was respectability, must have writhed under the gibes and sneers of the free-born. Freed-

1 Dio, liv. 23.
2 Suet. *Claud.* 24.
3 Suet. *Nero*, 15.
4 App. *B. C.* I. xxxiii. 2.
5 Dio, liii. 27: *καί τις Γάϊος Θοράνιος αἰτίαν ἀγαθὴν ἔσχεν, ὅτι δημαρχῶν τὸν πατέρα, καίπερ ἐξελεύθερόν τινος ὄντα, ἔς τε τὸ θέατρον ἐσήγαγε καὶ ἐν τῷ δημαρχικῷ βάθρῳ παρεκαθίσατο.*
6 Pliny, *Epp.* iii. 14.
7 Dio, lxxi. 22: *τοιαῦθ' ὁ τλήμων πόλεμος ἐξεργάζεται.* Cf. Eur. *Suppl.* 119.

men enjoying wealth and prosperity always presented a repulsive sight to the writers of the Silver Age.[1] Rich and ostentatious freedmen are reminded that servile birth is no birth at all. Martial[2] with evident relish tells a certain Diodorus that, however sumptuously he may celebrate his birthday, no one supposes that he ever was born, free birth being the only kind of birth that really matters. Similarly he gibes at another freedman, who is evidently obtaining privileges for his possession of children. He may get all the rights of a father of seven children, but his parentage is servile, and therefore for society he has no father and mother at all.

> O Zoilus, get thy rights as sire
> Of seven children free,
> So long as mother and father
> Shall ne'er be given thee![3]

However, it must not be supposed that freedmen were incapable of returning the contempt. They had worked their way up from the ranks and were proud of their progress; for rich dandies who never worked with brain or hand they must often have conceived a most intense scorn. A friend of Trimalchio speaks of his rise to freedom as an achievement worth achieving; 'as for being born free, it's as easy as saying "come along," '[4] is his contemptuous conclusion. But retaliation did not give equality, which was what many a freedman must have yearned for in vain.

The caste division was noticeable even in ordinary hospitality. At a dinner party there were often three grades, and the fare was most generous for the highest and most frugal for the lowest rank. Naturally the lowest grade was occupied by the freedmen among the guests.

[1] Cf. *infra*, Pliny's indignation at the insolence of Pallas, *Ep.* viii. 6.

[2] Mart. x. 27, 4. 'Nemo tamen natum te, Diodore, putat.'

[3] xi. 12. 'Ius tibi natorum vel septem, Zoile, detur,
Dum matrem nemo det tibi, nemo patrem.'
See also ii. 29; xi. 37.

[4] Petr. *Sat.* 57: 'Enatavi; haec sunt vera athla; nam in ingenuum nasci tam facile est quam "accede istoc".'

Pliny the Younger, who was of a less exclusive spirit, partook of the same food and at the same table as his freedmen; and his guests fared alike, whether illustrious or obscure.[1] Augustus excluded freedmen from the imperial board altogether, a course which saved the freedmen the humiliation of being present 'to be seen and not heard,' but which on the contrary was thought more hostile to *libertini* than the usual custom.[2]

If nobles and intellectuals alike despised the ex-slave, he found nevertheless a more genial welcome among the lower classes. During the early Empire, the proletariat was filled to such an extent by freedmen and their descendants, that, while some may have found contempt for the freedman a convenient way of hiding their own servile extraction, such feeling cannot have become at all general. In the trade *collegia* slaves, freedmen and free-born mingle freely with one another, and there never seems to have been any line of cleavage between the *ingenui* and their colleagues of lower rank.

Moreover, in the municipalities of Italy and in the provinces even the upper classes did not look upon freedmen with such heartfelt contempt as in Rome. The Roman spirit lost much of its exclusiveness when it left the confines of the capital. Prominent freedmen are honoured in a way which would scandalize Roman sentiment. At Suessa, C. Titius Chresimus celebrates games in honour of Antoninus Pius, is given a special seat in the theatre, is allowed the use of the municipal water-supply in his house and is granted the privileges of the local Senate. His son is to enter the Senate without paying the usual honorarium.[3] An imperial freedman is granted the decora-

[1] *Ep.* ii. 6. [2] Suet. *Aug.* 74.

[3] *I. L. S.* 6296: 'C. Titio Chresimo Aug. $\overline{II}$. Huic ordo decurionum quod pro salute et indulgentia imp. Antonini Pii Felicis Aug. et ex voluntate populi munus familiae gladiatoriae ex pecunia sua diem privatum secundum dignitatem coloniae ediderit, honorem biselli quo quis optimo exemplo in colonia Suessa habuit, et ut aquae digitus in domo eius flueret commodisque publicis ac si decurio frueretur, et Titio Chresimo filio eius ob merita patris honorem decurionatus gratuitum decrevit.' It

tions of a municipal senator at Puteoli for his constant interest in the city.[1] C. Silius Felix is voted a funeral at the public expense, and his son is given the title of *decurio et duumvir*, honours corresponding in the *municipia* to those of senator and consul at Rome.[2] At Formiae a freedman waxes so bold as to dedicate an inscription to a knight with the words *amico incomparabili*, and his friend is no ordinary knight. He had been commander of the smiths, cohort-commander, military tribune, imperial procurator and patron of the colony of Minturnae.[3] At Rome a knight with such honours as these would never have allowed a freedman to use the familiar term 'friend'. Similarly in the provinces, while the rule debarring *libertini* from the municipal Senate was faithfully observed, individual freedmen who had conferred some benefit on the city were often honoured with the senatorial decorations.[4] Two Spanish inscriptions supply examples of how freedmen were granted the utmost honours that could legally be bestowed on men of their station.[5]

There is another consideration to set against the disabilities of freedmen and the contempt they had to endure from literary and aristocratic circles. Whatever their social inferiority to free-born citizens in Rome and Italy, they were in a higher grade than the conquered provincials. Freedmen in Rome had tasted Roman civilization

is practically certain that Chresimus was a freedman. Had he been free-born, he would have been given a seat in the municipal Senate and not merely accorded the privileges without the name of senator.

[1] *I. L. S.* 1678: 'Aurelio Symphoro Aug. lib. oficiali (*sic*) veteri a memoria et a diplomatibus, exornato ornament. decurionalibus, ordo splendidissim. civi ob amorem et instantiam erga patriam civesque.'

[2] *C. I. L.* xiv. 415. The son of Felix, however, preferred to defray the funeral costs himself. 'C. Silio Epaphrae l. Felici Maiori, Augustali. Hunc d(ecuriones) f(unere) p(ublico) efferundum cens(uerunt). Nerva filius honore usus impensam remisit.'

[3] *I. L. S.* 6295. 'Praefectus fabrum, praefectus cohortis, tribunus militum, procurator Augusti, patronus coloniae Minturnensium.'

[4] e. g. *C. I. L.* iii. 1079. Cf. p. 137.

[5] *C. I. L.* ii. 1944: 'omnibus honoribus quos libertini gerere potuerunt honoratus.' (*I. L. S.* 6914 has 'genere' wrongly.) Cf. *I. L. S.* 6915.

at its fountain-head, albeit through slavery; in Italy they had tasted it where it had first established itself beyond its source. In virtue of this experience freedmen ranked nearer to the lords of the world than the subject peoples of the Empire, the bulk of whom had yet to learn Rome's lesson. If a slave was freed by a Roman citizen he generally became a Roman citizen. He was thus better off than his countryman who was free-born but lived in an unprivileged part of the world. Indeed so highly did provincials value the Roman franchise that in a few cases they might go into voluntary slavery in the hope that freedom and citizenship would be the ultimate prize. One of Trimalchio's friends says, 'Of my own free will I gave myself up to be a slave. I wasn't going to pay tribute; better to be a citizen of Rome'.[1] Under the early Empire Italy was sharply divided from the provinces. All Italians, *ingenui* and *libertini* alike, were exempt from the poll-tax and the land-tax[2] which fell upon the rest of the Empire. Tacitus upbraids Clodius Quirinalis, prefect of the fleet at Ravenna, because with his self-indulgence and cruelty he oppressed Italy as if it were a mere subject land.[3] With all its freedmen, Italy was still Italy for the first emperors and the poets whom they patronized. With all its foreign blood it was for them a land apart, of infinitely greater worth than the nations it had conquered—'a mighty mother of fruits and heroes, the land of Saturn'.[4]

[1] Pet. *Sat.* 57. 'Ipse me dedi in servitutem et malui civis Romanus esse quam tributarius.'

[2] 'Tributum capitis' and 'tributum soli.'

[3] *Ann.* xiii. 30: 'velut infimam nationum Italiam luxuria saevitiaque adflictavisset.'

[4] Virg. *Georgics* ii. 173–4:

> 'Salve, magna parens frugum, Saturnia tellus,
> Magna virum.'

V
GRADES OF FREEDMEN

I. Creation of the class of *dediticii* — their status — their numbers.

II. The *Latini Iuniani* — whom this class comprised and why — status of the class — how its members could rise to full citizenship — by the permission of the patron — by service of the state — numbers of *Latini Iuniani*.

III. The *ius anuli aurei* — the rights it conferred — its history in relation to freedmen.

IV. The *restitutio natalium*.

IN the last two chapters we have seen firstly how the liberty of a freedman was limited by his obligations towards his patron, and secondly how his rights as a citizen were curtailed by the disabilities which his past servitude involved. The status thus defined belonged to the ordinary freedman, the man who was formally freed by his master in normal conditions. Usually a freedman's civil rank would follow that of his patron. If the latter were a Roman citizen the former would become a Roman citizen. If he had only Latin rights or, lower still, was a mere *peregrinus*, the freedman would in the same way acquire no more and no less than his patron's status. But the early Empire created two lower grades—*dediticii* and *Latini Iuniani*—to comprise those freedmen who, although their patrons might be Roman citizens, nevertheless failed to fulfil certain conditions in respect of their character, their age, or the circumstances of their manumission.

I. The lower of these classes was that of *dediticii*, created by the *Lex Aelia Sentia* in 4 A. D. It has already been shown what measures Augustus took to restrict the frequency of manumission, and his reasons were the gradual Orientalization of the city and the elevation of totally unworthy persons to the Roman franchise. Of these two features of the last century of the Republic the latter throws most light on his policy with regard to the *dediticii*. Much of the crime and terrorism of the epoch which his own triumph had effectually closed was due, in his opinion, to slaves of desperate character who had escaped from their masters' homes or from the rural *ergastula* to enlist under revolutionary banners. Conscious of wrongs inflicted upon them and of the injustice of their position, slaves had let their passions run riot not only in servile insurrections, but also in civil strife when adventurers like Milo, Antony, or Sextus Pompeius[1] enrolled them for their own warfare against the state. Augustus had therefore contracted a wholesome dread of the criminal contagion which slaves when freed might introduce into society, and decided that, if such slaves did attain their freedom, they should at any rate live far away from his capital and should be for ever debarred from entering the ranks of Roman citizens.

Consequently he enacted with reference to all slaves who had been condemned for some crime, or who had been fettered by their masters as a punishment, or who for bad conduct had been sent from domestic service to the mill or the rural estate,[2] that, if subsequently freed, they were to belong to the class of *dediticii*; their status was assimilated to that of conquered peoples who had fought to the last and had finally been compelled to surrender at discretion. They were in the lowest rank that could be found above slavery. They had none of the rights of Roman citizens. The *ius commercii* and the *ius conubii* were alike denied them. They could not make wills or receive bequests;[3] and besides this they were compelled by law to reside not less than one hundred miles from Rome. If they transgressed this law, they were to be sold into slavery with a proviso that they were never to be freed again.[4]

However, at the death of a *dediticius*, his possessions did not always pass in their entirety into the hands of his

[1] Caes. *B. C.* iii. 22; Cic. *Ad Fam.* XI. x. 3; *Mon. Anc.* v. § 1–2.

[2] The ancient equivalent for 'being sent down South' in U.S.A.

[3] Gaius, i. 25.

[4] Gaius, i. 27.

patron. The regulations varied according to the conditions that attended manumission. If the slave had been manumitted by such a form and in such circumstances that, had not his character already determined his status as that of *dediticius*, he would have become one of the *Latini Iuniani*[1]—the category between the *dediticii* and the *cives Romani*—then the control of the succession, as in the case of *Latini Iuniani*, lay entirely in the hands of the patron. But if he had been freed by such a form and in such circumstances that he would have become a full Roman citizen, had not his moral record prevented it, then the patron was only allowed the same share in the succession as in the case of freedmen who were full Roman citizens.[2] How then is it that these *dediticii* have not the right of making their own will? Gaius says that if the *dediticius* be of the higher class the patron has not the whole control over the disposition of his goods; and yet he qualifies his statement by saying that in no case have *dediticii* of either class the *ius testamenti factionis*. Gaius himself is puzzled by the paradox, no doubt because in his day the regulations as to the dedititician category had already ceased to be enforced. Probably the *dediticius* of the higher class could not at death dispose as he wished of the share on which his patron had no claim. He must settle it on his actual descendants, and could not leave it to any former partner in crime that he might choose. If he had no descendants, the portion of the estate from which the patron's claim was excluded either went to the patron or more probably was swept into the imperial coffers.

The number of *dediticii* in the Empire can never have been very large. It was not a frequent event that a slave having once disgraced himself succeeded in winning his liberty. Criminal and badly-behaved slaves were little likely to obtain manumission unless they were sold by the master who had punished them to another into whose graces they could eventually contrive to worm them-

[1] See p. 75 ff. [2] Gaius, iii. 74–6.

selves. And this was almost impossible; for if the imperial authorities knew a slave's record—and it seems they did, if they knew when to put him in the dedititician category—it is very likely his later masters were also aware of it. At any rate, either very few slaves of the criminal type were freed, or else many such who were manumitted escaped into one or other of the higher categories. Justinian found the class a mere legal expression. It had fallen entirely into desuetude, and he suppressed it by a special constitution which he inserted in his Code.[1]

II. Such is our knowledge of this small class of freedmen who, on the grounds of their moral character, were finally and irrevocably debarred from attaining higher rank. Between the *dediticii* and the *liberti cives Romani* was another class of freedmen who, having a partial franchise, were called 'Latins', and their 'Latinity' was qualified by the name of the consul Iunius who defined their status. Accordingly they went by the name of *Latini Iuniani*. This class was composed of slaves who were freed before they appeared to be qualified to bear full civic responsibilities, or whose manumission, being *minus iusta*,[2] lacked the formal ceremonies necessary for the complete franchise. It was not a case of moral delinquency; it was simply that the legislator entertained doubts whether certain slaves were deserving of entire Roman rights. The grade was really for those who were in the probationary stage—a fact shown by the number of avenues open through which the Latin, unlike the *dediticius*, could attain full citizenship.

Who then occupied this category? In the first place, until the passing of the *Lex Iunia* (probably 17 B.C.[3]) which created the class, there had existed a number of freedmen whose legal status was vaguely and improperly defined. Those who had been informally freed were not admitted to Roman citizenship; indeed according to the

[1] *Cod. Iust.* vii. 5: 'Sit penitus deleta: quia nec in usu esse reperimus, sed vanum nomen huius libertatis circumducitur.'

[2] See p. 21.

[3] On the date of the *Lex Iunia*, see appendix I.

strict letter of the law they were still slaves; but the praetor had to a great extent throughout the Republic refused to allow their masters to annul a manumission once made.[1] Yet they had no official recognition of their rank; they mixed in free society not legally free, though generally confident that their freedom could not be taken away from them. On this class the *Lex Iunia* took compassion. It did not indeed make them Roman citizens, but it recognized their freedom[2] and defined their civic rights and directed them on the path by which they could obtain the full franchise.

This legalization of informal manumission may appear inconsistent with the general policy of the first emperor. Augustus tried to check manumission, yet here the law is facilitating manumission by recognizing as free a class that it has hitherto considered enslaved. But in two respects the *Lex Iunia* was a serious restriction on the freeing of slaves. In the first place, it made manumission, by whatever means accomplished, final and irrevocable. Before this law masters had still some reason to hope that they could revoke an informal gift of freedom. Certainly praetorian jurisdiction is said by Gaius to have protected the informally freed slave from being re-enslaved by his former master, yet citizen naturally favours citizen, and in all likelihood a very slight pretext was sufficient to encourage the praetor to oblige the patron and allow the grant of freedom to be withdrawn. Moreover, many a freedman of this lower class, when his patron was seeking to revoke his liberty, must have known the fact that he was legally still a slave, but not the further fact that he could appeal to the praetor for protection. By the *Lex Iunia*, however, his legal status as a *libertinus* was recognized; he was further separated from the slave class below him than from the ranks of the *ingenui* above him. Accordingly, thoughtless manumission by the less legal forms must have been somewhat restrained. After the passing of this law masters were not able to lavish freedom recklessly among

[1] Gaius, iii. 56. [2] Gaius, i. 22.

their slaves, speculating on the possibility of recalling the step if they subsequently should come to repent it. Henceforward owners had to consider beforehand whether they could afford the loss of a slave's services perpetually, and such enforced consideration alone must have acted as a slight, though not negligible, check upon the freeing of slaves.

There was a second factor in the recognition of informal manumission which tended to restrict the emancipation of slaves. Before the *Lex Iunia*, manumission *inter amicos* &c. probably did not involve the paying of the five per cent. tax. But when these informal modes were acknowledged to have a legal value there is no reason to think that they were still exempted. Thus by rendering all manumission, by whatever form accomplished, liable to taxation, the imperial government not only considerably increased the national revenue, but also gave a slight discouragement to the practice of freeing slaves.

In 4 A. D. another important category of freedmen were made *Latini Iuniani*. The *Lex Aelia Sentia* denied full citizenship, but granted Latin rights to slaves liberated before the age of thirty years, unless their case was approved by the Manumission Council.[1] This measure had been introduced by Augustus together with his other regulations limiting manumission. It was not a direct restriction, because it withheld not liberty but the franchise; yet it must in many cases have postponed the emancipation of those who aspired not only to be free but also to be Roman citizens.

The other sources from which this new class of Latins recruited its members are not important. One, however, deserves a passing mention. It has been said that Claudius declared a sick slave abandoned by his master to be free, and that Vespasian took the same course with regard to female slaves prostituted by their masters.[2] In the former of these cases and probably also in the latter, when liberty

[1] Gaius, i. 18; Ulp. i. 12.

[2] *Dig.* XL. viii. 2; *Dig.* XXXVII. xiv. 7, *pr.*

was given as the master's punishment, the liberated slave acquired only Latin rights.[1] The number of slaves who thus received their liberty can never have been great, but their exclusion from full Roman privileges helps to illustrate the theory which regulated the enfranchisement of freedmen. It seems to have been held in principle that a master by formally freeing his slave pronounced him fit for Roman citizenship, and on his tacit recommendation Roman rights were to be granted. On the other hand, informal manumission implied that such recommendation was withheld, while, when a slave received liberty from the state and not by the direct act of his master, this personal guarantee was naturally not forthcoming. Failing this implicit testimonial on the patron's part, the freedman had to prove his fitness for the franchise by other means, such as the service of the state in spheres which will be indicated below.

The privileges of the *Latini Iuniani* were much the same as those of the Latin Colonists. They had the whole *ius mancipationis*, and could therefore buy and sell land, slaves and cattle in the full legal forms; but a great part of the *ius testamenti factionis* was denied to them. They could be witnesses to a will, but they were not authorized to make their own will; except under the form of *fideicommissa*, which for a long time carried no more than a moral obligation, they could not even receive bequests.[2] While they could exercise the *tutela*, they were not permitted to appoint *tutores* by will, and, more serious still, they could not reap the great advantage which the *tutela* conferred, namely succession to the estate of him over whom they exercised it. Likewise when a Latin died, the patron had the full control over his estate.[3] On the death of a Latin his goods reverted entirely to the patron, and it was only by the courtesy of the latter that anything

[1] Justinian enacted that a sick slave abandoned by his master should be not a Latin but a full Roman citizen. *Cod. Iust.* VII. vi. 1, § 3.

[2] Gaius, i. 24; ii. 275; Ulp. xx. 14.

[3] Gaius, iii. 56. In Egypt the *fiscus* occasionally intervened. See appendix V.

went to his relatives.[1] The *ius Latinorum*, the patronage of Latin freedmen and the right to their estate, was therefore a lucrative possession. Moreover it could be given and received, bought and sold, bequeathed and inherited, by any Roman citizen whatever. In alienating the *ius Latinorum*, the possessor need not see that the receiver is of his own family or even remotely connected. Thus Pliny mentions as a valuable gift the patronage of a friend's Latins which he has inherited from him.[2]

Intermarriage between Latins and Romans must have been frequent at all times; it is not clear what status the children of such marriages received in the first century; but from the reign of Hadrian onward the condition of the mother was followed; if she was Roman her children possessed the same status; but however truly the father was Roman the offspring of a Latin mother was at birth always Latin.[3] Yet these regulations cannot often have had any important effect. As will be seen later, possession of a one-year-old child enabled one class of Latins, and after 75 all Latins, to obtain full Roman citizenship for themselves and their family. Consequently, if the necessary formalities were complied with, the child of a Roman-Latin marriage could never after 75 have had more than a year of Latinity.

The institution of the *Latini Iuniani* did not introduce any rigid caste-division among the freedmen. The gulf between Romans and Latins could always be bridged. At his first creation the Latin found open to him many avenues of access to the Roman citizenship, and these tended to increase in number as time went on. It has already been pointed out that in theory the Roman government held that an ex-slave asking for the franchise should produce some evidence that his master thought him fit for it. If he was under thirty years of age he was

[1] In view of the regulations by which Latins could advance to Roman citizenship by the possession of children, this provision seldom meant that the family of a Latin was left destitute.

[2] Pliny, *Ep.* x. 104.

[3] Gaius, i. 30, 56, 80; Ulp. v. 4 and 9.

on that score alone considered unfit, unless he justified his claim or his master justified it for him before the Manumission Council. If his master did not free him *vindicta* or *testamento*, he was deemed to be withholding his testimony to his fitness. Suppose then a slave has been freed either informally or before the age of thirty. He has no guarantee to offer that he deserves Roman citizenship, and has therefore become a Latin. He now considers by what means he can rise to the higher privileges. Obviously there are two alternatives; either he can procure a testimonial from his former master, which will be of no effect unless he is thirty years of age, or he can prove his claim by his services to the state, whether military, social, or economic. To take the former alternative first: it was always open to a Latin, whether he owed his inferior rank to his youth at the time he was freed or to the informal circumstances of his manumission, to ask his former master to repeat the ceremony of emancipation by the legal forms or at the legal age. This, the simplest means of converting one's status, was naturally of great frequency at all times.[1] Suppose, however, the patron was ready to give his consent to *iteratio*, as this formal repetition was called, but was disinclined to go to the trouble and expense of the legal ceremony. Even in that case, if the Latin had a friend with influence at court, he could obtain full citizenship by the indulgence of the Emperor (*beneficio principis*). Several examples illustrate how Pliny obtained privileges for his friends and clients from the Emperor Trajan. Now it is an equestrian friend for whom he asks senatorial status,[2] now it is an Egyptian physician whom he wishes made a Roman citizen,[3] now it is some freedmen with Latin rights whom he desires to possess full Roman privileges.[4] In all these cases the Emperor courteously complies with the request—indeed, on the last-mentioned occasion, not only is his temper unruffled by the entreaty, but he encourages Pliny to make more applications of the

[1] e. g. Pliny, *Ep.* vii. 16.

[2] Pliny, *Ep.* x. 5, 6.

[3] Pliny, *Ep.* x. 4.

[4] Pliny, *Ep.* x. 104, 105.

same nature. Yet Roman emperors limited their grants of the franchise by one rule which they faithfully observed. If a Latin freedman applied for the full franchise he had to do it with the knowledge and consent of his patron, provided the latter were still alive. If citizenship were acquired *beneficio principis* without the knowledge of the patron, the grant indeed was not annulled, but at his death the freedman was considered a Latin, and therefore he was bound to make his patron his heir, although he could substitute another heir in the event of the patron declining the estate.[1] It is not difficult to see why the patron's assent was required. In the first place, he might have some good cause for not considering his freedman deserving of citizenship; and, secondly, emperors realized that, by granting the Roman franchise, they were depriving the patron of a large part of his control over the succession.

We come now to a second class of alternatives. The Latin might prove that he had contributed to the welfare of the state and in virtue thereof had a claim to be numbered among its citizens. In this case the patron's consent was not required. By his service the Latin had merited citizenship; the patron's right to his estate was overridden by the Latin's right to the franchise. We should have expected the requisite service to be of a conspicuous or exceptional character, if the patron's rights were thus wantonly abrogated. But curiously enough the reverse is the case. When the Latin can show one child, of either sex, a year old, born to him by a Latin or a Roman wife, not only he himself but also his wife and child become Roman citizens.[2] At first such means of acquiring full rights were only available for that class of Latins who had been freed before they were thirty years of age. But in 75 A. D. those who had been informally manumitted were also allowed to make use of such means.[3]

[1] After Trajan: Gaius, iii. 72.

[2] *Lex Aelia Sentia*, Gaius, i. 29; Ulp. iii. 3. If the mother was Roman, the child was Roman at birth, and only the father had to wait till the child's first birthday to obtain the franchise.

[3] Gaius, i. 31.

This generous opening of the doors to the Roman *civitas* may be referred by some to the efforts made by the government of the early Empire to arrest the decline in the population. Yet this view is hardly tenable. If this had been the object, surely the qualification would have been higher than one child. When families of at least three or four children were required to supply the deficiency left by those who remained unmarried, this law would have tended to limit families to one; for having obtained all that they wanted by one child, parents would have pleased themselves whether to have more. No, this measure, like so many others, must be assigned to the campaign against manumission in general. Augustus foresaw that, when he refused the franchise to slaves freed under the age of thirty, his measure might not always have the effect he desired. In some cases, no doubt, it would postpone manumission. Slaves would wait till they were thirty before they asked for their liberty in return for their *peculium*. But in other cases a master might deliberately free large numbers of slaves before the age of thirty in order that the slaves thus freed might not have the right of making their will, and that he himself or his male descendants might inherit their whole estate. Augustus took skilful steps to avert this. He facilitated access to Roman citizenship in the very law in which he refused it to this class of freedmen. By so doing he made the fact appreciated that, at whatever age he had been freed, the slave could ultimately rise to full rights without the sanction of his master. The latter therefore was forced to remember that he probably surrendered at manumission most of his claim on the slave's estate, and that he must think seriously of his finances before manumitting him.

Augustus did not extend the same opportunity of winning full Roman rights to those slaves who had been informally freed. Indeed, as mentioned above, it was not till 75 A. D. that they could claim Roman citizenship in respect of one child. This inequality of prospect between two classes of Latins is certainly surprising. Augustus with characteristic foresight prevented masters from freeing slaves before the age of thirty in order to retain the control over their estate, but apparently he never realized that a similar advantage might be taken of the rules regarding informal manumission—in other words, that masters for the sake of the succession might free informally. He may have considered that his legislation[1] imposed sufficient restrictions on *manumissio minus iusta*, and that he therefore did not need to open the franchise to informally freed slaves in order to discourage it. On the other hand, the inequality may be due to sheer neglect. The *Lex Aelia Sentia*, so far as we know, never directly concerned itself with the recipients of *manumissio minus iusta*: apart from indirect restrictions,[2] it treated informal manumission as a subject definitely closed by the *Lex Iunia*. Accordingly, when its own measures were being drawn up, slaves freed *inter amicos* &c. may have been omitted.

Several provisions, however, had been made before Vespasian's time by which any Latin, whatever the cause of his status, could rise to the higher rank. The *Lex Visellia* of 24 A. D. allowed Latins to become Roman citizens after six years' service in the *vigiles*, the police and fire-brigade of Rome.[3] Later, the period of service necessary to qualify for citizenship was reduced to three years.[4] Evidently the work of the corps was never attractive, and enlistment had to be encouraged.

In Claudius' reign the nationalized corn-trade was not going as well as it might have gone, and private enterprise had to be fostered. The inducements of Roman citizenship were offered to any Latin who would build at his own expense a ship to hold 10,000 *modii* and who would participate for six years in the provision of corn for the

[1] The *Lex Iunia* restricted informal manumission by legalizing it; the *Lex Aelia Sentia* indirectly limited it by prescribing *causae probatio apud consilium* followed by *manumissio vindicta* when the master was under twenty years of age, and by ordering the same procedures if a slave under thirty was to become a full Roman citizen.

[2] See previous note.

[3] Gaius, i. 33; Ulp. iii. 5.

[4] Ulp. iii. 5.

capital.[1] Here, too, conditions were made easier in after time. Perhaps the particular talent of the Latin did not lie in over-sea trade; then he might confine his activities to Rome and establish a mill there. If for three years he ground a hundred *modii* of corn per day, his public service was considered to have merited Roman citizenship.[2] After the great fire in the reign of Nero, the housing question became acute, and in this sphere also private enterprise had to be encouraged. If a Latin possessing a fortune of 200,000 sesterces (£2,000) spent half of it in the building industry in Rome, he also was to be rewarded with the full franchise.[3] In all these cases it was held that the Latin had merited Roman citizenship by his public service, but the real position was that the need of help in these various departments was so urgent that co-operation had to be invited. Service in the *vigiles*, offering little besides constant danger and severe discipline, was never tempting. Rome, like ancient Athens and modern Britain, depended for most of her food-supply on foreign parts, and the widest precautions were necessary in case the African or Egyptian harvest failed. Lastly, when a large part of the capital was 'at one fell swoop' destroyed by fire, every effort was necessary to rebuild the city with speed. No wonder, then, that inducements of equality were offered to an inferior class, especially as its inferiority was after all felt to be only probationary.

It may be asked what was the number of *Latini Iuniani*. There is not much on which to found a conjecture. The increasing facility of proceeding from Latin to Roman rights both reduced the average period of a freedman's Latinity and discouraged, as we have seen, manumission in general. Nevertheless, inscriptions of young freedmen under thirty years of age are very numerous, and informal manumission must have retained some of its popularity by reason of its freedom from awkward ceremony. What

[1] Suet. *Claud.* 19; Gaius, i. 33; Ulp. iii. 6.
[2] This dates from the time of Trajan. Gaius, i. 34.
[3] Gaius, i. 34.

might be held a greater indication of their numbers is the fact that it was thought worth while to legislate for the very small proportion who had a fortune of over 200,000 sesterces. If we take into consideration the comparative purchasing power of money, this sum represents in our money about £10,000. If the number of Latins possessing this fortune was considerable enough for the government to legislate about them, then surely the Latins among the poorer classes must have numbered several thousands. This argument, however, is weak; for the legislation in question refers to all persons of Latin rank and not only to Junian Latins, just as all the above-mentioned avenues to the full franchise, except *iteratio* and *anniculi probatio*, were open to Latins whether Junian or not.

III. It remains to speak briefly of two other grades of freedmen which had not less but more privileges than the ordinary class of *Liberti cives Romani*. One of these grades comprised freedmen who had obtained from the Emperor the *ius anuli aurei* or right to wear the gold ring.

Their position is well summarized by Lemonnier.[1] 'L'ancien esclave, une fois l'anneau d'or obtenu, cesse d'être un *libertinus*, mais demeure un *libertus*.' In relation to society he is deemed to have free birth,[2] but in relation to his former master he is still his freedman. The *anulus aureus* renders a freedman immune from the disabilities that servile parentage entails. All the offices open to the free-born are now open to him.[3] Nothing now debars him from the Roman priesthoods; he is no longer disqualified from municipal office; and, if he wishes, he can enter the legions or the praetorian guards. At the same time all the privileges of the patron abide. The *obsequium* and *officium* are to be as faithfully observed as in his first freedman days.[4] The regulations governing the succession are

[1] *Op. cit.*, p. 239.

[2] 'Ingenuus intelligitur,' *Dig.* XL. x. 6; cf. XXVII. i. 44, § 3; XXXVIII. ii. 3, *pr.*

[3] 'Omnia ingenuitatis munia habet,' *Dig.* II. iv. 10, § 3.

[4] 'Puto eum reverentiam patrono exhibere debere.' *Dig.* II. iv. 10, § 3; cf. XXVII. i. 14, § 2.

the same as in the case of an ordinary freedman.[1] No mention is made of the *operae* in this connexion, but there can be no doubt that here too the patron's rights remained intact.

The first grant of the gold ring was probably that made by Sulla to the comic actor Sextus Roscius.[2] Augustus gave it to certain freedmen who had rendered eminent service to his person. Antonius Musa, a physician who saved Augustus' life, was rewarded with the gold ring.[3] Pallas, one of the props of Claudius' throne;[4] Icelus, first to announce to his patron Galba the news of Nero's death;[5] Asiaticus, Vitellius' favourite;[6] the father of Etruscus, *a rationibus* under Vespasian;[7] all received the gold ring from their imperial masters. In their cases the *ius anuli aurei* was the avenue to much greater honours, such as equestrian status, to which, without obtaining ingenuity through the gold ring, they were unable to proceed. But large numbers of humbler freedmen, not necessarily servants of the Emperor, obtained the right in both the first and second centuries.[8] Their ambition was not the *equus publicus* and knightly rank, but the municipal decurionate and the dignity of free birth.

IV. The *ius anuli aurei*, then, did not annul any of the patron's rights. That could only be done by an exceptional process called the *restitutio natalium* or complete restoration of ingenuity.

Like many other institutions of Roman law, this process was a fiction. It was derived from the official emancipation from his master's or patron's authority of a slave or freedman who had been illegally enslaved. As is implied in two epigrams of Martial cited above, the

[1] *Dig.* XXXVIII. ii. 3, *pr*: 'vivit quasi ingenuus, moritur quasi libertus.'

[2] Macrob. *Sat.* III. xiv. 13: 'is est Roscius qui etiam L. Sullae carissimus fuit et anulo aureo ab eodem dictatore donatus est.'

[3] Dio, liii. 30.

[4] Plin. *Ep.* viii. 6.

[5] Suet. *Galba*, 14, 22; Tac. *Hist.* i. 13; Plut. *Galba*, 7.

[6] Suet. *Vit.* 12; Tac. *Hist.* ii. 57.

[7] Stat. *Silv.* III. iii. 143–5.

[8] *Cod. Iust.* ix. 21; Plin. *N. H.* xxxiii. 32–3; *I. L. S.* 1899, 5631.

slave or the freedman was supposed by law never to have been born; consequently, when it was recognized that his enslavement was illegal, such recognition was accomplished by a 'restoration of his birth'.

If persons legally free were kidnapped by brigands and sold into slavery, they could on proving their case win their release by the *natalium restitutio*. Under the Republic, when both Italy and the provinces were so unsettled, there is no doubt that many of these cases occurred. In Sicily alone, towards the end of the second century before Christ, when the Senate ordered an investigation, more than eight hundred proved their right to liberty in the course of a few days.[1] In the revolutionary period and even after the Principate had brought the *pax Romana*, travellers still ran the risk of being kidnapped and imprisoned as slaves in *ergastula*. Augustus and Tiberius and probably later emperors organized inspections of *ergastula* from time to time, and freemen who had been wrongfully enslaved were set at liberty by the *restitutio natalium*.[2] On these recognitions of freedom were based the fictitious ceremonies by which freedmen shook off all the disabilities of their servile origin.

The first case, perhaps, is that of Menas, who was rewarded by Augustus for his treachery towards Sextus Pompeius with the rights of free birth. Cassius Dio only says he received the gold ring, but Suetonius claims that he was *adsertus in ingenuitatem*, which is the term used in the *restitutio natalium*.[3] The slave's advocate is said to be an *assertor in ingenuitatem*. Later, Nero granted free birth to his favourites. Paris, the actor, was a freedman of the Emperor's aunt, Domitia. Nero determined to reward his talents with the full status of an *ingenuus*.

[1] Wallon, *Hist. de l'esclavage dans l'antiquité*, vol. ii, p. 303.

[2] Suet. *Aug.* 32; *Tib.* 8. Cf. Plin. *Ep.* vi. 25, where a traveller has mysteriously disappeared, a fact which suggests that *suppressio* or kidnapping was still a very real danger.

[3] Dio, xlviii. 45; Suet. *Aug.* 74. As Menas' patron was dead, his position would be the same, whether he received the gold ring or obtained the *restitutio natalium*.

Domitia, with praiseworthy but futile temerity, persisted in clinging to her privileges as patroness. No doubt Paris was fulfilling on the stage the *operae fabriles* he owed her. Nero suborned witnesses to attest the free birth of the comedian, and the case naturally went against Domitia. Insult was added to injury; for Paris drew the logical conclusion from the issue of the process, and claimed with success from Domitia the sum he had paid for his liberty.[1] Similarly Nero emancipated Acte from his own patronal authority by procuring witnesses to testify to her royal extraction.[2]

These cases are outside the law. They are high-handed and exceptional acts on the part of monarchs, and the legal ceremonies restoring free birth to a freedman have not yet passed into Roman practice.[3] Very much later we hear of them. Scaevola, who flourished under M. Aurelius, is the first to mention the fictitious *restitutio natalium* as an official act.[4] No doubt, in the later half of the second century, prominent freedmen could in exceptional circumstances obtain this supreme privilege from the Emperor. But as it even annulled the patron's rights, the latter was always consulted.[5] No grant of complete free birth could be made unless the patron had first signified his consent to the loss of his privileges.

1 Tac. *Ann.* xiii. 27; *Dig.* XII. iv. 3, § 5.

2 Dio, lxi. 7; Suet. *Nero*, 28.

3 Suetonius (*Vesp.* 3) mentions the case of Flavia Domitilla, a Latin freedwoman, who was about the year 39 A. D. declared a free-born Roman by a 'recuperatorium iudicium' and who afterwards married the future emperor, Vespasian. Either Domitilla had been wrongfully enslaved and no legal fiction was employed, or else, if a fictitious *restitutio natalium*, it was quite exceptional and probably due to Vespasian's influence with Caligula.

4 *Dig.* XL. xi. 3.

5 *Dig.* XL. xi. 2 and 4–5.

VI

FREEDMEN IN PRIVATE LIFE

Freedmen in domestic service — in trade and agriculture although still dependent on patrons — as clients — relations between patrons and freedmen — examples in literature — provisions made by patrons for freedmen's burial — legacies left by patrons to freedmen — statues and inscriptions set up by freedmen in patrons' honour and by patrons in freedmen's honour — freedmen as actors, charioteers and gladiators — Roman prejudice against trade and industry — freedmen and their descendants predominant in these fields — the *collegia* — liberal professions — law — medicine — teaching — painting — architecture — sculpture — minor arts — wealth of freedmen — Trimalchio's account of his career — his ignorance and vulgarity — outlet for freedmen's riches — in luxury and ostentation — in prudent benevolence.

OUR survey of a freedman's legal status is now complete. He was handicapped by obligations towards his patron and by disabilities in society, and he might be in one of two inferior classes whose liberty and equality were not even so fully realized as those of the ordinary ex-slave. We have now to demonstrate how the freedman contrived to circumvent those handicaps, how he made a living in Rome, Italy and the provinces in spite of them, and how the patronage of his former master or his own artistic, scientific or commercial ability stood him in good stead, and enabled him to contend with success against the disadvantages of his position.

After being freed, the slave would, more often than not, continue in the same situation as before manumission. If he had been placed in business or trade, he would pursue the same occupation on such terms as the master imposed in the form of *operae fabriles*. If, on the other hand, he had been employed in domestic service, he would continue to perform the same function as before, or perhaps, if the Roman aristocrat's hierarchy of servants offered a vacancy in its higher ranks, he might be promoted to it.

Domestic service was always a frequent occupation with freedmen. Many slaves became attached to a house and felt that freedom was no reward if it meant they were to leave their master and mistress and fellow-slaves. Masters, for their part, entertained great affection for their confidential attendants, and, fearing new and untried service, made every effort to retain the slaves they freed. At any rate, the frequent legislation about freedmen in their patron's household shows that it was not uncommon for them to be employed there in considerable numbers. Several passages in the literature of the Silver Age bear like testimony. When Libo Drusus commits suicide in his house, it is his freedmen who rush to his aid thinking he has been murdered.[1] When Paullina tries to commit suicide at the same time as her husband Seneca, not only his slaves but also his freedmen are on the spot to prevent her at the orders of the imperial soldiers.[2]

Epigraphy shows what kind of offices such freedmen filled. In the first place there is the *procurator*, who combines the function of supervising the slaves with that of representing his patron in law. He is always a freedman. The sixth volume of the *Corpus Inscriptionum Latinarum* gives the epitaphs of miscellaneous tradesmen and domestic servants together. All the *procuratores* there are freedmen.[3] Under him are some financial secretaries, *dispensatores*,[4] *tabularii*[5] and *arcarii*,[6] who are mostly slaves, though the *dispensator* in the *Cena Trimalchionis* seems from his air of authority to be a freedman.[7] Another overseer, the *lorarius*, who has the unpleasant duty of inflicting corporal punishment, is often a freedman,[8] while we hear of servants, *decuriones*, who have a number of slaves (not necessarily ten) under them, but whose sphere of service is not specified. They too are mostly ex-slaves.[9] Further the cook (*cocus*, *coquus*),[10] the head-waiter and meat-carver (*structor*),[11] the keeper of his lordship's bedchamber (*cubicularius* or

[1] Tac. *Ann.* ii. 31. [2] *Ibid.* xv. 64. [3] *C. I. L.* vi. 9830–38.
[4] *Ib.* 9319–72. [5] *Ib.* 9921–26. [6] *Ib.* 9146–48.
[7] Petr. *Sat.* 30. [8] *C. I. L.* vi. 9528.
[9] e. g. *C. I. L.* vi. 4421, 4487. [10] *Ib.* 9263, 9270, 9271.
[11] *Ib.* 9905, 9906, 9910.

a cubiculo),[1] the reminder of social duties (*nomenclator*),[2] the private secretary (*a manu, amanuensis*)[3] and the tutor or attendant of the children (*paedagogus*)[4] are frequently freedmen. Moreover there is a host of other offices which were nearly always domestic in Roman times, but which one would never dream of filling to-day out of one's private staff. In Rome it was the ambition of each plutocrat to be self-sufficing;[5] it did not matter how many slaves and freedmen hung about his mansion doing nothing most of the day, so long as he did not suffer the indignity of having to supply his needs from outside. Thus many a household had its own doctor, its own banker, and its own barber, while spinning and weaving were still essentially home occupations. The latter branch of domestic life was left to slaves, but the other attendants mentioned were generally freedmen. Of those doctors whose names are recorded together in the sixth volume of the *Corpus*[6] quite a large number are freedmen, and many of these no doubt started life as the private physician of some wealthy Roman. Of the *argentarii* or bankers[7] a fair proportion are freedmen, and of these one is mentioned as a private banker, while the others yield no certain conclusion on this point. Of the freedmen barbers,[8] more than half mention the masters whom they served.

Outside his patron's house the freedman might still remain in his service. For instance, he might carry on a trade in direct relation to his former master. Very often this would merely be a continuation of his employment during slavery. A master frequently set up his slave in business, lent him capital, and the slave paid him interest;[9] or the master made his slave his agent, took the profits for himself and encouraged the slave with wages or presents.[10]

[1] *C.I.L.* vi. 7370.
[2] *Ib.* 9689, 9692.
[3] *Ib.* 9540, 9542.
[4] *Ib.* 4718, 6327–31.
[5] Petr. *Sat.* 38. A friend of Trimalchio says with admiration: 'omnia domi nascuntur: lana, credrae, piper, lacte gallinaceum si quaesieris invenies'.
[6] *C.I.L.* vi. 9562–617.
[7] *Ib.* 9155–85, esp. 9172.
[8] *Ib.* 9937–41.
[9] *Dig.* XIV. iv.
[10] *Dig.* XIV. iii.

In either case the slave might receive his freedom by free gift or by a commercial transaction, but continue in the same occupation after as before manumission. At other times, however, it was not a slave but a freedman that was set up. Having earned his freedom in the house he then entered his master's commercial service. One inscription, for instance, commemorates the life of a freedman jeweller, who in all likelihood was supplied by his patron with the materials of his trade, but who furnished the labour himself.[1] Either before or after manumission, his master must have settled him in a shop, where he both produced his goods and supplied his customers.

In industries where the factory system prevailed, capitalists made their freedmen overseers, while the rank and file of the workmen were slaves. In this connexion we cannot have better evidence than the rough inscriptions on bricks. Many a brick bore not only the name of the maker, but also that of the foreman under whose direction it was made. The inscriptions on bricks in the city of Rome have been collected in the *Corpus Inscriptionum Latinarum*, volume xv, part I. Domitius Afer and his two sons succeeded in establishing a practical monopoly in the brick-making industry, and the names on bricks are frequently those of their slaves and freedmen. Often from one brick we find the maker is a slave; on a later brick the same man appears as a freedman. Agathobulus appears first as a slave with at least two *vicarii* under him. Later he is a freedman; the two *vicarii* are now his own slaves, and indeed two more have been added. As a slave he was evidently a man of some authority—when he was freed that authority was doubtless extended. One subordinate of Agathobulus, Trophimus, receives his freedom from his master, and later he possesses as many as five slaves. Indeed of the twenty-four freedmen whose names occur, about half appear elsewhere as slaves; no doubt the others would also, if our supply of ancient bricks were less limited.[2]

[1] *I. L. S.* 7695.

[2] cf. *C. I. L.* xv. part i, pp. 265–75.

In factories, then, many slaves by industry and intelligence obtained their liberty and became departmental directors in the business. No doubt some of the overseers were slaves, but in such responsible positions it was easy for a slave to win his liberty. Probably the majority of foremen in these manufactures had obtained their freedom, while most of the rank and file were still slaves; but of course manumission and promotion in the industry were not necessarily simultaneous.

In agriculture freedmen in their patrons' employment were not so common. At the head of the *familia rustica* was a bailiff (*vilicus*) who together with his wife was either a slave or an ex-slave; and the rest of the *familia* have generally been supposed to be slaves. Yet one-third of the employees on pastoral estates had to be free labourers; this was enjoined by a law during Caesar's dictatorships.[1] Doubtless the spirit of his law was carried out to a wide extent, and free Italians reaped the benefit. But many must have found an opportunity to evade its spirit while obeying its letter. In order to keep a closer control over the labour on their estates, they would free some of their slaves and fill with freedmen the proportion reserved for free labour.

In another way the agricultural population became interspersed with freedmen. Rich landed proprietors, on freeing their slaves, often gave them a small farm on their estate. The freedman thus became a tenant of his patron and paid him a yearly rent; or, if the latter were particularly generous, he would make a free gift of the land to the freedman, who thereby would become an independent proprietor. As we shall see later, the probabilities are that this practice was commoner than has been usually supposed.

It was, however, in the ceremonial sphere that the relation of freedman and patron was most typically Roman. A freedman who failed to find employment on land, in trade, or in his master's home, might help to swell the ranks of those dependants on his patron who, whether

[1] Suet. *Iul.* 42.

manumitted or born free, were engaged as his *clientes*. For adding to his patron's dignity and for acting as an instrument of his ostentation, the client received a small pittance each day and in the midst of great privations was able to support a precarious existence. The principal function was the morning call (*salutatio*), which was as useless to the patron as it was irksome to the client. Rising in the small hours from his bed, in winter and summer alike, the client would don the cumbersome *toga*,[1] and trudge, it might be for miles, to wish his patron good morning. At his patron's house he would encounter the insolence of the domestics and perhaps might have to give a gratuity in order to secure admittance.[2] But here the freedman client was probably better off than the free-born. He would be known to his patron and in all likelihood to the servants of the house too. Juvenal draws an amusing picture of praetors and tribunes clamouring for admittance and being forestalled by a freedman.[3]

When at last the great man appeared and welcomed his callers, he dismissed some with a small payment, but retained others to attend him during the day.

Wherever he went in the fashionable capital, he went in full aristocratic pomp. If legal business took him to the *forum*, his retinue, both freedmen and free-born, followed him thither and heard him plead.[4] No doubt as *claqueurs* they were useful, and at a sign from their lord burst into loud applause of some point whose subtlety they had failed to notice. Sometimes it was not judicial pleading but a literary recitation that they had to try to appreciate. After robbing them of sleep, their duties now forced them to sit wearily through a reading of some dull unoriginal epic or drama and to keep sufficiently wide awake to laugh

[1] Mart. ix. 100; iv. 26. [2] Juv. iii. 184–9; Sen. *De Benef.* vi. 34.

[3] Juv. i. 99–102: 'iubet a praecone vocari
Ipsos Troiugenas, nam vexant limen et ipsi
Nobiscum. "da praetori, da deinde tribuno."
Sed libertinus prior est.'

[4] Mart. vi. 48.

or applaud at the right place.[1] One thing which the Roman aristocrat to his credit could never forgo was his bath in the middle of the afternoon. Clients attended their patrons to the bathing establishment, but conventional circles would have been horrified if they had used the same baths as he. While my lord reclines easily in the luxurious *Thermae Agrippianae*, his clients must take a hurried wash in the humbler baths of Titus.[2] They must at all costs, even at that of cleanliness, be ready to attend their patron, as soon as it pleases him to finish his ablutions or his conversation and proceed on his way. Sometimes the patron had a call to pay, often on some childless widow on whose wealth he cast longing eyes; on such occasions too, the clients would have to come;[3] their presence would help to make an impression; indeed it would be disrespectful to come unattended.

More valuable services were at times rendered by clients. A chosen few would accompany their patron abroad[4] or canvass for him at municipal elections.[5] At other times even dangerous enterprises were entrusted to them. The freedmen of Domitius Ahenobarbus, acting no doubt as his clients, were employed by him to defend Massilia against Caesar in the Civil War, 49 B.C.[6] Tacitus records how in Nero's reign Silana employed two of her clients, Iturius and Calvisius, to bring charges against the Empress-mother Agrippina.[7]

In return for such services the patron was supposed to protect the legal interests of his client, a duty which he too often neglected.[8] If the client's rights were infringed in any way, it was the patron who had to act as solicitor and sometimes as barrister also. Further, if the client fell in need, the patron was expected to tide him over his

1 Mart. x. 10.
2 *Ib.* iii. 36.
3 *Ib.* ix. 100.
4 Hor. *Ep.* I. vii. 75–6.
5 e. g. electioneering notices at Pompeii, *I. L. S.* 6419 f: 'Cuspium Pansam aed. Popidius Natalis cliens cum Isiacis rog.'; cf. *I. L. S.* 6411 d; *C. I. L.* iv. 593, 933, 1016.
6 Caes. *B. C.* i. 34.
7 Tac. *Ann.* xiii. 19–21.
8 Mart. ii. 32.

difficulty by advancing capital.[1] But the old-world idea of the patron as father of his clients was now not much more than a legal fiction. It produced enactments, as we have seen, on the relations between freedmen and their former masters; but those freedmen, and still more those free-born citizens who were in the position of clients, were now regarded by their patron as mere dressed-up flunkeys hired by him to produce a good effect. Many plutocrats treated their dependants with marked scorn and took no trouble to show interest in their welfare. Under Nero it could even be made a matter of accusation that the Stoic Paetus Thrasea concerned himself with the affairs of his clients and made no sycophantic efforts to compass the ruin of supposed traitors like Silanus and Vetus.[2] Too many patrons thought that their duties ended when they had paid the wages for ceremonial attendance. Even these were barely sufficient to support life. The sum of six and a quarter sesterces (1*s.* 3*d.*) is mentioned by Martial as the value of the dole.[3] Whether this was for the *salutatio* alone or for a full day's service we do not know. It may be suggested that those who went only to the *salutatio* had opportunities of employment during the rest of the day. Perhaps so; but woe betide any man who has another engagement when his patron claims his further presence. That would end the paltry benefits that his monotonous labour has earned. The daily wage, however, might be supplemented by gifts. One client receives some cast-off clothing,[4] another a piece of land.[5] Sometimes the patron rises to the occasion and gives a dinner to his clients. 'But what a dinner!' says Juvenal with eloquent brevity. The account of that repast, and the distinctions observed between host and guests in the attendance, the wine, and the food down to the very bread, are too well known to be quoted here.[6] Probably for a year or two in Domitian's reign patrons rewarded their clients with daily invitations

[1] Mart. x. 18. [2] Tac. *Ann.* xvi. 22. [3] Mart. x. 75.
[4] Pers. i. 54. [5] Juv. ix. 59.
[6] Juv. v. 24 ff. 'Qualis cena tamen!' etc.

to dinner instead of a payment in money.[1] Then of course, if they failed to find other employment, their existence would be precarious in the extreme.

That in many cases the client's was a dog's life we cannot doubt. The dominant feature in the accounts of Martial and Juvenal is the patron's meanness. He was not above feigning illness in order to avoid giving employment and wages to his clients.[2] Martial complains that he only got a hundred and twenty sesterces (24*s.*) in the whole year.[3] The most generous patron is 'the best of a bad lot'.[4] 'No one', exclaims Juvenal, 'asks now what Seneca used to send to humble friends; no one asks now the bounties that good Piso and Cotta used to lavish.'[5]

This last passage suggests that conditions were better during Nero's reign than a generation later. And it may fairly be questioned whether the whole account is not overdrawn; for to overdraw is the part of a satirist. A kindly interest in his less prosperous fellow-townsmen was shown by the younger Pliny.[6] He at any rate was free from the vulgarity which Juvenal exposes in his fifth satire. He did not feast himself on the choicest fare, while common and even putrid food was served up to his guests.[7] He and his humane circle of friends, and many more whose names are not bequeathed to us, must have appreciated to the full the moral duties of a patron.

Moreover, all these grievances apply rather to the freeborn than to the freedman. In the latter, who once had served him in his home, the patron would take a more generous interest than in the hirelings who chose to depend upon him for daily bread. Indeed one of the com-

[1] Allusions to the replacement of the *sportula* by invitations to dinner occur only in Book III of Martial, e. g. *Epig.* 7, 30, 60.

[2] Mart. ix. 85.

[3] Mart. iv. 26.

[4] 'Optimus malorum,' Mart. xii. 36.

[5] Juv. v. 108–10: 'Nemo petit modicis quae mittebantur amicis
A Seneca, quae Piso bonus, quae Cotta solebat
Largiri.'

[6] e. g. his efforts to found a school at Novum Comum and his generous contribution thereto. *Ep.* iv. 13.

[7] Plin. *Ep.* ii. 6.

plaints mentioned above is that the ex-slave received more courteous attention than the free citizen reduced by poverty to the client's profession. Any distinction that was made was probably in favour of the freedman. It was he that could be trusted; it was he whose ability had been tried. Further, in some cases we can hardly blame the patron if he was liberal only in his contempt. It was not so much a depression in trade as a disinclination for commerce and manual labour that nerved the poorer citizen to suffer patiently the indignities to which a client was subjected. It is well known how both Greeks and Romans despised those who worked with their hands at anything but war and agriculture. Many made this prejudice a justification for looking to the state for most of their food and to some wealthy citizen for the rest of their necessities. No wonder that the haughty senator despised such parasites. Knowing that money was all they wanted, he tossed it to them with an air of indifferent scorn and cared not to inquire of their other affairs.

Since the relations we have just detailed held less of freedmen than of free-born, it would be well to survey what is known about the actual relations between patrons and freedmen. It has been shown above how unsafe it is to draw dogmatic conclusions from legislation about freedmen who violated the *obsequium*. Such a vast proportion of the legislation which penalized a patron's or a freedman's offences consisted of mere replies to individual questions, that the cases calling for imperial decisions must represent the exception rather than the rule. Undoubtedly acts of cruelty on the one side and of disloyalty on the other occasionally took place. Nero's father flew into a rage with a freedman who refused to drink as much as he was ordered, and killed the temperate offender on the spot.[1] The freedman Milichus is notorious for his dastardly betrayal of his patron and the Pisonian conspirators.[2] More importance should be attached to the debate in the Senate on ungrateful freedmen, because it

[1] Suet. *Nero*, 5.

[2] Tac. *Ann.* xv. 54.

is evident that at that time freedmen's infidelity had created a scandal.[1] On the other hand, the list of faithful freedmen is a long one. In the proscriptions which preceded the establishment of the Principate, freedmen exposed themselves to danger in order to save their patrons from the soldiers of the triumvirs. One was rewarded by Augustus (possibly himself the baffled triumvir) for hiding his patron.[2] In a survey of the proscriptions Velleius Paterculus awards the palm for loyalty to wives; freedmen are second, and slaves third, while sons distinguished themselves by displaying the basest treachery.[3] In the reign of Nero a freedman took the blame of a murder in order to shield his patron.[4] When Octavia was accused of adultery with a slave, her servants were tortured for evidence; with the exception of one or two who gave way under the pain, all testified bravely to their mistress's purity.[5] These were slaves, but the incident shows the sterling faith at least of potential freedwomen.

Patrons no less could show a benevolence which often passes unnoticed by those who generalize about the harshness of a Roman master. There are two men in Roman history whose private life we know perhaps more thoroughly than that of all other Romans put together —Cicero and the younger Pliny. Both of these were faultless patrons. Cicero's affection for his freedman and secretary Tiro is one of the most delightful features of his letters.[6] Nor is Pliny behind his great model. For Zosimus his comic actor and for Encolpius his reader he shows the most tender solicitude.[7] He rewards the long and faithful service of his nurse by presenting her with a small farm for her declining days.[8] Towards his servants in general this best of pagans displays a broad humanitarian feeling which would have put to shame many a

[1] Tac. *Ann.* xiii. 26, 27.
[2] Suet. *Aug.* 27.
[3] Vell. ii. 67: 'id tamen notandum est fuisse in proscriptos uxorum fidem summam, libertorum mediam, servorum aliquam, filiorum nullam.'
[4] Tac. *Ann.* xiii. 44.
[5] Tac. *Ann.* xiv. 60.
[6] *Ad Fam.* xvi.
[7] Plin. *Ep.* v. 19; viii. 1.
[8] *Ib.* vi. 3.

so-called Christian planter in the Southern States. He is genuinely distressed by the illness and death of some of his slaves;[1] he encourages his slaves to make wills and honours the provisions therein, although by law the *peculium* passed to the master at the slave's death.[2] As St. Paul interceded with Philemon on behalf of Onesimus, so Pliny intercedes with a friend whose freedman has wronged him but has repented;[3] in a sincere desire to promote the welfare of freedmen he urges another friend to take the opportunity offered by the presence of a magistrate and to improve the status of informally freed slaves by manumitting them *vindicta*.[4] What is more important, he is not ashamed of his humanitarian views. He is not a master who secretly indulges his servants fearing that others will scoff at him. Rather he assumes that his correspondents are capable of appreciating his conduct and that they follow the same rules in their own lives. Genuine charity, therefore, must have been a living force throughout the whole society with which he was intimate.

Various customs which obtained in Roman history bear additional evidence to the cordial relations which subsisted between patron and freedman. For a long time freedmen and freedwomen were buried together with their patron and his wife in the family tomb. Indeed the form *libertis libertabusque posterisque eorum*, which the dying patron directed to be inscribed over his tomb, became so common and conventional that in the second century it was declared invalid.[5] A freedman accordingly could no longer claim, on the score of this formula alone, to be buried with the patron. Perhaps the custom of admitting freedmen to the family vault was universal only in the early days of the Republic, when slaves were few in number, and when those who were freed remained very much dependent on their patron. When the numbers and average intelligence of slaves increased with the gradual conquest of the Hellenistic East, when freedmen launched

[1] *Ep.* viii. 16 and 19. [2] *Ib.* viii. 16. [3] *Ib.* ix. 21.
[4] *Ib.* vii. 16 and 32. [5] *Dig.* XI. vii. 6, *pr.*

VI. A TOMBSTONE ERECTED BY FREEDMEN

Sepulchral slab with portrait busts of Antistius Sarculo and Antistia Plutia his wife and probably his freedwoman; erected by two of their freedmen. Cf. p. 101, n. 4. Now in British Museum (No. 2275)

forth in trade and industry and became self-supporting, then the patron by degrees absolved himself from the responsibility of giving his multitudinous freedmen a share in his own grave. But it is probable that the patron generally took upon himself the duty of providing for the last remains of at least his domestic freedmen. It was in the case of house-servants that the tradition of burying freedmen in the patron's tomb must have lingered longest. At any rate, favourite freedmen were often buried with their patron. Dasumius provided in his will that a certain number of his freedmen should be buried with him.[1] So too a cook (who is himself a freedman) records on an inscription that the monument has been raised to him along with several slaves whom he has freed.[2] Other patrons built *columbaria* where their slaves and freedmen, after cremating their dead fellows, might deposit their ashes in an urn and leave thereon a brief record; or a patron might even go the length of giving his freedman a separate tomb. Reciprocally the freedman often showed his fidelity by paying the last honours to his patron's remains and perpetuating his memory by an inscription.[3] He might even arrange for a statue or a bust of his late master and inscribe below an account of his life and the offices he held.[4] A slightly different case is of frequent occurrence. The words *sibi et patrono* are often found in inscriptions.[5] Here the freedman has purchased the tomb and arranged for the memorial to his patron and himself. The mere fact of such arrangements bears testimony to the cordial relations which prevailed between patron and freedman. Evidence more convincing still is to be found in the wording of the epitaphs. Brief memorials of patron's benevolence or freedman's loyalty abound among inscriptions.

[1] *Testamentum Dasumii*, *C. I. L.* vi. 10229, lines 103–7.

[2] *C. I. L.* x. 5211; cf. xii. 4481, 4627; *I. L. S.* 7602.

[3] e. g. *I. L. S.* 2868; *C. I. L.* vi. 9177; x. 3420; xi. 108; xii. 4490.

[4] e. g. *I. L. S.* 5010: 'Rufus l., Anthus l., imagines de suo fecerunt patrono et patronae pro meritis eorum.' Cf. plate vi and Mrs. Arthur Strong, *J. R. S.* iv. 147; e. g. also *I. L. S.* 7769; *C. I. L.* x. 1782.

[5] e. g. *C. I. L.* xii. 4586, 4588.

In scores of cases a patron is called *bene merens*;[1] and that hackneyed phrase is often replaced by more glowing tributes; *optimus*, *dulcissimus*, *indulgentissimus*, *rarissimi exempli*, *honestissima et optime merita* are found.[2] One grateful freedman says: 'To a patron inimitable and most generous, whose deeds are beyond all narration.'[3] Freedmen receive from patrons similar panegyrics. *Libertus bonus* and *libertus gratissimus* are found;[4] the freedman jeweller above mentioned was eulogized by his patron in no uncertain terms: 'During his life he spoke ill of no one; he did nothing without the consent of his patron; in his hands there was always much gold and silver, but he coveted none of it. In his art, Clodian engraving, he surpassed all.'[5] A freedwoman receives the following praise: 'Most sweet in her affection, her duties and her tasks; she loved her patron.'[6] Of another her patron says: 'She never caused me pain save by her death.'[7]

In various wills that are recorded we have striking testimonies of friendship between patrons and freedmen. Among inscriptions and in the Digest such evidence abounds. In the former we often come upon the words *liberti et heredes*, *libertus et heres*, &c.[8] So, in the Digest, a patron leaves fifteen freedmen a small farm and a shop attached.[9] Elsewhere the freedmen of a household receive their master's estate; in another case they are left a daily

[1] e. g. *C. I. L.* vi. 18048, 18061, 18109, 18133, 18156, 18188.

[2] e. g. *C. I. L.* ix. 3922; xi. 3892; vi. 18156, 18072; xiv. 171; xii. 2956; ii. 4405.

[3] *I.L.S.* 6348: 'patrono inimitabili largissimo cuius facta enarrari non possunt'.

[4] e. g. *C. I. L.* ix. 265; x. 4142.

[5] *I. L. S.* 7695: 'Hic in vita nulli maledixit, sine voluntate patroni nihil fecit, multum ponderis auri arg(entique) penes eum semper fuit, concupiit ex eo nihil unquam. Hic arte caelatura Clodiana evicit omnes.' On Clodian engraving see Pliny, *N. H.* xxxiii. 139.

[6] *C. I. L.* x. 4142: 'gratissima adfectu et officis (*sic*) et impendis (*sic*): patronum dilexit.'

[7] *C. I. L.* x. 8192: 'stomachum mihi nullu(m) uncquam (*sic*) fecit nisi quod mo(rtua est).'

[8] e. g. *C. I. L.* ii. 496, 4347, 4390; vi. 9672.

[9] 'Praediolum cum taberna', *Dig.* XXXII. xxxviii. 5.

wage.[1] In Spain a knight combines municipal patriotism with liberality to his freedmen. He leaves to the town of Barcelona a sum of money which can be spent in games and distributions of oil and other necessaries; but he stipulates that in return any of his own freedmen who are elected to the Augustal sevirate shall be exempted from all duties in that office which involve expense.[2]

Such is our brief survey of relations between patrons and freedmen. Of grateful and ungrateful freedmen or of generous and ungenerous patrons exact statistics are naturally not forthcoming; but, though the evidence is not conclusive, on the whole we feel the tendency was for relations to improve. After that memorable occasion in Nero's reign we never hear again that freedmen's ingratitude becomes a subject of debate in the Senate, while patrons for their part responded generously to the appeal of Stoic and Christian, and, far in advance of legislation, treated slaves and freedmen as fellow-citizens in a world-wide commonwealth.

We now leave the patron and follow those freedmen who went forth into the world without a protector and without obligations, ex-slaves who had become independent citizens, either immediately after manumission, or when their patron died and his heir took no interest in them, or when their public services had won exemption from the *operae*. Such freedmen took their place in the population armed only with their ability and such capital as they had not expended in attaining their independence. Yet their intelligence in general and their indifference to the indignity attending trade won them and their descendants a place in Roman history which should never be forgotten. It was freedmen and their descendants who

[1] *Dig.* XXXI. lxxxviii. 6; XXXIII. i. 20, § 1.

[2] *I. L. S.* 6957: '. . . do lego darique volo X̶ $\overline{\text{VII}}$ Đ, ex quorum usuris semissibus edi volo quodannis spectac. pugilum . . . et . . . oleum in thermas public. populo praeberi et lecta praestari ea condicione volo ut liberti mei item libertorum meorum libertarumque liberti quos honor seviratus contigerit ab omnibus muneribus seviratus excusati sint.'

ministered to the amusement of the public, who supplied most articles of daily use and consumption, and who in the liberal professions competed not unsuccessfully with free-born immigrants from the East.

As actors, charioteers and gladiators, slaves and freedmen dominated the stage, circus and arena. Whether as the employees of their masters or as independent citizens who offered their services, it was they pre-eminently who engaged in these professions. How strong was the prejudice of Romans against such occupations is shown by execrations hurled against Nero when he forced nobles to perform in public and eventually followed in their wake himself. Certainly Nero inflamed the wrath of the aristocracy as the murderer of his mother, his wife, and many a wealthy or influential citizen; yet it was no less as the man who made senators disgrace their dignity by dancing, acting and singing in public, and who dragged in the mire the honour of the Caesars by doing so himself, that he earned his title to infamy among all Romans of native stock.[1] Consequently it was left to slaves and freedmen to occupy the stage, circus and arena. The most famous actors in Roman times were freedmen of the imperial house, who were useful both in amusing the court and in any performances with which emperors sought the favour of the proletariat. Several imperial freedmen of the names of Paris, Pylades and Apolaustus won great celebrity on the stage,[2] and Agilius Septentrio in the time of Commodus was called by the citizens of Lanuvium 'the first pantomime of his day'.[3] Among the less famed of freedmen actors many no doubt performed in their patron's employment either privately for his entertainment[4] or

[1] Cf. the words of Subrius Flavus, who was condemned in connexion with the Pisonian conspiracy: 'I began to hate you when you revealed yourself as the unnatural murderer of mother and of wife, as a charioteer, an actor and an incendiary.' 'Odisse coepi, postquam parricida matris et uxoris, auriga et histrio et incendiarius extitisti,' Tac. *Ann.* xv. 67.

[2] Friedländer, *op. cit.*, vol. i, p. 62; Eng. trans., vol. i, pp. 59, 60.

[3] *I. L. S.* 5193–4: 'pantomimo sui temporis primo.'

[4] e. g. Zosimus, the *comoedus* of the younger Pliny.

publicly for his profit. But when their patron was dead, or when they were no longer under any obligation to him, numbers of freedmen who had made their mark as actors must have hired themselves to companies and as independent citizens have contracted to serve certain employers.[1]

If they had no taste or ability for drama, freedmen might yet win a great popularity as charioteers or as gladiators. As the champion of one of the four factions which spectators supported, charioteers made the circus a road not only to fame but also to wealth, since the winners of bets liberally rewarded the man on whom they had put their money.[2] So also in the amphitheatre, though gladiators were too often 'butchered to make a Roman holiday', many a brave or skilful warrior became the people's favourite and made untold profit in the rewards which successful gamblers showered upon him. Both these professions were practically reserved for men of servile extraction or for free-born aliens. Freedmen when entering them were no doubt sometimes merely serving their patrons, performing the *operae* in other words; but others, when independent, voluntarily enlisted or continued in these occupations, and found in them their most lucrative and most congenial way of earning a living.[3]

Nor was the pre-eminence of freedmen and their dependants less marked in trade and industry. How they entered into every phase of commercial life is well shown by Lemonnier in his account of the freedmen's rôle in Roman society. He gives examples of how they competed in nearly every sphere of money-making—as farmers, builders, food-merchants, clothiers, slave-dealers, bankers, metal-workers, doctors, artists and teachers.[4] Trade and industry they not only shared but dominated. Work with the hands was left to slaves, freedmen and their

[1] Some inscriptions of freedmen actors: *I. L. S.* 5212, 5213, 5236; *C. I. L.* vi. 10102, 10108. A freedman dancer, *C. I. L.* vi. 10144.

[2] Freedmen charioteers, *I. L. S.* 5282, 5286; *C. I. L.* vi. 10061.

[3] Freedmen gladiators, *I. L. S.* 5105, 5129; *C. I. L.* vi. 10196, 10200.

[4] Lemonnier, *op. cit.* pp. 273–84.

descendants: a true Roman would have none of it. In a Roman's mind it was less disgraceful to depend idly on the state or on a patron for subsistence than to earn it by sordid labour. War and agriculture were the only work to which he might put his hands. In two invaluable sections of the *De Officiis* Cicero admirably strikes the keynote of the Roman prejudice against manual labour. As it was this prejudice which gave the freedman his opportunity, the sections may be quoted in full.[1]

'Public opinion divides the trades and professions into the liberal and the vulgar. We condemn the odious occupation of the collector of customs and the usurer, and the base and menial work of unskilled labourers; for the very wages the labourer receives are a badge of slavery. Equally contemptible is the business of the retail dealer; for he cannot succeed unless he is dishonest, and dishonesty is the most shameful thing in the world. The work of the mechanic is also degrading; there is nothing noble about a workshop. The least respectable of all trades are those which minister to pleasure, as Terence tells us, "fishmongers, butchers, cooks, sausage-makers." Add to these, if you like, perfumers, dancers, and the actors of the *ludus talarius*. But the learned professions, such as medicine, architecture and the higher education, from which society derives the greatest benefit, are considered honourable occupations for those to whose social position they are appropriate. Business on a small scale is despicable; but if it is extensive and imports commodities in large quantities from all the world and distributes them honestly, it is not so very discreditable; nay, if the merchant, satiated, or rather satisfied, with the fortune he has made, retires from the harbour and steps into an estate, as once he returned to harbour from the sea, he deserves, I think, the highest respect. But of all sources of wealth farming is the best, the most agreeable, the most profitable, the most noble.'

From this it is seen how narrow the Roman outlook was. All manufacturers are despised; the merchant only frees himself from the stigma of commerce when he settles down on the land, and the liberal professions, which are

[1] Cic. *De Off.* i. 150–51. The translation is that of G. B. Gardiner, *Cicero De Officiis*, London, 1891, reproduced by permission of Messrs. Methuen and Co., Ltd.

admitted to confer a great benefit on society, are said only to dignify 'those to whose social position they are appropriate'. On none of these ways of earning a living, however essential they may be to the state, can the upper classes pride themselves. Agriculture and direct service of the state are the only occupations fit for a gentleman. The causes of the prejudice must be sought in the history of the Republic. When patriotism was the greatest of virtues, it annoyed good citizens to see a class whose trade did not afford it time to take an interest in public affairs. They made allowances for the farmer. He lived away from the centre of things and his enthusiasm could not be expected to bring him all the many miles from his farm to the city. But here were men, they complained, in the capital working at their trades when affairs of great moment were happening under their very noses. They never stood for office, and seldom, if ever, attended meetings of the assemblies, because, forsooth, their private affairs were too pressing! Surely such occupations were for subject races, not for the lords of the world.

Moreover it was agriculture and not business that produced sturdy warriors who could do the state good service.[1] The yeomen of Italy won Rome's victories in the third and second centuries B.C. Even after agriculture fell largely into the hands of slaves and freedmen, poets and statesmen yearned for the bygone age when peasant proprietors throughout Italy reared a heroic stock for the Roman legions. Toil in stuffy workshops enfeebled the body and unskilled labour dulled the brain. Such work could be left to slaves; it was not for the citizen.

When therefore the great influx of slaves began in the second century B.C., industrial labour and domestic employment were the channels into which it was first directed. At the same time art and science were brought to Rome by the more brilliant of her captives, and were left wholly in the servile hands. Industry, medicine, architec-

[1] Cf. Cato the Censor (*apud* Plin. *N. H.* xviii. 26): 'Fortissimi viri et milites strenuissimi ex agricolis gignuntur minimeque male cogitantes.'

ture and similar occupations became increasingly connected with slavery, and the prejudice against them was correspondingly intensified.

Very soon, however, captive labour was applied to agriculture. Vine and olive estates or vast cattle-ranches increased at the expense of arable land, and it was found most profitable to work them by gangs of slaves. Even in the cornfields that still remained foreign slaves came to be employed to a great extent, and tillage ceased to be the occupation *par excellence* of the Roman and the Italian. In spite of this the favour shown to agriculture remained; though slaves worked in the fields, it was not considered dishonourable for a citizen to work there also. The veterans of Sulla, of Pompey, of Augustus, and on some occasions the unemployed in the capital, clamoured for landed allotments. When other spheres of employment were staffed with slaves, Romans and Italians were content to leave them so; but in the case of agriculture they deplored the new tendencies. Deeds wrought by peasant ancestors were still remembered; possession of land was a mark of nobility; agricultural labour was no degradation; but to traffic in sea-borne commerce, to engage in retail trade, to study the physician's lore, or to emulate the greatest artists, was to lower oneself to the level of the conquered races.

With such forces at work, no wonder if the scions of the Italian stock held aloof from trade and industry. Greeks, on the other hand, and still more the semi-hellenized peoples of Syria and Egypt, now had no antipathy to such toil. The Greek spirit had once been almost as much against manual labour as the Roman was now. But with the extinction of political independence and self-government, politics, hitherto the all-absorbing occupation of the ancient Greek, had lost their ascendancy. So he turned to trade with a will; and, when the Roman subjected Hellas, not only in literature and art did 'captive Greece lead her captor captive', but her industry conquered on the conqueror's own soil.

Before we proceed to statistical evidence of the freedman's industrial record, some words of caution are necessary. Our statistics will be based on inscriptions, and certain factors prevent us following unreservedly a law of averages in the province of epigraphy. For instance, slaves are naturally less fully represented than freedmen, whether we take the evidence of epitaphs or the markings of makers' names on manufactured articles. A slave was often buried without an inscription, while, if he did receive one, it seldom recorded the work he performed; the free labourer had greater liberties than the slave in the matter of inscribing his name on the lamps or pipes which he made. Moreover, many persons who were slaves for a large part of their lives meet us in funereal inscriptions as freedmen. We know of them only as freedmen, yet in reality their servitude may have been of longer duration than their liberty. So, although the mass of industrial workers must have been slaves, epigraphical evidence tends to minimize their importance.

On the other hand, free-born Italians are not proportionately represented. They did not take the same pride in their work as the Orientals did; consequently they were less apt to have their trades mentioned on their tombstones or to inscribe their names on the articles their hands produced. However, this last reservation is not of very great importance. If Italians had engaged in trade and manual labour in large numbers, such numbers would have emboldened them to make no secret of their occupation.

Bearing in mind these qualifications, we may proceed to the statistics given us.

Who made those thousands of little clay lamps that meet the eye in every archaeological museum? In the fifteenth volume of the *Corpus Inscriptionum Latinarum*, pp. 782–870, are collected the inscriptions on all the lamps found in Rome. Those showing the maker's name (pp. 793–858) I have divided in the following manner. First the inscriptions with only one name were taken and divided into Greek and Latin, and then the Latin were subdivided into those which were pre-eminently the names of slaves and freedmen and those which more often belonged to free-born citizens. The following were the results:—

Cognomina only.

Greek.	Latin but servile.	Ingenuous Latin.	Total.
60	32	17	109

Next, those which gave the gentile name and the *cognomen* were taken and divided in the same way.

Cognomina with gentile name attached.

Greek.	Latin but servile.	Ingenuous Latin.	Total.
61	13	14	88

The division of the Latin names has inevitably been of a somewhat arbitrary character, and often it has been necessary to follow impression in deciding whether a name is commoner among slaves and ex-slaves or among the free-born. *Cognomina* which were borne by prominent men under the Republic have always been classed with the ingenuous Latin names. Twenty examples of each kind will furnish some idea of the methods followed.

Names taken as servile.	Names taken as ingenuous.
Agilis	Aquila
Amandus	Bassus
Auctus	Capito
Communis	Carus
Donatus	Celer
Faustus	Crescens
Felix	Crispinus
Fortunatus	Fortis
Ianuarius	Fronto
Lascivus	Frugi
Marinus	Gratus
Possessor	Iustus
Primigenius	Lucanus
Primio	Marcellus
Restitutus	Maximus
Rufio	Princeps
Salvius	Probus
Successus	Romanus
Vitalis	Saturninus
Vividus	Secundus

From these lists it will be seen how unsafe it is to draw hard and fast conclusions from epigraphical statistics. Almost every one of the names in the second list somewhere can be found belonging to a freedman, and yet they are, to a great extent, *cognomina* of prominent Republican families who would have been the last to be suspected of servile descent.

The proportions are similar in the private manufacture of pipes. While pipes needed for the supply of the public fountains and the imperial palaces and grounds were produced in Caesar's own factory by his slaves and freedmen, householders who obtained the right of tapping the imperial water-supply made their own arrangements for the bringing of water to their houses. The stamps upon their pipes show whom they employed.[1]

Cognomen alone.

Designated as slaves.	Greek.	Latin but servile.	Ingenuous Latin.	Total.
5	17	6	4	32

Cognomina with gentile names attached.

Greek.	Latin but servile.	Ingenuous Latin.	Total.
59	38	19	116

Sometimes on the pipe is inscribed the name of the artisan in whose workshop (*officina*) it has been produced. Such *officinatores* must have been in a position of authority. Either they were the owners of their several workshops and had advanced the capital by which their business was supported; or else they were foremen appointed by unmentioned employers to be responsible for the work of so many men. The ten recorded *officinatores* are as follows:—

Greek.	Latin but servile.	Ingenuous Latin.	Total.
1	5	4	10

From these statistics what conclusions are to be drawn? Taking firstly the single names alone and adding together

[1] Those examined are contained in *C. I. L.* xv., pp. 932–64.

both the statistics of lamps and those of pipes, we obtain the following results:—

Designated as slaves.	Greek.	Latin but servile.	Ingenuous Latin.	Total.
5	77	38	21	141

A solitary name is never a sure criterion of actual servitude, and probably only about half of these 141 are slaves. All the rest are either freedmen or their descendants with the exception of those who bear good Latin names. And even of them a considerable number have libertine blood in their veins. It has been shown above how fond freedmen were of giving their children good Latin names like *Maximus*, *Proculus* and *Silvanus*, which were not in themselves a badge of servile extraction.

The *cognomina* which have a gentile name attached yield the following statistics, when the figures both of lamps and of pipes have been joined:—

Greek.	Latin but servile.	Ingenuous Latin.	Total.
120	51	33	204

As before, the Greek names are over half the total number. Slaves of course do not figure in this list, as they only possessed one name. But practically the whole[1] of the first two groups may be confidently asserted to be freed-

[1] Do any of the Greek names represent *peregrini* or their descendants? Provincials migrated to Rome or Italy only if they had conspicuous advantages over those with whom in their calling they would have to compete. The Sidonian glass-blowers had such advantages in the possession of an industrial secret. A number of the more celebrated doctors, teachers and artists had such advantages in that their pre-eminent skill placed them above competition; by a law of Julius Caesar (Suet. *Iul.* 42) Roman citizenship was granted to members of some of these professions, if they migrated to Rome. But few *peregrini* would go to the expense of removal to Italy in order to compete in the crowded fields of retail trade and industrial labour, especially since their vocation would not qualify them to benefit under Julius' law. Free-born provincials therefore are absent from lists of such workers in Italy. Descendants of alien immigrants or of those provincial veterans of the *classes praetoriae* (cf. p. 141) who on retirement settled in Italy may be found in trade and industry to some small extent, but most of them would tend to engage in their ancestors' professions.

men or their descendants; and not all the thirty-three sound Latin names belonged to men of pure Italian stock.

Other trades may be briefly noticed. In the pottery industry, whose centre was Arretium, two classes of persons, factory owners and pattern-designers, appear in the inscriptions. The designer was often a freedman or a slave; *a fortiori*, then, the mechanical labourer, whose name is not given, was probably a slave also. Owners were free citizens; yet many of their *cognomina* in the inscriptions are Greek, and in some cases servile or libertine designers seem to have risen in course of time to the ownership of factories.[1] In the brick industry the Domitii, as we have seen, gradually acquired something like a monopoly which ultimately fell to the inheritance of Marcus Aurelius; in these brickyards the labour was supplied by slaves and ex-slaves.

Interesting figures are forthcoming with regard to the goldsmiths and jewellers found among inscriptions.[2]

	Slaves.	Freedmen.	Free-born.	*Ingenui* or *libertini.*	Total.
Rome { Imperial	15+1*	7+1*	—	—	24
Rome { Private	11+5*	33+11*	2+4*	22	88
Rest of Italy .	3+2*	11	2+1*	11	30
Total . .	29+8*	51+12*	4+5*	33	142

* Assignment is only probable.

This industry, ministering not to the needs of the whole population but to the luxury of the rich, only flourished after the influx of wealth and the arrival of talented slaves. Romans had neither the skill nor the wish to engage in such work, which was consequently left in the hands of slaves and freedmen.

Glass manufacture was mainly in the hands of Orientals. Here, however, some free-born provincials competed with advantage. Certain Syrians invented a new method of

[1] Cf. Tenney Frank, *An Economic History of Rome*, 1st ed., Baltimore, 1920, pp. 166–9; 2nd ed., London, 1927, pp. 220–4.

[2] Gummerus in Pauly-Wissowa, *Real-Encyclopädie*, *s. v.* 'Industrie und Handel', col. 1504.

glass-blowing. The secret was well guarded, and the Sidonians took the foremost place in the industry. Their agents in Rome and other cities were probably Syrians.

Next the epitaphs of tradesmen and artisans in Rome may be considered. In the sixth volume of the *Corpus Inscriptionum Latinarum* all Roman inscriptions referring to occupations, exclusive of those of imperial servants and those in the *columbaria*, are recorded together.[1] Now, if obviously late inscriptions and all those which mention domestic offices are omitted, the following figures are obtained for the tradesmen, artisans and members of the liberal professions in Rome itself:—

Slaves		15
Freedmen		171
One name only:		
Greek	54	
Latin but servile (Optatus, Davus, &c.)	26	87
Ingenuous Latin (Cinna, Gratus, &c.)	7	
Two or more names:		
Greek *cognomen*	120	
Latin but servile *cognomen*	53	213
Ingenuous Latin *cognomen*	40	
		486

Similar statistics on a smaller scale may be found in other large towns of the Roman Empire:—

		Puteoli.		Capua.		Narbo.
Slaves		—		—		—
Freedmen		5		19		29
One name only:						
Greek	6	9		—	–	1
Latin but servile	3				1	
Two or more names:						
Greek *cognomen*	10		5		5	
Latin but servile *cognomen*	2	14	1	7	5	12
Ingenuous Latin *cognomen*	2		1		2	
		28		26		42

[1] *C. I. L.* vi. 9104–10007.

The first two classes in each list speak for themselves. As for the third class, its two first sub-divisions, that is eighty out of eighty-seven in the former list and ten out of ten in the latter, must in the main represent slaves and freedmen and a few *ingenui* of libertine descent. In the fourth class the two first sub-divisions again heavily outnumber the last; in other words, this class is mainly filled by freedmen and their descendants. Even among those whose *cognomina* seem unimpeachable, many may have had freedman blood in their veins.

In smaller towns, too, striking examples of how freedmen dominated commercial life can be found. At Ulubrae,[1] for instance, an inscription gives a list of ten bakers, and nine of these are designated freedmen. In the same city a guild of miscellaneous tradesmen had seventeen members. One name is indecipherable, but all the rest except one are freedmen.[2]

In the older provinces of the West, such as Baetica and Gallia Narbonensis, slaves, freedmen and their posterity enjoyed almost the same monopoly in industrial undertakings. Newer provinces, on the other hand, like Belgica, Pannonia and Britain, had not developed a large servile (and therefore not a large libertine) population; nor were the native inhabitants sufficiently Romanized to disdain manual labour. In these districts, therefore, the free provincial was the usual labourer. Nor had freedmen the same commercial importance in the Hellenized East. Slaves no doubt were numerous, but manumission (though probably commoner than in fifth and fourth century Greece) was still less frequent than in Rome and Italy. Business owners were their own managers, and the freedman set up in trade was a comparatively rare figure.

The industrial masses in the Roman Empire, slaves, freedmen and free-born, grouped themselves together in guilds. Their constitution was democratic. Each year the members elected a president (*magister*) and every fifth year the president (*quinquennalis*) reviewed the list

[1] *C. I. L.* x. 6494. [2] *I. L. S.* 7483.

of members. Some prominent man in the district acted as the patron of the society and was supposed to take an interest in its affairs in return for the honour which members paid him.

These guilds were arranged according to trades, when a town contained enough members of the same trade to make a guild; but, unlike those of medieval times, they were not organized primarily for the purpose of controlling their respective industries. Their object was at once social and religious. At frequent intervals these *collegia*, as they were called, met for a common meal and for mutual entertainment. They always welcomed excuses for a dinner. One *collegium* made it a rule that any slave member who obtained his liberty should celebrate the occasion by giving an *amphora* of good wine to his colleagues. The same guild (and probably many others too) demanded a dinner from all the officers it elected and stipulated that good wine should be provided. Any quarrel or disturbance that interrupted the merriment of the proceedings was punished with a heavy fine. Members were supposed to keep their disputes for private life and not to spoil the whole guild's enjoyment by bringing them up at social meetings.[1]

A *collegium* might take some spiritual power as its protector. Often it would merely be the *genius* of the guild,[2] at other times that of its patron[3] or of Augustus.[4] More often some deity would be selected. Thus the carpenters (*fabri tignarii*) and the woodcutters (*sectores materiarii*) took Silvanus[5] for their tutelary god, while the corn-measurers placed themselves under the protection of Annona or of Ceres.[6] Frequently no special connexion between the god and the trade can be seen. Jupiter Optimus Maximus is worshipped by workers in iron, butchers

[1] *I. L. S.* 7212.
[2] e. g. *C. I. L.* v. 4211; vi. 243; xiii. 1734; xiv. 10.
[3] *C. I. L.* v. 7469.
[4] *C. I. L.* xiii. 941.
[5] *C. I. L.* xiii. 1640; *I. L. S.* 3547.
[6] *I. L. S.* 3816, 6146; *C. I. L.* xiv. 2.

and perfumers;[1] Minerva by fullers and hemp-makers;[2] Hercules by carpenters, clothiers and bakers.[3] In many cases altars were erected by guilds or *magistri* in honour of their divine protectors.[4]

The most important function of the *collegium* was to secure burial for its members. One of the things of which ancient peoples were most afraid was the possibility of being left to rot unburied. If some friend was at hand to cremate or entomb the body and to care for his last remains, the citizen of the ancient world died content. Consequently when petty tradesmen were so poor and had often paid their last penny to secure their liberty, they found it convenient to use a *collegium* as a system of burial insurance. Members of a guild could thus be confident that their dust would be tended by their fellows. However poor they were, they could die in peace.

It is in these *collegia* that the bulk of independent freedmen are to be found. Here they mingled without restraint among the free-born, and cheap gibes at their servile origin did not vex them. *Libertini* often became masters of their colleges.[5] They were equals among equals, for their fellow-members could not count far up their family tree without coming across a freedman.

Such then was the state of Roman industry. It recruited its labourers almost entirely from slaves, freedmen and their children. Yet the enterprise of these classes did not limit itself to the industrial field. The liberal professions, too, to a great extent fell into their hands; men of servile origin made livelihoods in law, medicine, teaching and art.

Among these professions it was in law that Romans

[1] *C. I. L.* xiii. 5474; xiii. 941; vi. 384.
[2] *C. I. L.* xi. 4771; *I. L. S.* 3129.
[3] *C. I. L.* v. 4216; *I. L. S.* 7315, 3417.
[4] Most of the examples just given are inscriptions upon altars.
[5] e. g. *C. I. L.* xiv. 299; v. 4449; *I. L. S.* 7283, 7243. Kühn in *De Opificum Romanorum Condicione* (p. 74) has found among the 166 *magistri collegiorum* 22 freedmen and 3 slaves. Of the rest only 10 can be certainly designated as free-born.

made their most serious bid for supremacy. Here indeed they occupied the highest positions. The greatest advocates were always Roman or Italian. In Trajan's reign Pliny and Tacitus were the most skilled barristers: law was a profession which could not sully the aristocrat's dignity, especially since, in theory at least, under the Republic cases were undertaken without remuneration. But at the end of the Republic and up to 47 A.D. the Cincian law forbidding an advocate to receive fees or presents was a dead letter. However, the fortunes thus made by advocates in defiance of the law created such a scandal that in 47 A.D. it was proposed to revive the Cincian law. A compromise had to be made between wealthy lawyers who practised not for riches but for fame and others who sought to improve their more moderate fortunes. A limit was finally set to counsel's fees at 10,000 sesterces (£100) for each brief.[1]

Even so the law could become a lucrative profession, since the legal limit was no doubt often exceeded in practice. The Roman, blocked by his pride in so many careers, found in the law a not dishonourable means of livelihood. But it is quite likely that the lower ranks of the profession were filled to some extent by freedmen and their descendants. We have seen that patrons often made their freedmen their private solicitors (*procuratores*); and, as rhetoric came from the East, there is no reason why Orientals, *ingenui* and *libertini* alike, should not have embarked on that career which offered rhetoric its widest scope.

A more promising field for the freedman was opened by the other liberal professions. Here in great measure Romans disdainfully withdrew from the lists. It will be remembered that Cicero characterized these occupations as 'honourable enough for those to whose station they are appropriate'.[2] They were not to be contemplated by the upper orders, the only class of Romans that had the brains and ability to compete with the Orientals. But in these

[1] Tac. *Ann.* xi. 5–7.

[2] 'iis, quorum ordini conveniunt, honestae', Cic. *De Off.* i. 151.

occupations a new competitor appeared in the form of the free-born immigrant. *Peregrini* did not come to Rome in any great numbers for the purpose of retail trade. It had been captured by the slave-descended population of the city. Merchants from the provinces possessed a large part of the carrying-trade—they brought a fair proportion of the imports of the East to Rome and Italy; but instead of setting up warehouses in various parts of the Empire they found it easier to sell their goods wholesale to the freedmen or natives of the ports to which they brought them.[1] As teachers, architects, artists and doctors, however, they came and settled in Rome and other towns of Italy in greater numbers. Julius Caesar offered citizenship to members of these classes who would take up their residence in Rome and practise their professions there.[2] Evidently the freedmen and descendants of freedmen in whose hands these occupations had been were deficient either in quantity or in quality or in both. Accordingly, natives of Athens, Pergamum, Rhodes, Antioch, Alexandria and other cities of the Hellenistic world came to Rome where higher remuneration and the Roman franchise awaited them. During the Empire they competed favourably with freedmen whose abilities had been cramped as a result of slavery.

For instance, the greatest doctors were nearly all free immigrants from the Greek East. Antonius Musa, the freedman of Antony and physician of Augustus, is a notable exception, but after him the Emperors nearly always drew their chief doctors from the ranks of free-born Orientals. Charicles, the physician of Tiberius, was probably a free alien;[3] this was certainly the case with P. Stertinius Xenophon of Cos and his brother in the time of Claudius,[4] with Andromachus the Cretan in Nero's reign,[5]

[1] This is substantially the conclusion of Pärvan, *Die Nationalität der Kaufleute im römischen Kaiserreich*, cited by Frank, *op. cit.*

[2] Suet. *Iul.* 42.

[3] Tac. *Ann.* vi. 50.

[4] *Bull. de Corr. Hellén.* v. (1881), pp. 461–76; *C. I. L.* vi. 8905.

[5] Galen, *De Theriaca ad Pis.* p. 470.

and with Galen of Pergamum at the end of the second century. But among the humbler practitioners, slaves, freedmen and their descendants bulked large. Of the fifty doctors classed together in *C. I. L.* vi. 2, only two (Nos. 9563, 9597) are certainly *peregrini*. On the other hand, twelve are designated freedmen outright, and thirteen have only one name, which suggests the condition either of a slave or a freedman. Of the rest fully half are probably the descendants of freedmen. From this we may generalize that among the doctors of Rome not more than twenty-five per cent. were free provincials or their posterity.

Among the teachers the same struggle between *libertini* and *peregrini* may be seen. The most eminent *iurisconsulti* (lecturers in law and assessors at trials) were nearly always *peregrini*. Gaius came from Asia Minor, Papinian from Syria, Ulpian from Tyre. The Hellenistic East was the home of Cervidius Scaevola, Modestinus, Callistratus, Marcian, and Tryphoninus. Salvius Julianus and Tertullian were from Africa.[1] A few Romans probably did not disdain to enter this profession (it was a short step to it from advocacy) and no doubt freedmen and their descendants occupied its lower ranks.

Among the grammarians men of servile extraction held the field. Suetonius in his treatise on famous grammarians mentions nine of the imperial age, and of these seven were freedmen. Where the grammarians are classified in *C.I.L.* vi. 9444–9455, most bear Greek or servile names, though only one is definitely said to be a freedman. In view of the poor remuneration that was everywhere the grammarian's lot,[2] provincials cannot have come to Italy in any great numbers to follow this profession, and on the whole it must have been left, for the little it was worth, to men of the freedman stock.

[1] Friedländer, *op. cit.* i. p. 185; Eng. trans. i. 165.

[2] Juv. vii. 215–43. 500 sesterces (£5) was the fee for a year of eight months: Schol. *ad* Juv. vii. 243. With thirty pupils the gross income would thus be only 15,000 sesterces (£150).

The professor of rhetoric was valued somewhat higher,[1] and therefore, in this capacity, the freedman and his descendants did not have the arena so much to themselves. Even Roman knights were not ashamed to embrace the profession, Blandus under Augustus being the first instance.[2] Nero's passion for oratory raised the rhetorician's rôle into still higher esteem among the aristocracy, and in Vespasian's reign Quintilian was the first to be appointed to a state chair of rhetoric. Most municipalities employed their own teachers of oratory by the middle of the second century,[3] and direct service of state or city was a thing no Roman of the bluest blood could scorn. When Pliny seeks a rhetorician for Comum, he asks Tacitus if any of his literary circle can fill the post.[4] He looks first, not among the Greeks, but among the young Romans who attend Tacitus' readings. Yet, even though Romans condescended to teach rhetoric, in sheer genius the Greeks easily outstripped them. Trained in the schools of Athens, Pergamum or Rhodes, the dwellers of the East swarmed into Italy and quickly vanquished native teachers in the unequal struggle. Against such competition freedmen had still less chance than the Romans; their descendants unhandicapped by slavery might have had some success and may have taught oratory in a modest way. But Romans were better off, and Greek *peregrini* best of all.

Of the arts, painting was probably the least despised by Italians of the old stock. In Diocletian's edict, which established a tariff for the control of industry, the portrait painter's wage was fixed at one hundred and fifty *denarii*, twice that of the stucco-modeller and three times that of the carpenter. Some examples of Roman painters are known. Turpilius, a Roman knight, painted at Verona.[5] The chief painters of the imperial age whom Pliny

[1] Juv. vii. 217. 2,000 sesterces was the yearly fee, Juv. vii. 186–7.

[2] Seneca, *Controv.* ii. *proem.* 5.

[3] *Hist. Aug.*, *Anton. P.* 11: 'rhetoribus et philosophis per omnes provincias et honores et salaria detulit.'

[4] *Ep.* iv. 13.

[5] Plin. *N. H.* xxxv. 20.

mentions in his *Natural History* all appear to be Romans. Studius or S. Tadius (the reading is doubtful) introduced a charming style of landscape painting. Famulus, or Fabullus, probably a Roman but possibly of freedman stock, was employed on Nero's Golden House, and, when Vespasian restored the temple of Honos and Virtus, Cornelius Pinus and Attius Priscus were entrusted with the decoration of the interior.[1] But it is unlikely that the upper classes embraced the profession. The aristocracy of the Empire treated the art as beneath their notice. Valerius Maximus expresses his surprise that under the Republic a Fabius should have stooped to painting.[2] Freedmen and their descendants no doubt competed with Romans and foreigners. Sometimes the painter's was a domestic post. From the *columbarium* of Livia comes an inscription of a slave or a freedman who was her painter.[3] In *C. I. L.* vi. 9786–94 are given the Roman inscriptions of painters; two of these (9786 and 9794) are freedmen, and the rest may well be of freedman extraction. An inscription of Southern Italy[4] affords another example of a freedman painter.

Architecture is claimed by Friedländer as an art in which the Romans excelled the Greeks. The only certain non-Roman architect of any prominence was Apollodorus of Damascus, who designed Trajan's Forum, Odeum and Gymnasium in Rome and that emperor's bridge over the Danube.[5] Severus and Celer were Nero's chief architects. Rabirius was employed by Domitian and Decrianus by Hadrian, while an apparently Roman architect, Costumius Rufinus, was even entrusted with the temple of Zeus Asclepius at Pergamum.[6] Yet a caution is necessary before we accept Friedländer's generalization. All of these may have been freedmen or their descendants or even *pere-*

1 Plin. *N. H.* xxxv. 116–20.
2 Val. Max. VIII. xiv. 6: 'sordido studio deditum ingenium.'
3 *C. I. L.* vi. 4008.
4 *I. L. S.* 7596: 'colorator.'
5 Dio, lxix. 4; Procopius, *De Aedif.* iv. 6.
6 Friedländer, *op. cit.* vol. iii, p. 105; Eng. Trans. vol. ii, p. 324.

VII. STATUE OF A HUNTER WITH A HARE

Capitoline Museum, Rome. The inscription on the right side of the plinth, 'Polytimus lib.', means either that the freedman Polytimus was the sculptor or (less probably, in view of the mention of no one else) that he had the statue erected in honour of his patron. Cf. H. Stuart Jones, *Catal. of Mus. Cap.*, Oxford, 1912, p. 292

grini who had adopted Roman names. One cannot say for certain either one way or the other. But the probability is that Greeks predominated in this field as in so many others. When Pliny asks Trajan to send him an architect to inspect plans for a theatre at Nicaea and for baths at Claudiopolis, the Emperor replies that in Bithynia he is in the midst of architects, for it is from the Greek East that they come to Rome.[1] Freedmen must have filled to some extent the lower ranks of the profession. Among the imperial freedmen in *C.I.L.* vi. is an architect,[2] and when among the miscellaneous trades and professions of this volume we come to architecture two at least of its four exponents are freedmen.[3] In Puteoli the only architect mentioned is a freedman.[4]

In sculpture, men of pure Roman blood withdrew from the lists. The only Roman sculptor of any note is Coponius.[5] The greatest sculptors of the imperial epoch were all Greek *peregrini*. The plastic decorator of the Pantheon was Diogenes of Athens, while the seven sculptors who filled the imperial halls on the Palatine with their works were all Greeks.[6] In this art also one or two freedmen made their mark. M. Cossutius Cerdo was a freedman, and Lollius Alcamenes most probably was of freedman descent.[7] Possibly the Avianius Evander who is mentioned by Pliny[8] was another freedman sculptor. But the humbler ranks of this art, as of painting and architecture, were recruited largely from ex-slaves and their descendants. Free provincials only faced the expense and uncertainty of migration to Rome if they had attained a considerable degree of proficiency in their own country and could therefore count on rising higher in their profession at Rome.

[1] Plin. *Ep.* x. 39, 40: 'Architecti tibi deesse non possunt. Nulla provincia est quae non peritos et ingeniosos homines habeat; modo ne existimes brevius esse ab urbe mitti, cum ex Graecia etiam ad nos venire soliti sint.'

[2] *C. I. L.* vi. 8725.

[3] *C. I. L.* vi. 9151–4.

[4] *C. I. L.* x. 1614.

[5] Plin. *N. H.* xxxvi. 41.

[6] *Ib.* xxxvi. 38.

[7] Ampère, *L'Histoire romaine à Rome*, pp. 79, 80. Cf. plate viii.

[8] Plin. *N. H.* xxxvi. 32.

Consequently it was the greater artists of the East that took up their residence by the Tiber; in the main, the lesser preferred to bear the ills they had rather than fly to others that they knew not of. The princes of art were free provincials from the Orient; the lowly craftsmen, who executed an order here and an order there for people who could not afford high remuneration, were freedmen and their posterity.

In the minor arts, which might nowadays be classed as artistic industries, men of servile origin enjoyed a practical monopoly. Among the urban inscriptions of carvers in metal or ivory (*caelatores*), metal-casters (*flaturarii*), jewellers (*gemmarii*), goldsmiths (*aurifices*), silversmiths (*fabri argentarii*) and workers in ivory (*fabri eburarii*), there are several freedmen.[1] The craftsmen who are not definitely said to be in that position at any rate bear Greek or servile names, showing that their ancestors at no very distant date had passed through servitude.

Thus predominating in trades and amusements, and partaking to no small extent in the liberal professions, many freedmen found opportunities of rising to considerable wealth. How the imperial freedmen enriched themselves will be shown in a later chapter. But it was not only they who attained prosperity. That ordinary freedmen in all parts of the world reached a high degree of affluence is shown by the fact that in many municipalities of all sizes in Italy and the Western provinces there was an Augustal sevirate of which the six annual tenants were freedmen. This office could become very expensive. Unless its holders had possessed at least a moderate income, they could not have celebrated the games in honour of the Emperor, which was the chief duty that fell upon them.

It was by commerce and banking that most of these fortunes were made. 'I buy wisely, I sell wisely,' says Trimalchio, the type of the successful freedman.[2] Still, it is doubtful whether many could have become rich

[1] *C. I. L.* vi. 9149, 9202–14, 9221–2, 9373, 9397, 9418–9, 9433–7.
[2] Pet. *Sat.* 75: 'Bene emo, bene vendo.'

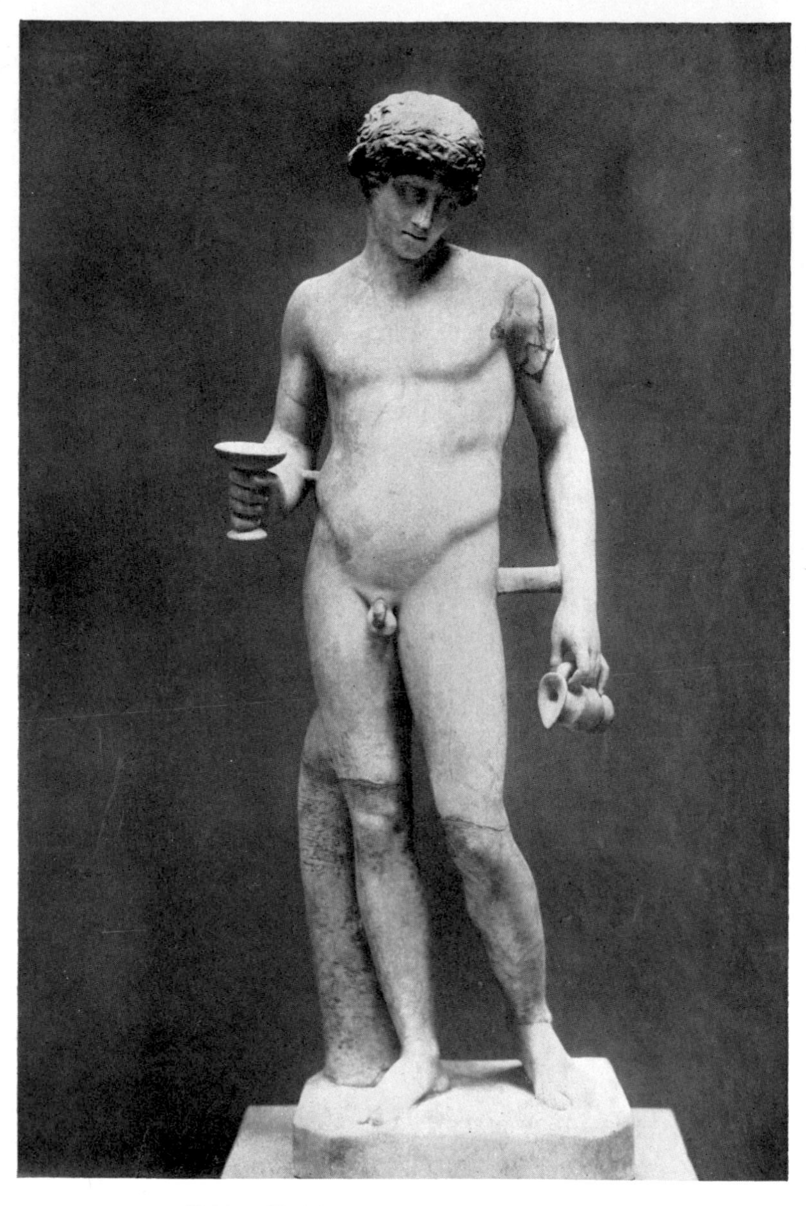

VIII. STATUE OF A YOUNG FAUN

BY A FREEDMAN ARTIST

This statue and another almost identical (British Museum Nos. 1666–7) bear the artist's name, M. Cossutius Cerdo. The inscription on one reads *Μάαρκος Κοσσούτιος Μαάρκου ἀπελεύθερος Κέρδων ἐποίει*

without external help; to embark in wholesale trade, a large capital was required, and many had spent most of their *peculium* in buying their freedom. But patrons often came to the rescue and advanced enough to float a business; and in other cases a freedman would be helped by a legacy from a friend or more probably from his patron. Once started, with average good fortune, he could rise rapidly.

It is interesting to note Trimalchio's account of his career.[1] With much vulgar ostentation he describes the ascent to his pinnacle of prosperity. As a slave he was quick to win his master's favour and confidence; he became his business manager and obtained absolute command of the house.[2] His master died and left him his freedom, if he had not freed him already. But more than this: Trimalchio and the Emperor were the only legatees, and the former received an inheritance fit only for a senator.[3] Not content with this, he conceived a passion for business and embarked on the wine trade. Despite severe loss from shipwreck on the first venture, he fitted out another cargo of wine, bacon, beans, perfumes, and slaves. This time fortune favoured him. He made 10,000,000 sesterces (£100,000) on one voyage.[4] Now he caught the Roman spirit. Like the merchant whom Cicero deigned to think respectable, he turned from commerce to agriculture. After buying up all the estates which had belonged to his patron and increasing them several fold, he retired from active business and began to finance freedmen.[5] No doubt, if the story had continued into their future, we should have seen the most favoured of these becoming Trimalchios in their turn.

The 'wealth of freedmen' became proverbial.[6] Of course the largest individual fortunes were in the hands of imperial servants, but high figures can be quoted of other

[1] Pet. *Sat.* 75 and 76. [2] 'Dominus in domo factus sum.'
[3] 'Coheredem me Caesari fecit, et accepi patrimonium laticlavium.'
[4] 'Uno cursu centies sestertium corrotundavi.'
[5] 'Sustuli me de negotiatione et coepi libertos faenerare.'
[6] 'libertinas opes,' Mart. v. 13, line 6; cf. Plin. *N. H.* xxxiii. 134.

freedmen. Demetrius, the freedman of Pompey, could boast 4,000 talents (£1,000,000)[1] and C. Caecilius Isidorus left an estate of 4,116 slaves, 3,600 oxen and 257,000 head of smaller cattle.[2] With this wealth went a certain amount of the boorish ignorance, vulgar ostentation and ridiculous lack of taste that are associated with the *parvenu* of modern times. We can picture the scorn with which the man of letters said that a man had the 'wealth and brains of a freedman'.[3] Trimalchio's excursions into mythology are merely ludicrous. The following is a typical example of how he jumbled the tale of Troy: 'Diomede and Ganymede were two brothers. Their sister was Helen. Agamemnon ran off with her and palmed off a deer on Diana!'[4] His manners were no better than his mythology. When he produces his wine he says, 'I give you real wine of Opimius' year; the stuff I uncorked yesterday wasn't half so good, and I had far finer folks to dinner'.[5] The whole banquet is one long series of ostentatious surprises. Every course contains some feat of human ingenuity. One dish is arranged so as to represent the signs of the zodiac; but this is only the top part of the dish. When the latter is lifted, fowls are revealed around a hare equipped with wings to look like Pegasus. At the corners are figures of Marsyas. Sauce runs from their wine-skins, thus providing a sea for the fish which are round the fowls.[6] Such artistic *cuisine* is excellent for one course, but it becomes tedious when repeated in different forms throughout the feast.

The self-indulgence of well-to-do freedmen was noticed by several authors. Seneca, speaking of the freedmen's baths, says, 'We have come to such a pitch of luxury that

[1] Plut. *Pomp.* 2. [2] Plin. *N. H.* xxxiii. 135.

[3] 'patrimonium et ingenium libertini,' Sen. *Ep.* xxvii. 5.

[4] 'Diomedes et Ganymedes duo fratres fuerunt. Horum soror erat Helena. Agamemnon illam rapuit et Dianae cervam subiecit.' Pet. *Sat.* 59.

[5] 'Verum Opimianum praesto. Heri non tam bonum posui et multo honestiores cenabant.' *Ib.* 34. Opimius was consul 121 B.C. So the wine would be nearly two hundred years old!

[6] *Ib.* 35, 36.

the very pavements we tread have to be jewels'.[1] So too, Martial after a wonderful description of a man's immaculate appearance—his deep purple mantle and spotless toga, his well-oiled hair and anointed arms, his scarlet shoe and brand-new latchet—mentions some patches that hide portions of his face. 'Do you know what he is? Remove the patches and you will read.'[2] The man had been a slave and had been branded by his master as a thief. After rising to wealth he spent his gains in luxury and self-adornment.

A great hole would be made in a freedman's capital if he were elected to the Augustal sevirate. In large towns the citizens holding this office would give spectacles as magnificent as their means allowed in order to impress the proletariat with their greatness. The richest of the rich would even be moved by their love of ostentation to give voluntary exhibitions of beasts and gladiators.[3]

But of course every freedman who rose to wealth was not a vulgar buffoon like Trimalchio. Many were men of culture and intellect, and indeed owed their manumission to these qualities. Supposing Cicero's secretary, Tiro, and Pliny's reader, Encolpius, to have inherited their patrons' estates, it is difficult to imagine them behaving with Trimalchio's vulgarity. Nor is it fair to suppose that, after attaining wealth, freedmen's sole aim in life was to parade it. Many a freedman helped a struggling *collegium* with his patronage.[4] Other examples of a like public spirit may frequently be found. One freedman left his city a legacy which, though it partly provided for the exhibition of gladiators, nevertheless was also designed for the upkeep of baths.[5] In Sulci, an island off Sardinia, a freed-

[1] 'Eo deliciarum pervenimus ut nisi gemmas calcare nolimus,' Sen. *Ep.* lxxxvi. 7.

[2] 'Ignoras quid sit, splenia tolle, leges,' Mart. ii. 29.

[3] e. g. Pliny, *N. H.* xxxv. 52: an imperial freedman gives a gladiatorial show; cf. Tac. *Hist.* i. 76: 'Crescens Neronis libertus (nam et hi malis temporibus partem se rei publicae faciunt) epulum plebei ob laetitiam recentis imperii obtulerat.'

[4] e. g. for an imperial freedman, *I. L. S.* 1909; for ordinary freedmen, *I. L. S.* 6985, 7323, and probably 6170, 6654, 6986.

[5] *I. L. S.* 6256.

man restored at his own cost the temple of Isis and Serapis.[1] At Neapolis two freedmen and two slaves together provided for the building of the *Lares Augusti*.[2]

There is more evidence to prove how the imperial freedmen used their wealth. A later chapter will notice in them the same love of pretentious display that we have met in their humbler brethren. But the building of baths and temples and other establishments of public utility will bear testimony to a wise and broad-minded benevolence. The Oriental freedman took his place as a citizen of Rome, and showed a patriotism that would have dignified an aristocrat of the purest blood.

[1] *C. I. L.* x. 7514: 'Templum Isis et Serapis cum signis et ornamentis et area . . . M. Porcius M. l. Primigenius magister Larum Augustorum restituit.'

[2] *I. L. S.* 3611 (quoted p. 17).

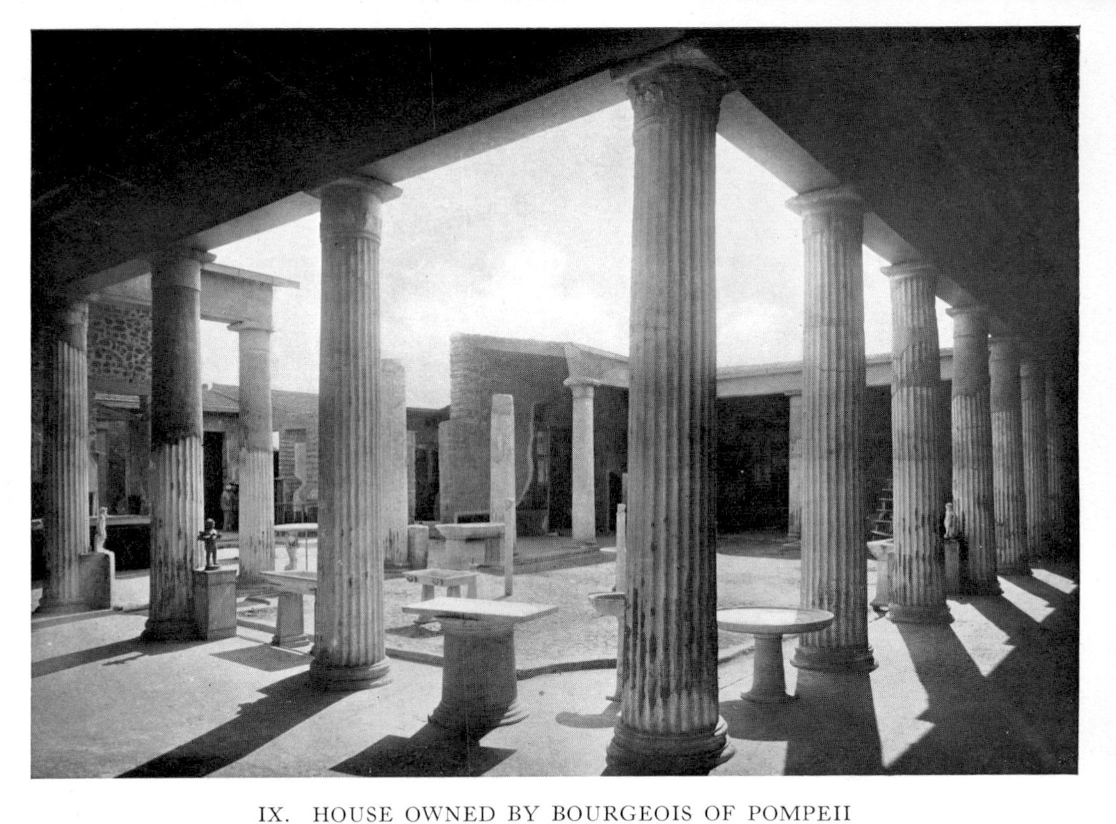

IX. HOUSE OWNED BY BOURGEOIS OF POMPEII

Peristyle of the House of the Vettii, Pompeii. The owners, A. Vettius Conviva and A. Vettius Restitutus, were merchants—freedmen according to Mau, but *ingenui* according to Della Corte. In the same house lived their freedmen Liberalis and Hilarus and their slave Verecundus

VII

FREEDMEN IN PUBLIC LIFE

I. Religious offices — priests of foreign deities — attendants on priests — superintendents of Emperor-worship — *magistri vicorum* — *Augustales*.

II. Municipal offices — secretaries and servants of magistrates.

III. Military openings — *vigiles* — imperial fleet — service in these forces never popular among freedmen.

IF we except for the present imperial freedmen, we may say that in every sphere of public life, religious, municipal and military, a freedman's past was against him. The highest positions were always denied him. Freedmen could not become directors of that system of government which worked so efficiently in the early Empire. But it was they pre-eminently who filled the lower ranks; without being in positions of high authority they kept the wheels of the imperial machinery going round; they gave the foundations on which greater men built.

I. In the province of religious worship, freedmen were excluded from the College of Augurs and from the priesthoods of old Roman deities except that of the *Bona Dea*. Though the Roman of the early Empire had not much faith in his ancient gods, he did not tolerate a foreign freedman offering sacrifice to the divine protectors of Rome. But he could not with reason prevent him becoming priest to those of his alien deities whom the state recognized. Freedmen could attain to the priesthoods of the Great Mother, Isis, Mithras, or any of the external gods in whose introduction into Rome they had been so largely instrumental. Thus freedmen were priests not only to the *Bona Dea*,[1] but also to Cybele, the Phrygian Mother of the Gods,[2] and to Mithras, the Persian lord of light;[3] while in addition a number of inscriptions refer to

[1] *C. I. L.* vi. 2240.

[2] e. g. *C. I. L.* vi. 2260. This is a priestess.

[3] e. g. *I. L. S.* 4270.

freedmen priests, but do not specify the deities whom they served.[1]

Among the attendants on priests even of time-honoured Roman gods, freedmen and their descendants bulked large. The lictors who formed the bodyguard of the priest were mainly citizens of the freedman stock. Inscriptions of priestly lictors show one or two freedmen, and, as for those who are not stated to be freedmen, their names betray their servile descent.[2] Similarly freedmen served as *calatores* (criers and general attendants) or as *viatores* (messengers).[3] The custodians of temples (*aeditui*) were often freedmen,[4] but this office was one which in Rome at least more frequently fell to imperial servants.[5] The Emperor, as *Pontifex Maximus*, had charge of several temples, especially of those which he himself or his predecessors had erected, and he therefore made it his custom to appoint temple guards out of his own freedman staff. Apart from employment as actual attendants, freedmen were probably numerous in the guilds of flutists, lyrists and choral singers,[6] who were responsible for the musical accompaniment in Roman religious worship.

However, freedmen in the capital found religious office open to them in the shape of the *magistratus vici*. Augustus divided Rome into *vici* or wards, which in the elder Pliny's day numbered two hundred and sixty-five.[7] In each ward were four magistrates elected by the citizens of the ward. Each group of four was responsible for public order in its own ward. The preservation of the *Lares Compitales* was likewise put under their charge. Some words are necessary as to the origin of these shrines. Each *vicus* had as its centre a place where roads met (*compitum*). At this point stood a pair of images under the name of *Lares Compitales*, which were honoured as the protecting spirits of

[1] e. g. *C. I. L.* vi. 2281, 2287, 2288, 2292.

[2] *C. I. L.* vi. 1885–94.

[3] e. g. *I. L. S.* 4973, 4978.

[4] e. g. *C. I. L.* vi. 2202 and 2215.

[5] *C. I. L.* vi. 8703–14.

[6] 'Collegia tibicinum fidicinum symphoniacorum.'

[7] Plin. *N. H.* iii. 66.

the *vicus*. Augustus placed between them a third image representing the *genius Augusti*,[1] and the *compitum* thus fell into symmetry with many a private house which had two *Lares* and a *genius domus*. During the Principate the regular name for the three images was *Lares Augusti* (the August Spirits). This designation had been known in the last century of the Republic,[2] but when the Emperor took the title Augustus and gave his own *genius* a place between the *Lares* the name *Lares Augusti* was felt to have gained in appropriateness and so became practically universal.

It was to superintend the worship and preservation of these *Lares* that the *magistri vicorum* were instituted in the years round 7 B. C.[3] In this connexion they were made responsible for the celebration of the *Ludi Compitalicii*, which Julius Caesar had suppressed because of the frequency of disorder, but which were revived by Augustus and were allowed to take place twice a year.[4] Moreover to the *magistri vicorum* was entrusted the worship of *Stata Mater*, the divine protectress of the city against fire.[5] Possibly at one time they had the supreme charge of the precautions against fire, but, with the establishment of the *Praefectura vigilum* in 6 A. D., they were practically confined to their religious functions.[6] On the occasion, however, of a fire in Claudius' reign they were used for marshalling the populace in the discipline calculated to render most effective aid.[7]

1 Ovid *Fasti*, v. 145: 'Mille Lares Geniumque ducis qui tradidit illos
Urbs habet, et vici numina trina colunt.'
and Horace *Odes* IV. v. 34: 'Laribus tuum miscet numen.'

2 *C. I. L.* v. 4087: *(A)UG LARIBUS DD*
(List of names)
C. IULIO / *M CALPUR* *COS*

3 We hear of a *magister vici et compiti* at Pompeii in 46 B. C., *I. L. S.* 6375. For 7 B. C. as the date of the institution or re-institution at Rome, see Dio, lv. 8, § 7. Cf. Suet. *Aug.* 30. But the *magistratus* did not begin for all the *vici* in the same year. *I. L. S.* 3617–20.

4 Suet. *Aug.* 31, § 4. 5 *I. L. S.* 3306–9. 6 Dio, lv. 26, § 4.

7 Suet. *Claud.* 18: 'Deficiente militum ac familiarium turba auxilio plebem per magistratus ex omnibus vicis convocavit.'

The wards were classified in regions. Presiding over each of the fourteen regions were a *curator* and his subordinate, a *denuntiator*. These were responsible for the control of the *magistri* in their regions and for seeing that their duties were scrupulously performed.

From a valuable fragment of a large inscription it may be discovered who filled these posts.[1] If the inscription had been preserved in its entirety, we should have been given the names of all the *magistri* serving at one time. However, time has left us two hundred and seventy-five names of *curatores*, *denuntiatores* and *magistri*, from which tolerably accurate conclusions can be drawn. Of these two hundred and seventy-five persons only thirty-seven are free-born and nine are doubtful. All the rest, two hundred and twenty-nine in number, are freedmen. Thus, eighty-six per cent. came from the ranks of ex-slaves. If this proportion remained constant throughout the imperial age, we have before us an office which was not only open to freedmen but almost reserved for them. Indeed, when this position was so overrun by freedmen, there cannot be any doubt that no pure-blooded Roman would attempt to enter it. Nor is it likely that those who were of servile extraction, but who could count some generations back before they came upon their libertine ancestors, would be found in company with so many men who had actually passed through slavery themselves. The small proportion of free-born *magistri vicorum* must have been almost entirely sons and grandsons of freedmen. More distant descendants, free from the legal disabilities of servile descent, would be eager to strive for social equality with Romans of unmixed stock, and would not be likely to compromise themselves by holding an office so peculiarly belonging to freedmen.

The title *magister vici* is rare outside Rome. At Ostia the officers charged with the *Lares* were *magistri vicorum*,[2]

[1] *I. L. S.* 6073.

[2] *I. L. S.* 5395. With the aid of the *duumviri*, the *magistri vicorum* erect a shrine at a *compitum*.

X. ALTAR DEDICATED TO THE *LARES AUGUSTI*
BY THE *MAGISTRI VICORUM*

Palazzo dei Conservatori, Capitol, Rome. The four *magistri* are represented standing two on either side of a sacrificial altar, to which the victims, a bull and a pig, are being driven. Cf. Mrs. Arthur Strong, *Roman Sculpture*, p. 73

but elsewhere in connexion with the August Spirits we find the simple title *magistri*, or more fully *magistri Larum Augustorum*.[1] Sometimes the mysterious adjective *Augustalis* is used.[2] Whatever the title, the majority of the officers are freedmen.

The subject of Emperor-worship naturally leads to the *Augustales*. The nature of the *Augustalitas*, which existed in many municipalities of Italy and the Western provinces, is still a very debatable question owing to the variety of the titles with which it is connected. Inscriptions mention in great numbers *seviri Augustales*, *seviri et Augustales*, *magistri Augustales*, *seviri* simply and *Augustales* simply. In general the title *sevir* is common only in North Italy, *seviri Augustales* (with or without the *et*) meets us in North and Central Italy and in Spain and Gaul, while the simple form *Augustalis* prevails in Central and South Italy, and in the central European provinces. With three exceptions,[3] *magistri Augustales* are confined to Italy. Almost all the *Augustales*, *seviri Augustales* and *magistri Augustales* and the majority of the *seviri*, are freedmen.

Generally, where *Augustalis* appears alone, it is but a common abbreviation for either *sevir Augustalis* or *magister Augustalis*. Probably the *magister Augustalis* was simply the *magister Larum Augustorum* under another title and thus corresponded to the *magister vici* in Rome.[4]

[1] *Magistri* at Verona and Neapolis, *I. L. S.* 3610–1; *magistri Larum Augustorum* at Sulci and Massilia, *C. I. L.* x. 7514 and xii. 406; *Larum Augustorum magister* at Singilia Barba, *C. I. L.* ii. 2013.

[2] e. g. 'seviro magistro Larum Augustali' at Tarraco, *C. I. L.* ii. 4304; 'Laribus Augustis G. Avittius Epaphroditus magister Augustalis' at Venusia, *C. I. L.* ix. 423.

[3] Carales in Sardinia and Napoca and Potaissa in Dacia, *C. I. L.* x. 7552; iii. 862, 912.

[4] See note 2 above. Additional evidence comes from *I. L. S.* 3627 = 6242: 'P. Flavius Sp. f. Cam. Decimus, P. Flavius Palestricus H(erculaneus) A(ugustalis), M. Trebienus Tiburtinus H. A., cur(atores), cultoribus domus divinae et Fortunae Aug(usti? / ustae?) Lares Augustos d. d.' Here the *Herculanei Augustales* (or the *magistri Herculanei Augustales*, as they are sometimes called) are the equivalent of the more usual *magistri Augustales*,

In those municipalities which employed them, *magistri* were frequently appointed in fours [1] (as in each Roman ward); but there is no need to suppose this number universal; in different cities different numbers of *magistri* may have been appointed.

Except in a very few towns *magistri* disappear after the reign of Augustus.[2] Where they had existed their place was taken by the *seviri Augustales*[3], who had already been

they are the *curatores* of the *Lares Augusti*, and they are recorded here as presenting the *Lares* to the worshippers of the imperial house and of the Fortune of Augustus. Of course there is the possibility that *cultores* means 'priests' and not 'worshippers'; in which case we must suppose two separate groups of officials to have existed in this town (Tibur) for the worship of the Emperor, and the *cultores*, not the *Herculanei Augustales*, to have had charge of the *Lares*. But in view of the word *cur(atores)*, which must surely mean *curatores Larum*, the first interpretation is the more likely.

[1] Four was the number at Nepet and at Falerii, *I. L. S.* 89, 5373.

[2] Except for *C. I. L.* iii. 862, 912, which are of the second century, all inscriptions whose dates can be inferred are of Augustus' reign.

[3] Between the systems of different towns and even in the same town at various times, we cannot postulate any strict uniformity. Some cities may have enjoyed the luxury of more than one grade of officials for Emperor-worship. Both *magistri vicorum* and *seviri* appear at Ostia (*I. L. S.* 5395; *C. I. L.* xiv. Index x, *s. v. Ostia*); *magistri Larum* and *seviri* appear at Massilia and Singilia Barba (*C. I. L.* xii. 400, 406, 409; *C. I. L.* ii. 2013 and *I. L. S.* 6915 = *C. I. L.* ii. 2026). The offices may have been parallel or one may have superseded the other. In the former case, the lower grade perhaps confined itself to religious rites, while the higher had more prominent duties such as the exhibition of games. Yet some general conclusions of fair probability may be drawn. Few towns (Brixellum, Carsulae, Florentia, Hadria, Parentium, Parma, and Pollentia) have inscriptions of both *magistri Augustales* and either *seviri* or *seviri Augustales*, and dated inscriptions of *magistri Augustales* after the reign of Augustus are rare. In those places where *magistri* only appear, either *magistri* continued the sole officers concerned with Emperor-worship, or else they gave way at some period to *seviri* of whom no record has been preserved; in the many places where no *magistri*, but only *seviri* or *seviri Augustales* or simply *Augustales*, are found, there it was to these officers that the cult of the *Lares* was entrusted; in the few places where both *magistri* and *seviri* appear, the latter probably took the place of the former; though at Florentia both terms (*magister* and *sevir*) were used together in the official title ('sevir magister Augustalis', *C. I. L.* xi. 1604, 1606, 1611). At Brixellum and Parentium both *magister* and *sevir* appear on the same inscription (*C. I. L.*

established in many other municipalities. The term *sevir* originally had no connexion either with freedmen or with the worship of the Emperor. In Rome and some cities of North Italy free-born officers called *seviri* existed from the reign of Augustus. In Rome they were members of the imperial house or sons of senators, and they commanded the equestrian companies at the annual review (*transvectio equitum*). In the other cities they were of humbler birth and marshalled military parades of the whole free-born youth of the municipality and district. Now, in many of the cities where these *seviri* existed, and in many others where they did not, a new *seviratus* came into being in the first generations of the Principate. This was the *seviratus Augustalis*, an office, as we have said, generally confined to freedmen. In some cities, therefore, there were two offices known as *seviratus*. In Mediolanum, for instance, the two sevirates continued—*sevir iunior* being the term for the free-born commander and *sevir senior* for the freedman *Augustalis*. The fortunes of the parallel offices varied in different towns. In many cities an amalgamation took place. *Ingenui* and *libertini* seem to have served together either as *seviri* or *seviri Augustales*; here therefore the titles came to imply the same duties. In Comum no libertine officials entered the sevirate. In other parts the free-born *sevir* disappeared, and there arose a sevirate almost reserved for freedmen.[1]

As was the case in trades, the *Augustales* and those who had been *Augustales* were organized into *corpora*, *collegia*, or *ordines*, with *curatores* and *quinquennales* as their presidents. This organization probably did not take place before the time of Trajan.

The *seviri Augustales* were certainly concerned in the worship of the Emperor. In some inscriptions they are

xi. 1029 and v. 336) and, to judge from the context, they cannot here denote the same office, and probably *magister* implies some position in the *ordo* or guild of *Augustales*.

[1] Cf. Miss L. R. Taylor in *Proceedings of the American Philol. Assoc.* 1914, pp. 231 ff. and *Journ. Rom. Stud.* 1924, pp. 158 ff.

definitely stated to have been entrusted with the *Lare Augusti*.[1] Out of the twelve relevant inscriptions which we know to belong to the reign of Augustus, half are dedications to that emperor.[2] Besides, in such an inscription as *Dis Manibus, Q. Insteio Diadumeno, Augustali, coluit annis XXXXV*, the word *coluit* distinctly implies a religious office.[3] It is probable that in most towns *Augustales* were expected to celebrate games, in addition to their more strictly religious duties.[4]

With the supreme magistracies and the local Senate in the municipalities closed to him, this office became the crown of a freedman's career. Imperial ex-slaves could rise to be secretaries of state, but freedmen outside Caesar's household wished for nothing better than the Augustal sevirate. If a citizen was relieved of the necessity of personal candidature and the office was presented to him in his absence, so much the better. It was an additional mark of the municipality's esteem. 'To this man was accorded the sevirate *in absentia*' dictates Trimalchio proudly when he is drafting an inscription for his tomb.[5]

The *Augustalitas* made a ruthless inroad into the capital of any who wished to fill it worthily. Games in most cities were expected, and on election successful candidates were usually required to pay an honorarium.[6] In the great trading centres, where individual fortunes were large, no doubt freedmen were competent for the task. But in small towns, where wealth was more evenly distri-

[1] At Histonium the only inscription concerned with *Augustales* or the *Lares* is *C. I. L.* ix. 2835, which gives 'sevir Aug. mag. Lar. Aug.'. At Tarraco no *magistri Larum* appear who are not also *seviri*.

[2] Miss L. R. Taylor in *Proceedings of Amer. Philol. Assoc.* 1914, pp. 231 ff.

[3] *C. I. L.* x. 1877 (Puteoli, 176 A. D.).

[4] e. g. *I. L. S.* 226 (Neapolis, 56 A. D.).

[5] Pet. *Sat.* 71: 'Huic seviratus absenti decretus est.'

[6] Trimalchio's friend says: 'Sevir gratis factus sum' (Petr. *Sat.* 57). He would not have said *gratis* if his case had not been an honourable exception to the usual rule. 2,000 sesterces was given for the sevirate at Assisium, *I. L. S.* 7812.

buted, many a citizen before his year was out must have rued the day he was elected. Accordingly sympathizers with the hard lot of the *sevir* sometimes left money to help him bear his burdens. We have already seen how in Barcelona a patron left a legacy to his city on condition that none of his freedmen, if elected to the sevirate, should be called upon to expend money in the performance of their duties. So too at the little town of Petilia money was left to help the *seviri* in their expenditure.[1]

Such was the part that freedmen played in the worship of the Emperor. It is plain what political purposes lay behind the institution of both the *magistri vicorum* at Rome and the *Augustalitas* in other parts of the Empire. Firstly, while he was bringing an Emperor-cult into existence, Augustus realized the importance of attracting to himself the loyalty of the freedman class; and secondly, he determined to apply that loyalty to exhibitions in the arena, that is, to the task of keeping the populace amused and contented.

II. In municipal government also freedmen played their humble rôle. In Rome they were excluded from the senatorial and equestrian *cursus honorum* and in other towns of the Empire from the magistracies and the local Senate. They might occasionally be presented with the decorations of the Senate and for some eminent public service be made honorary members without seats. At Senia in Illyricum a freedman received such honorary membership; at Puteoli an imperial freedman was so honoured; at Ostia another was accorded these decorations.[2]

In the subordinate posts of the senatorial civil service and as attendants upon magistrates, freedmen found ways open for advancement. As secretaries (*scribae*) of quaestors, aediles and tribunes, they secured not only good

[1] *C.I.L.* x. 113.

[2] *I. L. S.* 7170, 1678, 1534: 'ornamenta decurionatus' or 'ornamenta decurionalia'.

remuneration but also an employment which was not held to be disreputable. Even Roman knights did not disdain to fill these posts.[1] It must not be supposed that freedmen had anything approaching a monopoly in this field. Epigraphy shows us some freedmen who became secretaries,[2] but the majority of these situations were reserved for the free-born.[3] The office of the *scriba* was one which the over-nice Roman spirit did not find reason to despise. Every effort was therefore made to obtain men of respectable birth for it.

The case was different with the attendants on magistrates. Their duties were too menial to be performed by any but the lowest born. In the early Republic it had been enacted that the lictors had to be plebeian citizens;[4] this meant that slaves were excluded, but freedmen might be admitted. Under the Empire the magisterial bodyguards consisted partly of freedmen and partly of freeborn citizens, but the surnames that appear in their inscriptions show that most came from the freedman stock.[5]

Another class of attendants on magistrates were the *accensi*.[6] Their duties must have been of a comparatively private character; for, while the lictors were employed by the state, the *accensi* were employed personally by the magistrates. Accordingly, whereas the lictors were a permanent body of officials who retained their situations while magistrates succeeded each other, the *accensi*, on the other hand, changed as the magistrates changed. According to Varro, they had the task of summoning the people to meetings of the Assembly and of publicly announcing the hours of the day.[7] They were mostly freedmen. Usually magistrates would have their own freedmen as their *accensi*.[8]

[1] *I. L. S.* 1883, 1893, 6188.

[2] *C. I. L.* vi. 1818, 1852; *I. L. S.* 1896, 1899.

[3] *C. I. L.* vi. 1802–68.

[4] Liv. ii. 55.

[5] *C. I. L.* vi. 1869–84 and 1895–1915.

[6] *C. I. L.* vi. 1960–7.

[7] Varro, *De Ling. Lat.* vi. 88, 89.

[8] e. g. *I. L. S.* 1946, 1952.

The messengers (*viatores*) were often freedmen. Among those known by their epitaphs, some are stated to be freedmen, while most of the others are betrayed by their names as citizens of libertine extraction.[1] The duties of a *viator* do not seem to have been exacting enough to prevent his having another occupation, unless the inscriptions referring to double professions mean that they were not exercised at the same time. For instance, one man calls himself a collector of debts and a messenger (*coactor argentarius*, *viator*); another records that he has been a dealer in clothes in addition to his municipal calling. Another has supplemented his earnings in public service by trade in Spanish oil.[2]

One last category remains and that the lowest in rank. Magistrates had heralds (*praecones*) to make proclamations and to preserve order in the Assembly. Many of these—probably about half—were freedmen; while the rest were nearly all their sons and grandsons.[3]

These various officials formed themselves into decuries according to their functions and according to the rank of the magistrates they served. The quaestorian secretaries, being fairly numerous, formed three decuries; other decuries would be formed by the consular messengers or the praetorian lictors. Every presidency of a decury was recorded with pride in a man's inscription. A public servant tells posterity that he was the president of the three decuries, that is, the principal quaestorian secretary;[4] another was president of the brotherhood of messengers;[5] another commanded at different times the decuries of the consular messengers and of the consular lictors.[6]

Of course it was possible to rise from a lower decury to a higher. Many a man, after being a herald or a mes-

[1] *C. I. L.* vi. 1916–42.

[2] *C. I. L.* vi. 1923, 1926; *I. L. S.* 7489.

[3] *C. I. L.* vi. 1943–56.

[4] *I. L. S.* 1923: 'magister III decuriarum'.

[5] *I. L. S.* 1918: 'magister conlegii viatorum'.

[6] *I. L. S.* 1910: 'exercuit decurias viatoriam et lictoriam consulares'.

senger, rose to the position of secretary. Inscriptions afford examples of interesting careers of this sort. A messenger of the quaestors, employed in connexion with the treasury, becomes a secretary to the tribunes; he ends as a member of one of the three decuries of quaestorian secretaries.[1] A freedman starts public life in a company of the lictors attending priests at a town of mythical prestige, Lavinium; next he is, in succession, messenger of the augurs, herald of the quaestors, herald of the consuls, secretary to the curule aediles, and finally seems to be employed as secretary both of tribunes and of aediles. In this capacity he wins the gold ring from the Emperor Commodus.[2]

III. Such was the share of the ordinary freedman in the civil service. Much higher posts were obtained by imperial freedmen; officials who were in theory personal servants of Caesar naturally tended to be his freedmen. But with these we are not for the present concerned. Our interest is still in the average freedman, the slave freed by the ordinary citizen. In one more sphere of public life could he play his humble part. In military service his rights were as much curtailed as in municipal and religious offices. He was excluded from the legions and the praetorian guard and even from the urban cohorts. On the other hand, *auxilia* might be recruited from freedmen; and the *cohortes vigilum*, the police and fire-brigade of Rome, were open to them. At its first formation in 6 A.D. this corps was reserved for freedmen;[3] but they do not seem to have been eager to enlist. As early as 24 A.D. inducements in the shape of Roman citizenship had to be offered to Latins who would serve[4]; and probably about this time the brigade was opened to ingenuous citizens. True,

[1] *I.L.S.* 1926: 'Q. Fabius Africani l. Cytisus viator quaestorius ab aerario, scr. libr. tribunicius, scr. libr. quaestorius trium decuriarum.'

[2] *I.L.S.* 1899: 'Marius L. lib. Doryphorus anulos aureos consecutus a divo Commodo, scrib. aedilic. et tribunic., scrib. libr. aedil. curul., praeco cos., [pra]ec. quaestorius, sacerdotal. viator augurum, [lict]or curiat. Laurens Lavinas. . . .'

[3] Dio, lv. 26, §§ 4–5.

[4] Gaius, i. 33; Ulp. iii. 5.

freedmen figure among the inscriptions of the *vigiles*, and most of the names are certainly servile in character. But, if we count the cases where a man's condition is stated on the inscription, the *ingenui* are far in excess of the *libertini*.[1]

Nor do freedmen appear to have thronged the imperial fleets at Misenum and Ravenna. At first the galleys were manned by imperial slaves and freedmen;[2] but, since nothing more than average capacity could be secured in this way, they were thrown open to the whole Empire. Free provincials from all parts were admitted; and if we examine the inscriptions freedmen are conspicuous by their absence. All the certain cases are *peregrini*. For the rest one cannot say; they may be foreigners who have not inscribed their nationality, they may be free-born citizens of Italy, or they may be freedmen; but it is most probable that in the main they also are *peregrini*.

Why are freedmen so rare in the fleet and in the fire-brigade? In the case of the fleet the reason is not difficult to find. Service was for twenty-six years, while many freedmen were past the prime of life before they obtained their liberty. Indeed, it is quite likely that in view of the length of naval service required an age limit was fixed at twenty or twenty-five beyond which no one could be admitted. Even if a slave won his liberty early in life, it was not probable that he possessed the qualities required. A free provincial was able to practise himself for a sailor's life in his youth; a freedman's youth was spent in domestic or industrial labour.

In fact, probably neither of these careers—neither the sailor's nor the fireman's—appealed to ex-slaves. So many of them found themselves provided for when they reached their liberty—so many of them secured comfortable

[1] *C. I. L.* vi. 2959–3091; for a freedman see e. g. 2990. Cf. *I. L. S.* 2163 (203 A. D.): of eighteen *vigiles* whose condition is certain, thirteen are ingenuous and five are freedmen.

[2] In the war with Sextus Pompeius 20,000 slaves were freed by Augustus in order to serve as rowers in the fleet: Suet. *Aug.* 16.

situations in their patron's house, or had good prospects in trade, or obtained work not too exacting in the service of the state magistrates, that they scorned the arduous toil in fleet and fire-brigade. To pledge oneself for a number of years in work that offered more hardship than comfort was a thing that few freedmen would do. Rather they would take their chance in the world; many fields the fastidious taste of the high-born Roman had left open to them; they would try these before entering an occupation whose recompense lay in hard knocks and weary limbs. The freedman was essentially a man of peace. Of all his many disabilities his exclusion from the legions and the praetorian guard was what he least resented; why then should he bestir himself to enter military and naval service which was more exacting and of less repute?

VIII

IMPERIAL FREEDMEN

I. Minute sub-division of labour best exemplified in the imperial household — officials concerned with dress — with furniture and plate — with the Emperor's table — the imperial chamberlain — the *procurator castrensis* — the *libertus a mandatis* — actors and concubines.

II. How freedmen came to be employed in powerful offices — origin of the great secretariates — the *a rationibus* — the *a libellis* — the *ab epistulis* — the *a studiis* and *a cognitionibus* — opportunities open to the holders of these posts — their transference to the knights — subordinate officials in these bureaux.

III. Treasuries at Rome — freedmen in the collection of direct taxes — in that of indirect taxes — in imperial domains — in the administration of miscellaneous sources of revenue.

IV. High positions which were closed to freedmen — the *procurator aquarum* — freedmen in the administration of the corn-supply — in charge of the mint — of the post — of libraries — of imperial shows — of Caesar's journal — the *a copiis militaribus* — all these departments in touch with the general and financial secretariates — clerks and accountants in the above bureaux.

V. The *praefectus classis* — exceptional positions given to freedmen.

VI. Power and wealth of imperial freedmen — freedmen under Augustus and Tiberius — their *saturnalia* under Gaius, Claudius and Nero — freedmen in the year of revolution — under the Flavians — their ascendancy destroyed in the second century — luxury and ostentation of imperial freedmen — perils besetting their careers — the life of the father of Claudius Etruscus — the good government of the Roman world.

WE now come to the freedmen concerning whom we have most information, those of the imperial household. Exercising a political influence hardly surpassed by senators themselves, the freedmen of emperors figure prominently in the histories of Tacitus and Suetonius; holding the keys of princely favour they receive flattering addresses from Seneca, Statius and Martial; rising to considerable wealth, they have left us ample inscriptions from which we can trace their career.

I. In the first place, a glance may be taken at the subordinate freedmen of the imperial household; for it is here that the absurdly minute division of labour in Roman society is best exemplified. It has already been noted how in aristocratic houses there were vast arrays of servants, whose duties must have been exceedingly light. A private barber presumably would spend ten minutes on shaving his master and the rest of the day would be his own. He might indeed from time to time be employed in cutting the hair of his master's freedmen, but on the whole he must have done a ridiculously small amount of work for his daily bread. In the imperial palaces examples of idle freedmen are even more striking. For instance, there was one freedman whose sole duty was to look after the white robe that the Emperor wore in triumphal processions. To the care of other individual freedmen were entrusted his military costume, his dress for occasions of royal state, his hunting attire and the clothes he wore at the theatre.[1] Another's duty was to supervise the purchase and keeping of the brooches used in the palace, while another had similar charge of the scents.[2]

While these servants were enjoying their easy positions, a bureau administered the purchase of clothing for the whole household. In view of the vast numbers of the prince's servants and dependants, this bureau's sphere of control was a very wide one. But it was doubtless amply staffed. One of its officials is met with among the imperial freedmen under the title of assistant accountant in the clothing bureau.[3]

Another large and well-staffed bureau was that of the imperial treasures. Its director was a freedman.[4] Under it were those who had charge of Caesar's furniture. To one freedman is entrusted the furniture of the Golden House;[5]

[1] *I. L. S.* 1763: 'praepositus vestis albae triumphalis'; *C. I. L.* vi. 8547: 'adiutor a veste castrense' (*sic*); *I. L. S.* 1758: 'a veste regia'; 1762: 'a veste venatoria'; 1764: 'praepositus vestis scaenicae'. The last may have been responsible for the dress of court actors, but the interpretation given in the text seems more probable.

[2] *I.L.S.* 1575: 'praepositum a fiblis' (*sic*); *C.I.L.* vi. 9098: 'ab unguentis'.

[3] 'adiutor tabulariorum rationis vestiariae', *C. I. L.* vi. 8544.

[4] 'procurator thesaurorum', *I. L. S.* 1738.

[5] 'a supellectile domus auriae' (*sic*), *I. L. S.* 1774.

another's sphere of service is narrowed down to the chairs of the palace.[1] Similar sub-division of labour is witnessed in the case of the imperial plate. The collections of gold dishes, of gold cups and of silver goblets have each their individual keeper.[2] To another are entrusted gold ornaments embedded with precious stones,[3] while vessels of glass are put under yet another servant.[4]

The Emperor's table demanded a similar throng of attendants and officials. The supreme charge of his dining-room was committed to a *tricliniarchus*[5], who doubtless had a number of servants under him. To another freedman fell the daily round of tasting all foods before they reached his master's mouth.[6] The purchase of wines for the imperial board was put under a special procurator, but side by side with him was another freedman who had to see that the wine required for each meal was duly placed on the table.[7]

The friends of the Emperor, a select body of senators and knights who lived at court, probably brought their own servants to dance attendance upon them. But an imperial freedman was appointed in addition, to see that they had everything due to them and to make known any requests or orders to the palace official whom it concerned.[8]

The most prominent and influential of the Emperor's purely domestic servants were the chamberlains.[9] Often a man's chance of being admitted to the Emperor's morning levée depended upon them or upon the *liberti ab admissione*[10] who were probably their subordinates. They were even able to sell their reports of the Emperor's mood.

[1] 'a sedibus', *C. I. L.* vi. 9040.

[2] 'praepositus auri escari', *I. L. S.* 1811; 'praeposito argenti potori', 1813; 'praepositus auri potori', 1812.

[3] 'praeposito ab auro gemmato', *I. L. S.* 1814.

[4] 'praeposito a crystallinis', *I. L. S.* 1575.

[5] *I. L. S.* 1792.

[6] 'praegustator', *I. L. S.* 1797.

[7] 'procurator vinorum', *I. L. S.* 1738; 'a potione', 1792.

[8] 'a cura amicorum', *C. I. L.* vi. 8795–9.

[9] 'cubicularii'.

[10] *C. I. L.* vi. 8698–702.

They could for their own ends circulate rumours of secrets that their master had confided to them. A special term, 'smoke' (*fumus*), came to be used of these reports. Among the dishonest ways of earning a living in Rome, Martial mentions the sale of 'empty smoke about the palace'.[1] So too Antoninus Pius is said to have taken precautions that his freedmen might make no profit through 'smoke'.[2]

If we except the case of Helicon under Caligula, the office of chamberlain does not seem to have extended beyond its normal sphere until the reign of Domitian. Before that time the power of imperial freedmen depended on whether they held a governmental office, and the purely domestic servants of the Emperor never exercised any social or political influence. Why Parthenius and Sigerus, the chamberlains of Domitian, became important personages is difficult to see. Probably the answer goes no deeper than the individual characters of the freedmen concerned. The great freedmen of Claudius and Nero—Narcissus and Epaphroditus and others who enjoyed full power in virtue of their secretariates—in all likelihood took due precautions that no upstart chamberlain gained their masters' ear. But Abascantus and the father of Etruscus, Domitian's secretaries, were perhaps more conscientious, devoting their energies to their imperial business and not to the jealous limitation of the chamberlains' influence. At the same time the character of chamberlains may have undergone a change. Those who served Claudius and Nero in this capacity may have been honest or timid men who scrupled to rise by dishonourable means or who feared the dangers of power at court. Parthenius and Sigerus, on the other hand, were probably men of soaring ambition, able to win the favour of their prince and determined to override every obstacle that barred their ascent. Whatever the reason, it is not from the annals of the reigns of Claudius and Nero, but from the epigrams of Martial contemporaneous with Domitian that we

[1] Martial, iv. 5: 'vendere nec vanos circa palatia fumos'.

[2] *Hist. Aug.*, *Anton. P.* 11 (quoted p. 182).

obtain our picture of the chamberlain's importance. Just as nobles and princes cringed to Bontemps, the valet of Louis XIV, so senators and knights anxious for offices in the civil service besought the chamberlain with bribes and compliments to put in a good word for them with the Emperor. Poets and men of letters, covetous of imperial patronage, courted him with fulsome adulation and would spend their last sesterce to obtain his mediation. Martial addresses three flattering epigrams to Parthenius. In the first he congratulates him on his child's fifth birthday, in a second he begs him to recommend his epigrams to his master, and in a third he bestows extravagant praises on a *toga* Parthenius has given him, ending with the hint that a cloak to match would not come amiss.[1] Throughout most of the second century, however, the chamberlains, and indeed freedmen in general, were held in check by strong and vigilant rulers. But under Commodus their power became as scandalous as in the worst days of the first century. The chamberlain, Cleander, gave away or sold seats in the Senate, military commands, procuratorships and governorships to whom he would. It is said that in one year he appointed twenty-five consuls![2]

One or two other domestic or quasi-domestic offices deserve to be mentioned, not because they became politically important, but because they illustrate a slightly different charge that might be entrusted to imperial freedmen. A servant of the Emperor might be engaged to superintend the imperial baths or the storehouses.[3] Another would be the caretaker of some past emperor's mausoleum, or the head-gardener in Caesar's parks.[4]

Over all imperial property in Rome was set a *procurator castrensis*, who was ultimately responsible for the adminis-

[1] Mart. iv. 45; v. 6; viii. 28.

[2] Dio, lxxii. 12: *Ὁ δ' οὖν Κλέανδρος, μέγας ὑπὸ τῆς τύχης ἀρθείς, καὶ ἐχαρίσατο καὶ ἐπώλησε βουλείας, στρατείας, ἐπιτροπείας, ἡγεμονίας, πάντα πράγματα· . . . καὶ ὑπάτους ἐς ἕνα ἐνίαυτον πέντε καὶ εἴκοσιν ἀπέδειξεν.*

[3] *C. I. L.* vi. 8676–8, 8681.

[4] *C. I. L.* vi. 8686, 8672–3.

tration of the palaces and grounds and for the judicious employment of the funds set apart for that purpose.[1] His office somewhat resembled that of the early Mayors of the Palace in Merovingian times, though the latter acquired a political ascendancy which never fell to the lot of the *procuratores castrenses*.

One other question presents itself before we leave the Emperor's domestic staff. Supposing Caesar wished to give an order in his own palace, how could he distinguish among all his multitudinous slaves and freedmen which was the proper official? This difficulty was solved by the creation of yet another post in the palace. A special freedman, *libertus a mandatis*,[2] was appointed, whose duty it was to take the orders of Caesar to the heads of the departments they affected. Probably there were a number of these; one for orders concerning the palace, another for orders to be sent to the secretaries of state; one for patrimonial, another for fiscal matters, and so on.

Apart from the chamberlains and the freedmen in the civil service, the only imperial ex-slaves whose names are at all important in history were the actors and concubines. Both these classes of imperial servants have been mentioned before. From time to time actors won the Emperor's graces by their talents or their good looks and became influential personages at court. Mnester, for instance, became the lover of Messallina; and, when that bad eminence involved him in her downfall, he defended

[1] This is the view of Hirschfeld. It is assailed by Mommsen, who argues that the name *castra* never was given to the imperial palace, and never could be, since the Principate tried to disguise the fact that it was a military despotism. He holds that the *procurator castrensis* was a superintendent of the Emperor's *vestis castrensis* and his camp and travel equipments generally. In favour of Hirschfeld's view it may be remarked that, firstly, the name *Imperator* applied to the sovereign is sufficient justification for the term *castrensis*, and, secondly, an inscription (*I. L. S.* 1567) shows the *procurator castrensis* to be a higher official than the *procurator aquarum*. The latter office, we shall see, was no mean one; so it is unlikely that such petty duties as Mommsen suggests should succeed it in the libertine *cursus honorum*.

[2] *I. L. S.* 1575.

himself on the ground that the intrigue had been forced upon him. This defence would have persuaded Claudius to excuse him, had not the Emperor's omnipotent freedmen refused to consider it.[1] At one time Nero was under the influence of Paris, who, though a freedman of his aunt Domitia, may yet be counted an imperial freedman. This companion in his debaucheries so enchanted Nero that in defiance of the legal rights of Domitia he gave him the privilege of free birth, only to execute him later in his reign.[2] Court actors in the second century are known to have won the favour of the Emperor and the public,[3] though the princes of this age saw to it that they attained no excessive social importance.

More powerful than the actors were the concubines of the Emperor. Even the great Narcissus had recourse to two of Claudius' mistresses in compassing the doom of Messallina.[4] Nero's passion for his freedwoman, Acte, all but made her his lawful wife. Consuls were ready, after being bribed by the Emperor, to attest on oath her royal descent from Pergamene kings.[5] Even a strong ruler like Vespasian was so much under the sway of Caenis that she was able to sell positions as governor or procurator, military commands, priesthoods and the legal decisions of the Emperor to the highest bidder. Popular gossip ran that Vespasian himself connived at it; for the sale of offices replenished the state-coffers which had been almost emptied by the licentious extravagances of past reigns.[6] Antoninus, a stern disciplinarian with his freedmen, was known to be influenced by a concubine; rumour had it that a praetorian prefect owed his position to her.[7]

1 Tac. *Ann.* xi. 36.

2 Tac. *Ann.* xiii. 19–22, 27; Suet. *Nero*, 54; Dio, lxiii. 18.

3 e. g. Pylades under Trajan and Hadrian, Dio, lxviii. 10; *I. L. S.* 5185; Apolaustus under Trajan, *I. L. S.* 5184; another Pylades under Marcus Aurelius and Lucius Verus, *I. L. S.* 5195.

4 Tac. *Ann.* xi. 29.

5 Tac. *Ann.* xiii. 12 ff.; Suet. *Nero*, 28; Dio, lxi. 7.

6 Dio, lxvi. 14; cf. Suet. *Vesp.* 3.

7 *Hist. Aug.*, *Anton. P.* 8: 'Repentinus fabula famosa percussus est, quod per concubinam principis ad praefecturam venisset.'

II. The greatest freedmen, however, founded their power on their position in the imperial civil service. One or two general considerations are necessary to show how freedmen came to be employed in such responsible posts. It is well known what efforts Augustus made to limit or to disguise the monarchy, how he posed not as the ruler but as the foremost citizen of Rome, and how he divided or pretended to divide the government between the Senate and himself, the permanent proconsul with tribunician power. The Empire was regarded as the joint rule of a body of ex-magistrates and of a pre-eminent but not sovereign individual. This theory of the Principate demanded that, while the senatorial sphere of administration should continue on Republican lines, the whole of the imperial sphere should be entrusted to Caesar and his personal servants. Naturally this preposterous corollary could not be obeyed in its entirety. Senators might resent serving Caesar instead of the state; but they would far more fiercely resent the placing of slaves and freedmen in command of legions and provinces. Augustus, therefore, had recourse to other logic. Under the Republic each proconsul had *legati* or lieutenants on his staff, and from 55 B. C. to the Civil War Pompey, while resident in Rome, had been governor of Spain, which province he administered through his lieutenants. Thus a precedent was found to justify Augustus in governing his many provinces through senators, who as friends rather than as servants administered them under the title of *legati Augusti pro praetore*. Similarly, a senator with Republican sympathies might be pacified when taking the command of a legion. Though Augustus was the commander-in-chief of the army, the legionary lieutenant was nominally not his subordinate but his representative.

Such fine distinctions were not likely to deceive the matter-of-fact Republican into thinking that the case was anything other than it was; but they pleased the logical mind of Augustus, and he liked to believe he was only remodelling the Republic and not laying the foundations of a monarchy. However, in several parts of the administration, an office was so closely attached to his own person or was one in which he himself was bound to be so constantly interfering, that he was convinced no senator could with propriety be asked to undertake it. Financial posts in the imperial sphere, the direction of the corn-supply, the command of the praetorians, the fire-brigade, Egypt and third-class provinces were branches of national service which he was anxious to control as directly as possible himself, and from which accordingly he excluded his senator-peers. To secure for himself the most effective control he must needs have performed these duties through slaves and freedmen. Yet positions of this kind carried with them such political importance that most of them could be given to none but free-born citizens. At the same time it was the ambition of Augustus to found a civil service upon the moneyed aristocracy, the *ordo equester*. Accordingly the greatest of these offices—Egypt, the praetorians, the *annona* and small provinces like Raetia and Noricum—were all entrusted to knights. Financial posts—the procuratorships of provinces, of certain indirect taxes, of various imperial domains—were divided between knights and freedmen.

But secretarial work at Rome was even more closely attached to Caesar's person. It could only be entrusted to his private servants. Even if knights could become the agents of the Emperor, they could not perform the work of his private secretaries. The sorting of petitions to Caesar and the management of his correspondence were naturally for his slaves and freedmen to perform. Money entrusted to the Emperor but belonging to the state could, in Rome at least, be administered only alongside of his private fortune; these two classes of money were in close relation, and the latter may have often subsidized the former. Augustus therefore found it most convenient to manage both through his personal servants. Thus all the spheres of secretarial work which were afterwards known as the bureaux *a libellis*, *ab epistulis* and *a rationibus* were from the first committed to freedmen and slaves of the Emperor.

Yet in the reign of Augustus freedmen never, as in later times, commanded great centralized bureaux. That prince had no thought of allowing such excessive power to his freedmen. He aimed at personally directing the work involved and at preventing any abuses on his freedmen's part. But in the following reigns congestion of business, the retirement of Tiberius to Capri, and most of all the incompetence of Gaius and the eccentricities of Claudius, threw more responsibilities on the freedmen; and the idea of Augustus that princes could control their secretarial staff was seen to be nothing but a fond dream when less able men than himself succeeded to his throne.

Such was the origin of the three great offices which under Claudius were held by that infamous and omnipotent triumvirate, Narcissus, Pallas and Callistus. It is uncertain when the posts took official shape. The *libertus a rationibus*, financial secretary to the Emperor, is known as early as Tiberius' reign,[1] though the *fiscus*, which this office controlled, had probably existed previously. The title *acceptor a subscriptionibus*, also Tiberian in date, corresponds to the later and better known one of *libertus a libellis*, secretary for petitions and grievances.[2] The department of the general secretary of state, *libertus ab epistulis*, was officially established at the latest in the reign of Claudius, under whom Narcissus held the position.

Other secretariates of political or social importance followed quickly in the trail of the three great offices. The *libertus a studiis*, chief librarian and literary adviser to the Emperor, probably originated in the time of Claudius. The *libertus a cognitionibus*, Caesar's legal secretary, must also have been created under that indefatigable hearer of cases, Claudius. Indeed, in the *Apocolocyntosis* written shortly after his death, the very term

[1] *C. I. L.* vi. 8409, 8412.

[2] *I. L. S.* 1676.

a cognitionibus is used of Claudius himself, when, as a double satire on his mania for hearing cases and his subserviency to his own freedmen, he is finally made the slave and law-clerk of Aeacus' freedman Menander.[1] Another central bureau, that of *beneficia* or imperial grants, was created by Trajan, but it seems only to have existed under him. Indeed the *a commentariis beneficiorum* can never have been more than a subordinate of the *a libellis*.

The three greatest of these offices were of such historical importance that the *loci classici* for the duties involved in them deserve to be quoted in full. From the poem of Statius addressed to Claudius Etruscus in memory of his father, who was *a rationibus* under the Flavians, we gather that he was the greatest financial officer of the Empire. He was in charge of the *fiscus*. Through his hands passed all the revenue from imperial provinces, from most of Caesar's domains, and from those taxes which did not belong to the senatorial or military treasuries. Similarly he controlled the expenditure for the army and navy, for the conveyance of corn, for the establishment and repair of public works, and for the general administration of Rome, Italy and the imperial provinces. But Statius will speak for himself.[2]

'And now the light of nobility entered thy loyal home, and with step unchecked exalted fortune passed therein. Now to thee alone is given the governance of our holy ruler's wealth. In thy sole charge are the riches all nations render and the vast world's tribute; the bullion that Hiberia casts up from her mines of gold, the glistening metal of Dalmatian hills; all that is swept in from African harvests or ground on the threshing-floors of sultry Nile or gathered by the diver in Eastern waters; the fatted flocks of Spartan Galaesus, transparent crystal, Massylian oak-wood and the stately Indian tusk. Sole steward, thou art charged with and directest what Boreas and fearsome Eurus and cloudy Auster waft into our coffers. Lighter than thy task would it be to number the

[1] Sen. *Apocol.* 15: 'adiudicatur C. Caesari; Caesar illum Aeaco donat: is Menandro liberto suo tradidit, ut a cognitionibus esset.'

[2] Statius, *Silvae*, iii. 3, lines 85–108.

forest-leaves or the rain-drops of winter. Thine eyes are on all parts and thy wits are shrewd.[1] With quick brain thou reckonest what sums are demanded by the Roman arms in every clime, by the tribes and the temples, by the deep channels of rivers, by the barriers set against the deep and by the far-flung chain of roads. Thou takest thought what gold must shine on our sovereign's lofty ceilings, what lumps of ore are to be melted in fire and shaped to the likeness of gods, and what metal is to ring aloud stamped by the fire of the Ausonian mint. So thou wast seldom at peace; thy heart was closed to pleasure; thy fare was meagre, and never did draughts of wine dull thy industry.'

The department *a libellis* was of narrower range and less political significance. Nevertheless its director was a man of considerable influence and activity. His duties were somewhat analogous to those of the modern Italian 'Ministero di grazia e giustizia'. The distinction between *libellus* and *epistula* has recently been expounded by Professor Wilcken.[2] A *libellus* was a note delivered into the hands of the person addressed[3] by the author or his representative. The recipient answered it by a *subscriptio*. He wrote his reply underneath the *libellus* and handed it to the presenter. An *epistula*, on the other hand, was sent by the imperial post or carried by a messenger not taken into the writer's confidence, and was answered, if necessary, by another *epistula*. Now a *libellus* presented to the Emperor was almost always a petition.[4] Suetonius uses the word for that which naturally conveys a request.[5] When the African *coloni* appealed to Commo-

[1] Reading: 'vigil usque animique sagacis Et citus evolvis. . .'

[2] *Hermes*, 1920.

[3] Sometimes in the case of *libelli* addressed to the Emperor they might be personally presented to provincial governors or other persons in authority who would forward them to him. Cf. Pliny, *Ep*. x. 60, 83 and 106.

[4] A petition might contain an accusation and hence a libel. Cf. Pliny, *Ep*. x. 60.

[5] Cf. Suet. *Aug*. 53, § 2: 'Promiscuis salutationibus admittebat et plebem, tanta comitate adeuntium desideria excipiens, ut quendam ioco corripuerit, quod sic sibi libellum porrigere dubitaret "quasi elephanto stipem".' Here the *libellus* obviously carries *desideria*.

dus against the injustice of the rent-farmers and the peculation of the imperial procurator, their address was called a *libellus*. It was answered by a *sacra subscriptio*. Later an *epistula* was dispatched with instructions based on the *subscriptio*.[1]

Accordingly through the hands of the *a libellis* would pass all applications to the Emperor. His concern would be with complaints against the misconduct of imperial officials, claims for the recognition of certain rights, and petitions for offices, priesthoods, citizenship and *ius trium liberorum*.[2] He examined the *libellus*, abbreviated it to a brief statement of what was desired and the grounds of such a desire, brought to the Emperor's notice any precedents or other circumstances likely to aid his decision, perhaps conferred with him on the merits of the case, wrote the *subscriptio* according to the Emperor's commands, obtained his signature and finally handed the *libellus* with the *subscriptio* to the person who presented it.

That this post was an important one is shown by the fact that Seneca, who afterwards satirized the subjection of Claudius to his freedmen, yet thought fit to win the graces of the favourite who had been appointed *a libellis*. In his flattering letter of consolation to him on the death of his brother, Seneca gives an idea of the nature and importance of the minister's work:

'You must hear so many thousands of men and decide so many petitions. You have to examine such a mass of problems streaming in from the four corners of the world, for the purpose of submitting them in their due order to the judgement of our supreme ruler. You, I repeat, must not weep. To be able to sympathize with the grief of so many, to be able to dry the tears of them who are in peril

[1] *I. L. S.* 6870, § 4.

[2] In Juv. xiv. 193 a boy is told to apply for a centurion's staff by means of a *libellus*: 'aut vitem posce libello'. Other *libelli* are mentioned in Pliny's letters to Trajan, though in these cases they are dealt with by the Emperor himself and not by the *a libellis*. Cf. Plin. *Ep*. x. 83–4, property is claimed in virtue of an edict of Augustus; x. 92–3, the city of Amisus requests the freedom to form societies (*erani*) on the grounds of its home rule; x. 106, a petition for citizenship is made.

and who seek to obtain the mercy of our most gracious sovereign, you must dry your own tears.'[1]

In all probability the most confidential and the most responsible minister was the general secretary of state. He had to receive reports and inquiries from all the imperial provinces as well as from Caesar's private estates. Similarly he had to dispatch the Emperor's orders to all parts of the Roman world. If Pliny had lived in the reign of Claudius, most of Book X would have been addressed not to the Emperor, but to the freedman Narcissus. This secretary would control negotiations with client and foreign princes. At the same time it was his duty to know about the capabilities of rising men in the army or civil service. Such was the congestion of business in this ministry that in the second century it was divided into two departments under separate officials, one for the Western half of the Empire where Latin was the official language, and one for the Eastern half where correspondence was carried on in Greek.[2] Statius gives a picturesque idea of the duties that devolve upon Abascantus, secretary of state to Domitian.[3]

'He (Domitian) bent those shoulders to the yoke; he laid upon them a huge burden, a weight that man could scarce support. In the Emperor's house there is no duty so vast. Thy husband's task[4] was to send far and wide into the great spaces of the earth the commands of the imperial successor of Romulus, and his hand was to control the forces which support and the canons which guide our rule o'er the world. For his attention come triumphal missives from the North, and the tidings from winding Euphrates, from the marches round Ister's banks, from the standards of the Rhine,[5] and

[1] Sen. *Cons. ad Polyb.* 6, § 5.

[2] *ab epistulis Latinis* and *ab epistulis Graecis*.

[3] Stat. *Silv.* v. 1, lines 83–100.

[4] Priscilla, the deceased wife of Abascantus, is apostrophized.

[5] The Latin is: 'quae laurus ab arcto,
Quid vagus Euphrates, quid ripa binominis Istri,
Quid Rheni vexilla ferant. . . .'
The subjunctive *ferant* is dependent on *tractare manu* in the preceding sentence. These words embrace the meanings of examining the correspondence from the North &c. and acting accordingly.

news of what submission has been made by the earth's uttermost parts, even Thule surrounded by the cadence of a refluent tide. For him is every message whether all our arms are crowned with joyful bays and never a lance darkened by the pennon of dishonour. Again, if our sovereign lord divide his trusty swords, he must make known who has the character to command a company and be a horseman among the foot, who is to lead a cohort, who merits the more eminent rank of illustrious tribune, and who is worthier to dragoon a squadron of horse. Again he must foreknow a thousand chances, whether Nile has flooded his fields or Libya sweated amid Auster's showers.'

The *libertus a studiis* was politically of much less consequence. Intellectual adviser to the Emperor, he directed his notice to rising poets and men of letters. What he lacked in political power he made up for by his influence in the literary and learned world. Ambitious authors courted him; it was their best way of securing the favour of Caesar. Lastly, the *a cognitionibus* would make enquiries in each judicial case that was brought before the Emperor and would advise him in his decision.

When we consider the nature of these freedmen's duties and the complete absence of responsibility to anyone but Caesar, it is obvious how powerful and influential they could become even under a monarch of average strength and vigilance. But when the Emperor was a weak-willed and unpractical antiquarian or a vain songster whose eyes could be closed to peculation by judicious flattery, they became the omnipotent rulers of the world limited only by each other. The financial secretary could easily play the unjust steward; the minister of petitions could please himself whether to pass on or intercept an application to the Emperor; the secretary of state could make or mar a man's career in the army or civil service; the secretary for legal affairs could sell justice to the highest bidder; and on the favour of the literary adviser depended the author's prospects of obtaining Caesar's patronage.

The infamous use made of these powers by freedmen led to strong protests. Otho and Vitellius courted aristocratic favour by giving to knights some of the chief offices.[1] Vespasian went back to the old system, but, like a true man of business, doubtless kept his underlings well in hand. The precedent, however, had now been set, even though it was by emperors of but a few months' reign each. Under Domitian, a knight, Titinius Capito, was invested with the general secretariate,[2] and Trajan employed an equestrian *procurator a rationibus*.[3] These cases, indeed, are still the exception rather than the rule. In the reign of Hadrian, however, the greatest blow was struck at the power of imperial freedmen. Far more than any emperor before him did Hadrian give preference to the knights in the departments which freedmen had hitherto dominated without serious equestrian competition. In view of examples noticed above, Spartianus is not quite correct in saying 'He first had Roman knights for his secretary of state and minister of petitions';[4] yet the fact that the mistake could be made shows at any rate that Hadrian was commonly regarded as the author of an epoch-making reform in the civil service. The three great offices, together with that of the literary adviser, henceforth went to the knights, and only in exceptional cases did freedmen ever fill them again. Alexander, who was secretary of state for Hellenic affairs (*ab epistulis Graecis*) under M. Aurelius, is an almost solitary instance.[5] The legal secretariate, however, probably remained in the hands of imperial freedmen until the closing decade of the century. The first known equestrian official *a cognitionibus* belongs to the period of Septimius Severus.

[1] Plutarch, *Otho*, 9: *Σεκοῦνδος ὁ ῥήτωρ ἐπὶ τῶν ἐπιστολῶν γενόμενος τοῦ Ὄθωνος*. Tac. *Hist.* i. 58: 'Vitellius ministeria principatus per libertos agi solita in equites Romanos disponit.'

[2] For a table of representative inscriptions showing how knights and freedmen contested with each other for the central ministries and for other posts in the civil service, see appendix III.

[3] R. Cagnat, *L'Année épigraphique*, 1913, no. 143 a and b. Cf. R. H. Lacey, *The Equestrian Officials of Trajan and Hadrian*, Princeton, 1917, p. 4.

[4] 'ab epistulis et a libellis primus equites Romanos habuit,' *Hist. Aug.*, *Hadr.* 22.

[5] *C. I. L.* vi. 8606.

The sweeping change which Hadrian made in the tenure of these offices, as well as the gradual transference of other positions from the hands of freedmen into those of knights, must not be put down entirely to freedmen's misconduct. The decline of the Stoic opposition to the Empire may have induced princes to rely upon the aristocracy even for service whose nature might have been thought more suited to personal attendants. Moreover, among equestrian officials known to us through inscriptions, there are many who bear the gentile names Claudius, Flavius, Ulpius, Aelius etc. Their origin is plain. They are descended from imperial freedmen. When, therefore, Hadrian made his reform he was no doubt at least influenced by the fact that the descendants of Claudius' and Vespasian's freedmen were of equestrian rank, and that it was unreasonable to exclude them from the positions held by their ancestors. So, later on, the grandsons of Trajan's and Hadrian's servants acquired offices which had gained in dignity, if not in importance, through being reserved for free-born knights.[1]

Each of these departments had its under-secretary[2] with a large staff of clerks and accountants.[3] Each staff was recruited from the slaves and freedmen of the Emperor, and the under-secretaries also were nearly always freedmen, even after the general transfer of the headships to the knights. Of course it depended on individual character whether much could be made of these subordinate posts. If the director of a department were both honest and vigilant, his under-secretary would find that he could not make any profit except that brought in by his salary. If the director however were unwary, his subordinate could carry on a vast illicit traffic; whereas, if he were dishonest, his subordinate would sooner or later learn his secret and make him pay a high price for his silence.

[1] For Hadrian's changes, cf. R. H. Lacey, *Equestrian Officials of Trajan and Hadrian, with some notes on Hadrian's Reforms*. Princeton (London: Milford).

[2] e. g. 'proximus a studiis,' 'proximus rationum,' 'a libellis adiutor.'

[3] e. g. 'tabularius a rationibus.'

III. In the financial direction of the Empire were several important posts, of which a fair proportion fell to imperial freedmen. There were four distinct treasuries at Rome in the first two centuries of our era. The oldest was the ancient Republican treasury called the *aerarium Saturni*, which for the greater part of this period was administered by certain senators appointed by Caesar.[1] At first it bore the administrative expenses in senatorial provinces, and supported the cost of the city prefecture and the curatorships of public works, roads, water-supply and Tiber banks. At the outset of the Empire it was maintained by the duty on the sale of slaves, and the direct taxes, and perhaps the *portoria*[2], of senatorial provinces. Later it declined in importance, losing to the *fiscus* both its provincial duties and its provincial revenue.[3] By 200 A.D. it was little more than the municipal chest of Rome, dependent mainly on the *fiscus* for its support.

A second treasury was the *aerarium militare*, which was controlled by three senators of praetorian rank and which provided the pensions for discharged soldiers. It was fed by the *vicesima hereditatum*, a five per cent. legacy duty, and by the *centesima rerum venalium*, a one per cent. tax on goods sold by auction throughout the Empire.[4]

[1] For the vicissitudes in the control of the *aerarium Saturni*, cf. Tac. *Ann.* xiii. 29.

[2] The *portoria* of senatorial provinces, if they ever belonged to the *aerarium* after 27 B.C., were very soon transferred to the *fiscus*. Nero treats all the *portoria* as in his own sphere of financial administration, when he has thoughts of abolishing them altogether (Tac. *Ann.* xiii. 50). The customs of Sicily go to the *fiscus* before the end of the first century; for a knight, clearly in the imperial civil service, is *promagister portuum Siciliae*, then fills a number of other posts and lastly is commemorated in an inscription of 104 A.D. (*I. L. S.* 7193–5). Imperial procurators are known to have been concerned with the *quattuor publica* of Africa from the time of Hadrian (*I. L. S.* 1408).

[3] The *fiscus* had claims on Sardis in the senatorial province of Asia as early as 17 A.D. (Tac. *Ann.* ii. 47). The *fiscus Asiaticus* (again showing non-senatorial claims on Asia) existed in the reign of Domitian (*I. L. S.* 1517).

[4] Caligula abolished the tax (Dio, lix. 9), but only in Italy (Suet. *Cal.* 16). Ulpian mentions it as a prominent source of revenue, *Dig.* L. xvi. 17, § 1.

Two other treasuries were the *patrimonium*[1] and the *fiscus*. The former was the private property of the *princeps*. Very soon it acquired the rank of a state treasury through the great number of legacies left to the emperors. Augustus himself received vast estates by inheritance; Agrippa's bequest of the Thracian Chersonese and Vedius Pollio's of Pausilypum are two prominent examples.[2] The normal revenues of the *patrimonium* therefore were two, the income from existing estates and the acquisition of fresh bequests. Confiscation also swelled the *patrimonium*; for, though the more constitutional emperors sent the *bona damnatorum* to the *aerarium* or *fiscus*, others played the high-handed despot and swept them into their private coffers.[3] The expenditure of this chest must always have been considerable and under extravagant emperors enormous. Besides paying its staff and agents in the provinces, it bore the expenses of the Emperor's court, bought his slaves and paid the salaries of his freedmen officials. Moreover the maintenance of the water-supply and the cost of public buildings, so far as these fell to Caesar, were defrayed by the *patrimonium*.[4]

The other treasury, the *fiscus*, consisted of all the state possessions entrusted to Caesar. To this chest accordingly belonged the revenue from the direct taxes of imperial provinces (and later from those of senatorial also), the *bona caduca*,[5] and the lands in the provinces which before the

[1] In the second century emperors marked off a portion of the *patrimonium* under the name of *patrimonium privatum*, the family property of the Emperor, as distinguished from the Crown property of the Emperor as such. Succession to the *patrimonium* followed the succession to the Principate; the *patrimonium privatum* could be bequeathed and divided as its owner willed. Septimius Severus completed the cleavage. The *patrimonium privatum* was organized as a separate treasury under the name of *res privata*; the *patrimonium* declined in importance and probably was soon merged in the *fiscus*.

[2] Chersonese: Dio, liv. 29. Pausilypum: Plin. *N. H.* ix. 167; Dio, liv. 23. Cf. Hirschfeld, *K.Vb.* 18, n.2.

[3] For the *bona damnatorum*, see *infra*, p. 167.

[4] Cf. Hirschfeld, *K.Vb.* 41.

[5] Property to which there was no legally qualified heir. By the *Lex*

Roman conquest had been the personal property of the previous rulers.[1] Some of the indirect taxes, namely the *vicesima libertatis* and the *portoria*, went to the *fiscus*, at least if gathered from imperial provinces. By the end of the second century the *fiscus* claimed these taxes even when collected from senatorial provinces; and it is quite possible that this had been the case from the establishment of the Principate. Except in the spheres covered by the *aerarium militare* and the *patrimonium*, the *fiscus* bore all the expenses of the army and navy and of the many-sided administration which Caesar directed.

The date of the establishment of the *fiscus* is still a matter of controversy, some following Mommsen in believing it to be Augustan, and others, with Hirschfeld, holding that it did not come into existence till the reign of Claudius. Without pretending to settle the question or discuss it in detail, one may remark here that the need for some central office for the state moneys entrusted to Caesar existed as much in the time of Augustus as in that of Claudius. The early emperors must have had a head department to co-ordinate accounts from provincial bureaux. So, in spite of the facts that Augustus never mentions the *fiscus* in the *Monumentum Ancyranum*, and that Suetonius,[2] speaking of Augustus' reign, refers to the departmental *fisci* rather than the central *fiscus*, the view that it was Augustan seems the more probable.

Although the *fiscus* was never legally the private property of the *Princeps*,[3] and was for the first two centuries always distinct from the *patrimonium*, it may have

Iulia de maritandis ordinibus, 4 A. D. and the *Lex Papia Poppaea*, 9 A. D., unmarried possessors of 100,000 sesterces, if male, or of 50,000, if female (*Gn. Id. Log.* 30, 32), could not inherit except from relatives within the sixth degree. Those married but childless could take half the legacy left them.

[1] e. g. mines which had belonged to the kings of Macedon. After Roman occupation their owner was the *populus Romanus* until the establishment of the Principate, when they were taken over by Caesar.

[2] Suet. *Aug.* 101: 'quantum pecuniae in aerario et fiscis.'

[3] Here Hirschfeld (*K.Vb.* 7 ff.) is more convincing than Mommsen (*Staatsrecht*, ii. 1000 ff.).

often been found convenient in the early Empire to administer both treasuries on parallel lines. Freedmen controlled directly by Caesar were at first in charge of them.

The control of the *fiscus* was naturally in the hands of the *a rationibus*, who, as we have seen, became thereby the most powerful financial officer in the Empire. The *patrimonium* was directed by procurators, who were at first imperial freedmen, and until the reign of Hadrian it was only on exceptional occasions that knights obtained the control of it. In the second century, on the other hand, equestrian procurators are the rule; no doubt, the change is to be attributed to the same measure which swept the freedmen from the court offices.

These were the central treasuries and their administrators. Freedmen never had any concern with either the *aerarium Saturni* or the *aerarium militare*, but, until the time of Hadrian, the two most important of the state treasuries were under their control. A consideration of the revenue which filled these chests will show what part freedmen played in its collection.

In the first place the direct taxes (*tributum capitis* and *tributum soli*) made a large contribution. In senatorial provinces, for a time at least, they were collected by the quaestor and went to the *aerarium Saturni*. In imperial provinces the *fiscus* claimed these taxes and the officers responsible were the *procuratores provinciarum*. These officials were generally knights, but instances are known of imperial freedmen exercising the office both before and after Hadrian. Their duties were not confined to the collection of tribute, for they existed not only in imperial but also in senatorial provinces. In the latter at first they were responsible for the Caesarian domains and beyond them had no authority. In the former they both collected the direct taxes and supervised the administration of the domains. However, as the *aerarium* declined and the *tributa* originally destined for it were gradually transferred to the *fiscus*, it fell more and more to procurators to collect the *tributa* of senatorial as well as imperial provinces. Finally, therefore, in both classes of province, the *procurator provinciae* was the supreme financial officer. His importance did not end there. Though of lower rank than the legate or proconsul in charge of the province, a procurator was often in a more favoured position. Generally it was the governor whose treason or rapacity the Emperor feared, and one of the unofficial duties of the procurator was to act as a check on his superior. The unrestrained and all but irresponsible power of the proconsul had ruined many a fair province under the Republic; the Caesars, however, encouraged their procurators to be on the alert for the first signs of misconduct on the part of governors. The procurator was not to be the mere tool of the legate; he was to be Caesar's trusted ally against a man who might prove dangerous to Caesar or injurious to his province.

The indirect taxation of the Empire was conducted through three principal channels: the *vicesima libertatis*, or five per cent. tax on liberated slaves; the *vicesima hereditatum*, or five per cent. legacy duty; and the *portoria*, or duty on imports.[1] The rate of the last varied in amount according to the customs district, which was usually larger than the average province. For each tax there was a central bureau in Rome under a procurator, who was generally a knight but in exceptional cases a freedman. The revenue brought in was passed on to certain treasuries, that of the *vicesima hereditatum* to the military chest and that of the others to the *fiscus*, except perhaps in senatorial provinces at first. The collection, to begin with, was left to societies of *publicani* or *conductores*, who bought the right to exact particular taxes. They paid lump sums to the central bureaux in Rome and gambled on the number of manumissions, the frequency of deaths and the vivacity of import trade. These societies were never allowed to pursue under the Empire the infamous career of extortion

[1] Either middlemen or public slaves collected the tax on *venalia mancipia*, which went to the *aerarium* at any rate at first (*I. L. S.* 203). No more is known of the collection either of this tax or of the *centesima rerum venalium*.

which had been theirs under the Republic. The bureau of each special tax had procurators as its representatives in all parts of the Roman world. Their duty was to control the activities of the tax-farmers and to see that they exacted no more than their due. These officials were generally knights but sometimes freedmen. The procurators of indirect taxes gradually came to have more extensive duties. If no society undertook to farm a tax in a certain district, then the nearest procurator had to arrange for its direct collection, or else another procurator was appointed for the task. By degrees the direct method of collection superseded the system of middlemen. From the reign of Hadrian onwards the legacy duty was collected directly by imperial procurators, and, in the case of the customs and the manumission tax, the last society of middlemen became extinct before the year 200.[1] The cause is probably to be found in the vigilance of the procurator. Till the end of the Republic tax-farming was one of the most lucrative professions owing to the deceptions which could be practised upon simple and ignorant folk. But in the imperial age the controlling officer did his work well. The trade of tax-collecting had never been a pleasant one to respectable citizens; it now lost its glamour in the eyes of everyone, when immoderate profits were out of the question.

Very similar was the case of the imperial domains. The revenues from most of these went to the *fiscus* and were received by the financial secretary. The lands could be exploited for very different purposes. Some could be used for cultivation, others for pasture. Many estates, again, consisted in mines, forests or quarries. As with the indirect taxes, the revenues from them could be collected either directly by imperial officials, or indirectly through middlemen who hired the right of administering the property. In the case of mines and quarries a procurator might be put in charge, and the workers would be imperial

[1] Cf. H. Mattingly, *The Imperial Civil Service of Rome*, Cambridge, 1910, pp. 78–80.

slaves or condemned criminals. The whole profits would thus go to the state. On the other hand, the state might not possess a sufficient number of labourers, and might not be in a position to afford the capital for purchasing more. Then the right of working the mine or quarry would be leased to a private capitalist, who would make what profit he could out of it. Imperial procurators in charge of mines, quarries and fisheries, were either freedmen or knights. Freedmen probably lost ground gradually to their equestrian rivals, though as late as Severus Alexander we find a freedman administering the purple fisheries in Achaea, Epirus and Thessaly.

Two systems were also in vogue for arable and pastoral lands. Either each separate domain (*saltus*) was under some imperial official who resided on the estate, and worked it partly by slaves and partly by small rent-paying tenants (*coloni*); or one or several domains might be leased to *conductores* who themselves worked them by slaves or tenants. But in this case also an imperial procurator was generally present to check oppression on the part of the *conductores*, a duty which sometimes he did not perform, as we learn from the appeal of the *coloni* to Commodus.[1] In provinces where the state-lands were of considerable area, as in Africa, the separate domains were grouped together in tracts or regions (*tractus* or *regiones*). For the supervision of each tract, whether this meant control of *conductores* or direct administration of the land, an imperial procurator was appointed. Ultimately, all the Caesarian domains in a province, whether they were lands, quarries, mines or fisheries, were placed under the authority of the *procurator provinciae*. As regards the condition of these various officials, the superintendents of separate estates must have always been imperial slaves or freedmen, those of tracts sometimes freedmen and sometimes knights, the latter gradually displacing the former; while, as we have seen above, the procurator of the province was generally, though by no means always, a knight.

[1] *I. L. S.* 6870.

Finally, the revenue of the Empire was continually being increased by the estates of persons who were condemned on a capital charge (*bona damnatorum*), who died without qualified heirs (*bona caduca*), or who made Caesar their heir (*hereditates*). In the case of the *bona damnatorum* for a long period no constant rule appears to have been observed. Though probably their general destination was the *fiscus*, there were several occasions on which they enriched one of the other treasuries.[1] The *bona caduca* almost certainly went regularly to the *fiscus*. Separate departments for these two items of revenue were not evolved until late in the second century. Then, however, the *bona damnatorum* and the *bona caduca* fell under the control of separate procurators, who were sometimes freedmen and sometimes knights. More important were the estates left to Caesar. Starting as a mere branch of the *patrimonium*, the bureau for *hereditates* in the time of the Flavian Emperors became an independent department under a procurator of its own, while the directorship of the *patrimonium* correspondingly declined in importance. Further, it must have had offices in the provinces as well as a central one in Rome. The procurators in charge at first were freedmen, but after the time of Hadrian knights were regularly appointed to these positions.

Such in brief outline were the revenues of the Empire. In the first century freedmen played a great part in the collection of them and, as the confidential servants of the Emperor, must have been personages of high importance. In the second century, however, especially after the accession of Hadrian in 117, their power was on the wane. Knights began to occupy regularly not only posts which had been shared between the two orders in the preceding century, but even the more important of those which had been the exclusive possession of the freedman.

IV. We now come to administration. If we except the court offices, the positions of the greatest importance

[1] Tac. *Ann.* vi. 2 and 19; *Hist.* i. 90; Plin. *Paneg.* 42; Dio, lv. 32; *Hist. Aug.*, *Hadr.* vii. 7, *M. Aurel.* xxiv. 9, *Avid. Cass.* vii. 6.

were never in freedmen's hands. All military commands were denied to them.[1] Senators invariably filled the post of *legatus legionis*[2]; young men of senatorial or equestrian birth became *praefecti alarum*, *praefecti cohortium* and *tribuni militum*. The *praefectus vigilum* was always a knight, and the *praefectus praetorio* sometimes a senator but usually a knight. The supreme governor of a province, whether senatorial or imperial, was regularly a member of the Senate, except in the case of Egypt and the third class provinces. Here knights were entrusted with the command. Moreover, senators received certain lesser appointments, such as the city prefecture, and the curatorships of roads, of public works and of the Tiber's banks.

However, in several departments of general utility, such as those concerned with food and water supply, the imperial post and mint, the public libraries, Caesar's journal and the games he gave to the people, freedmen climbed high up the ladder of preferment. The case of the water-supply had better be taken first, because it was controlled by two separate bureaux between which a clear distinction must be made. On the one side was a public department which kept in repair the aqueducts supplying Rome, and which provided that water ran freely into the fountains of the city. This bureau was under the *curatores aquarum*, who were senators, and their *adiutores*, who were either senators or knights. On the other side was a Caesarian department which organized the manufacture of pipes for the transfer of water from the aqueducts to the imperial palaces and official buildings, and which issued licences to those citizens who wished to tap the imperial water supply. This bureau was under a *procurator aquarum*, a freedman in the earliest times of the Empire.

[1] A freedman military tribune is attacked by Horace (Epode iv). The context implies his position to be unconstitutional or at least unusual. This equestrian office was probably his reward for some exceptional service. The Scholiast says Menas, betrayer of Sextus Pompeius, is meant; a certain Vedius Rufus, possibly connected with Vedius Pollio, is also suggested.

[2] Equestrian *praefecti* commanded all legions stationed in Egypt and also the Parthian legions of Septimius Severus.

It was a well-paid office, in the third century worth 100,000 sesterces a year,[1] and the procurator would also have the frequent opportunity of accepting bribes from those who applied for water. In this bureau it is clearly seen from the evidence of the pipes themselves how the knights gradually gained upon the freedmen, though they never succeeded in ousting them altogether. In the *Corpus Inscriptionum Latinarum*, vol. XV. ii. p. 907, are collected the names of the officers under whom the pipes were made. Now the pipes which show such names yield results which fall into four main classes. A pipe may have been made under a freedman *procurator*; or under an equestrian *procurator*; or, again, the officer in charge is not called *procurator* at all, and is probably in the senatorial department of the *curatores aquarum*—Caesar may have been out of pipes at an urgent time and may have sent an order to the senatorial factory;[2] or, lastly, no official is mentioned, and the pipe is merely said to be provided by the Emperor's *patrimonium*. For the purposes of studying the office of *procurator aquarum*, the last two classes may be omitted. Accordingly, the following table shows the libertine and equestrian procurators who are known from the inscriptions on pipes.

Reign.	*Freedmen.*	*Free-born (probably knights).*
Nero	1	—
Domitian	8	—
Trajan	4	1
Hadrian	2	3
Antoninus Pius	*1	1
M. Aurelius	**5	2

* Combined with a free-born officer called *rationalis*.

** In two of these cases the *procurator* is combined with a *rationalis* whose name and condition are unknown.

[1] *I. L. S.* 478: 'procuratori aquarum centenario'.

[2] e. g. *I. L. S.* 8685 gives 'sub cura Aemili Frontini'. Now Frontinus is known to have been *curator aquarum*. Cf. *C. I. L.* xv. 7278, 'sub cura M. Arricini Clementis', and 7302, 'sub cura Silii Deciani et Memnii Rufi(ni)'. Clemens, Decianus and Rufinus were probably all *adiutores curatoris aquarum*. Cf. Lanciani, *Le Acque* (*Atti dei Lincei*, *Ser. III*, vol. iv, 1879–80, p. 530–4).

From this it may be seen that during the first century the office was entirely under freedmen of the Emperor. The knights first gained a foothold under Trajan, but their best time was under Hadrian and Antoninus Pius. Under M. Aurelius, freedmen seem to have regained some portion of their ancient prerogatives.

The corn supply was from the first under the superintendence of a knight who bore the title of *praefectus annonae*. He too had to be in constant touch with the financial secretary to Caesar, because it was from the bureau of that official that he obtained the capital necessary for the performance of his duties. He had several officers under him, such as an assistant prefect of the corn supply, a procurator for the Ostia department of the corn supply, and a procurator of the port of Ostia.[1] Freedmen are known to have held all these posts, but in the second century they are constantly filled by knights. Probably it was Hadrian who expelled the freedmen even from these subordinate positions.

The same emperor, or his predecessor Trajan, deprived the freedmen of their authoritative offices in the imperial post and mint. During the first century a freedman directed the post under the title of *a vehiculis*. Afterwards the postmaster general was dignified with the title of *praefectus vehiculorum*, and the office was henceforth filled by knights.[2] Similarly, in the case of the mint, freedmen probably directed it at first,[3] though they did not hold the title *procurator monetae*. In the reign of Trajan, however, we come across an equestrian *procurator monetae*. The directorship has passed to the knights, and only the subordinate positions can now be held by the Emperor's servants.

[1] *adiutor praefecti annonae* or *subpraefectus annonae*, *procurator annonae Ostiensis*, *procurator portus Ostiensis*. See appendix iii.

[2] Under Antoninus Pius a freedman was *praefectus vehiculorum*. But he had been presented with the *equus publicus* and therefore had become a knight, *I. L. S.* 1740.

[3] Even slaves were in charge of it under Julius Caesar, Suet. *Iul.* 76.

Inscriptions mention a number of officials in charge of libraries. Almost certainly the Palatine librarian and the literary adviser were one and the same person; the duties of both seem to be performed by the Sextus whom Martial entreats to find a place for his epigrams in the imperial library.[1] But there were in addition a number of state-endowed libraries whose supervision was entrusted to other officers. To be in charge of one of the minor libraries, or even to have the general responsibility for them all, did not bring one into such close connexion with Caesar as did the court office of literary adviser, but it carried with it some social dignity, since the state, recognizing the need, was putting more and more money aside for the endowment of education. Accordingly the superintendence of libraries, at first committed to slaves or freedmen, was transferred, probably by Hadrian, to men of a higher rank, namely the knights.

The secretaries for organizing the games and spectacular shows given by the Emperor, and the editors of the imperial journal, were sometimes freedmen and sometimes knights. The former never seem to have been excluded from these posts, which probably did not give much opportunity for bribery or embezzlement. Confined to imperial freedmen at first, they were thrown open to knights in the second century, but they never were the exclusive possession of the equestrian order. Another title is found among inscriptions, *a copiis militaribus*;[2] this officer was either the director of a recruiting bureau, or else a departmental official in the financial secretariate entrusted with the funds for army expenses. The position certainly started in the hands of freedmen, but there is not enough evidence to determine when, if at all, it was transferred to the knights.

The directors of all these administrative departments must have been in close touch both with the general secretariate and with the *fiscus* or the *patrimonium*. From the former they received imperial orders; to one or other

[1] Mart. v. 5. [2] *I. L. S.* 1571.

of the latter they sent in annually their accounts for the past year and their estimates for the coming one; since it was only from one of the finance bureaux that they could obtain the capital they needed.

So much for the chiefs of departments; each had an ample staff put under his authority. Inscriptions show accountants and chief accountants (*tabularii*, *principes tabulariorum*), clerks (*a commentariis*), treasurers (*arcarii*) and paymasters (*dispensatores*) serving the procurators mentioned above. These were always imperial slaves or freedmen. For the sake of efficiency emperors preferred to have permanent employees; so they filled such posts with their own dependants. They would have none of the free-born citizen who might come and go as he pleased. Indeed even in senatorial bureaux, the departments for public works, roads, metropolitan administration (under the *curator operum publicorum*, *curator viarum*, *praefectus urbis*), imperial freedmen sometimes occupied the lower positions. The share of imperial freedmen in the civil service was therefore very extensive. Certainly many high offices were never open to them; others, which they at first monopolized or shared with the knights, they gradually forfeited. But the humble clerks and accountants who were indispensable to the imperial system, the lowly employees who were largely responsible for its efficiency, the men whose labour never won the renown of the highly placed, but who were nevertheless the bulwarks of the Empire,—these were the slaves and freedmen of Caesar.

V. Posts in the army were never given even to imperial freedmen, though the permanent fleets at Misenum and Ravenna were sometimes under their charge. Generally speaking, up to the reign of Nero, the prefect of the fleet (*praefectus classis*) was a freedman. Under that emperor a knight commanded the fleet at Ravenna and a freedman that at Misenum.[1] The last freedman to hold the office was Moschus during the brief reign of Otho.[2] Henceforth the command was regularly entrusted to knights. The

[1] Tac. *Ann.* xiii. 30; xiv. 3. [2] Tac. *Hist.* i. 87.

post was one of high rank and dignity; it often came at the end of a long series of procuratorships, as in the case of the elder Pliny.[1] It seems to have been invested even with some jurisdiction in the environs of the naval base. Clodius Quirinalis had opportunity to make his authority hated round Ravenna.[2]

One or two exceptional positions, to which individual freedmen attained, deserve mention. The governorship of Egypt, with three legions under Augustus and two until Hadrian's reign, was, with the exception of the praetorian prefecture, the highest prize of a knight's career. But on one occasion during the reign of Tiberius this important charge was committed temporarily to a freedman.[3] Another instance is more familiar. It concerns Felix, the brother of Pallas, and governor of Judaea during part of St. Paul's captivity in Caesarea. Small provinces like Judaea, Sardinia, Raetia and Noricum were not considered important enough to be placed under the command of a senatorial proconsul or a Caesarian legate. Procurators regularly of equestrian rank were accordingly given the direction of them. Felix, however, was a freedman of Claudius.[4] He made abundant use of the exceptional favour shown him. Even from a poor prisoner like St. Paul he hoped to accept a bribe, and for the sake of popularity he retained him under arrest, and finally on quitting the province 'left Paul bound', though he well knew there was no legal charge against him.[5] Tacitus has left an epigrammatic account of his reign. 'With all manner of brutality and lust, he exercised the power of a monarch in the spirit of a slave.'[6]

VI. Such in outline were the offices which gave the imperial freedman his opportunity. It has already been shown

[1] Pliny, *Ep.* iii. 5; vi. 16. Suetonius, *Vita Plinii Secundi.*
[2] Tac. *Ann.* xiii. 30.
[3] Dio, lviii. 19.
[4] Suet. *Claud.* 28.
[5] *Acts of the Apostles*, xxiv, esp. vv. 26 and 27.
[6] 'per omnem saevitiam ac libidinem ius regium servili ingenio exercuit,' Tac. *Hist.* v. 9.

how unique were the prospects of amassing large fortunes from the great secretariates. Similarly in the provinces and imperial domains freedmen could, if they were clever enough to conceal it from other officials, reap vast profits either by direct extortion or by coming to an agreement with the farmers of taxes. But, apart from this, many a freedman exercised an influence over the Emperor which even his office did not warrant. Apparent good service lulled an unwary sovereign into what was often a false security. Reposing entire confidence in his freedman, he would allow him to assume imperial responsibilities totally outside his office. Besides, many emperors of the first century were men of such weak character that they were easily swayed by gracious and winning manners. Indeed the favourites of Galba and Vitellius excited homosexual passions in their masters' minds.[1] Thus, partly because of their official powers and partly because of their excessive influence over certain emperors, imperial freedmen gained an ascendancy in the Empire the like of which has never in another nation fallen to a series of low-born upstarts. Isolated cases may come from Byzantine and Russian annals,[2] but the Roman Empire enjoys an unenviable distinction. She possesses the longest list of menials who rose to guide the destinies of a state.

To these omnipotent parvenus nobles of senatorial rank cringed as if they themselves were the bondmen. While in exile Seneca, as already indicated, was careful to flatter the freedmen of Claudius;[3] the terms he employed have come down to us in the *Consolatio ad Polybium*. It was through

[1] Suet. *Galba*, 22; *Vitellius*, 12.

[2] e. g. in the Eastern Empire, Eutropius, minister of Arcadius; Narses, general of Justinian; Theodora, consort of that emperor; and, in modern Russia, Menshikov, minister and general of Peter the Great; Razumovski, consort of the Empress Elizabeth; Koutaissoff, barber of the Emperor Paul; and, in our own day, Rasputin.

[3] Dio, lxi. 10: *Τὴν Μεσσαλῖναν καὶ τοὺς τοῦ Κλαυδίου ἐξελευθέρους ἐθώπευεν ὥστε καὶ βιβλίον σφίσιν ἐκ τῆς νήσου πέμψαι ἐπαίνους αὐτῶν ἔχον, ὃ μετὰ ταῦτα ὑπ' αἰσχύνης ἀπήλειψεν.*

Narcissus that Vespasian obtained the command of a legion in Germany.[1] The whole Senate thought fit to abase itself before Pallas. It offered him the praetorian insignia together with 15,000,000 sesterces; and a public vote of thanks was offered to one who, sprung from Arcadian kings, thought less of his own ancestry than of the public service and permitted himself to be numbered among Caesar's servants. Pallas sent Claudius to tell the Senate that he accepted the honour but declined the financial assistance, preferring to abide in his former poverty. Forthwith the multi-millionaire was commended for his old-fashioned frugality![2]

Nobles of a later age, when freedmen were not so prominent in politics, were moved by their pride to express the disgust they felt. Pliny gives vent to the most violent indignation at the insolence of Pallas and the servility of the Senate. He is enraged to think that Pallas contemptuously refused the Senate's gift, but one is compelled to feel that his anger would have been the same had it been accepted.[3] So too he holds that great freedmen and little emperors go together.[4] Tacitus also resented the interference of freedmen in politics. He observed that national calamities and the ascendancy of freedmen run concomitantly. 'For even they play a political role during the misfortunes of the state.'[5]

Of course the destinies of freedmen always depended on the character of the sovereign. Under strong princes their

[1] Suet. *Vesp.* 4: 'Claudio principe Narcissi gratia legatus legionis in Germaniam missus est.'

[2] 'Additum a Scipione Cornelio grates publice agendas, quod regibus Arcadiae ortus veterrimam nobilitatem usui publico postponeret seque inter ministros principis haberi sineret. Adseveravit Claudius contentum honore Pallantem intra priorem paupertatem subsistere: et fixum est aere publico senatus consultum quo libertinus sestertii ter milies possessor antiquae parsimoniae laudibus cumulabatur.' Tac. *Ann.* xii. 53.

[3] Plin. *Ep.* viii. 6, § 9.

[4] Plin. *Paneg.* 88: 'Scis enim praecipuum esse indicium non magni principis magnos libertos.'

[5] 'Nam et hi (liberti) malis temporibus partem se rei publicae faciunt,' Tac. *Hist.* i. 76.

opportunities for peculation were never so great, and their insolence in aristocratic society could never proceed to such wanton excesses. A brief review of the fluctuations in the fortunes of imperial freedmen from reign to reign will shed incidental light on the uses they made of their power. During Augustus' reign they were kept well in check.[1] The first emperor, anxious to conciliate prominent Republican families, was not the man to allow undue liberties on the part of his freedmen. Yet even in his time exceptions occurred. Licinus, a Gaul, was given a procuratorship in his native country and was allowed to pillage it at will.[2] In Juvenal he figures with Pallas as the type of the freedman who has made his fortune by questionable means.[3]

Tiberius was by nature a disciplinarian. His cautious adherence to the policy of Augustus was likely to prevent excesses among his freedmen. Tacitus gives him the credit of administering his palace through a small number of freedmen.[4] Towards the end of his reign, however, a change took place. A freedman became temporarily prefect of Egypt.[5] Freedmen began to decide state issues. M. Julius Agrippa the Elder (the Herod of Acts xii) thought it advisable to bestow lavish presents on the freedmen of the Emperor.[6]

These cases were still isolated exceptions. Freedmen may have had influence in the reign of Tiberius; they never dominated the Empire. It was in the succeeding reigns that their power reached its zenith. Hitherto the character of the Emperor had been against them; now they had a series of princes from whom, with adroit flattery, they could obtain their heart's desire. An infatuate butcher, a weak-willed pedant, and a distracted aesthete, were

[1] Suet. *Aug.* 67: 'Patronus dominusque non minus severus quam facilis et clemens.'

[2] Dio, liv. 21.

[3] Juv. i. 109.

[4] 'Intra paucos libertos domus,' Tac. *Ann.* iv. 6.

[5] Dio, lviii. 19.

[6] Josephus *Ant. Iud.* xviii. 6. 1: *τὰ πλεῖστα δ' εἰς τοὺς Καίσαρος ἀπελευθέρους ἐτετέλεστο ἐλπίδι πράξεως τῆς αὐτῶν.*

powerless to resist the influence of men who were ready to aid them in crime or soothe their troubles with adulation. From the reign of Caligula dates the ascendancy of Callistus. 'He wielded a power nothing short of absolute through his vast possessions and the general fear with which he was regarded.' Such is Josephus' description of this creature.[1] Seneca had seen the first master of Callistus vainly beg admission at the house of his former slave.[2]

The court of Claudius, as previously shown, was dominated by freedmen. The only checks upon them were the wives and mistresses of the Emperor.[3] Indeed the person who counted for least in the palace was probably Claudius himself. Seneca describes in the *Apocolocyntosis* how the deceased prince absent-mindedly gave an order in heaven. 'You might have thought they were all his own freedmen; so little notice did they take of him'.[4] The two most favoured of these freedmen were Pallas and Narcissus. They acquired enormous sums by dishonest means.[5] Pallas had amassed three hundred million sesterces before the death of Claudius,[6] while his rival in crime died worth four hundred millions.[7] When Claudius' treasury was low, it was wittily suggested that an easy remedy would be found if he took these two freedmen into partnership.[8] This pair joined Callistus, and the three formed what was perhaps the most infamous triumvirate in Roman history. Commanding the three great secretariates among them, they,

[1] Josephus, *Ant. Iud.* XIX. i. 10: *Οὐδὲν ἄλλο ἢ ἰσοτύραννον εἶχε τὴν δύναμιν φόβῳ τε τῶν πάντων καὶ μεγέθει χρημάτων.*

[2] Sen. *Epp.* xlvii. 9: 'stare ante limen Callisti dominum suum vidi, et eum, qui illi inpegerat titulum, qui inter ridicula mancipia produxerat, aliis intrantibus excludi.'

[3] Suet. *Claud.* 29; Tac. *Ann.* xi. 29.

[4] Sen. *Apocol.* 7: 'putares omnes illius esse libertos: adeo illum nemo curabat.'

[5] Suet. *Claud.* 29.

[6] Tac. *Ann.* xii. 53.

[7] Dio, lx. 34. The number he gives is 100,000,000, probably reckoned in drachmae.

[8] Suet. *Claud.* 28: 'tantum praeterea adquirere et rapere, ut querente eo quondam de fisci exiguitate non absurde dictum sit, abundaturum, si a duobus libertis in consortium reciperetur.'

together with Messallina, distributed broadcast offices and commands, pardons and punishments, in the name of their imperial master. The nefarious traffic was carried on in such a way that Claudius in obeying their wish or whim often acted in ignorance.[1] This emperor's gauche enquiries after persons he had put to death have generally been ascribed to absent-mindedness. Often, however, he may have really been kept in ignorance till he asked the awkward question. After Narcissus has compassed the ruin of Messallina, we find a contention between the all-powerful trio as to who is to be Caesar's next consort. Indeed it is only because their opinions are divided that any other party has any say in the matter; and then it is not Claudius but the powerful senator Vitellius who, choosing between the three alternatives, adopts that of Pallas, and elevates Agrippina to the throne of an empress.[2]

The reign of Nero saw no abatement in the power of imperial freedmen. When Agrippina was accused of treason, freedmen were present to hear her defence. After her acquittal the conspirators against her were punished; but Paris, the freedman and actor who belonged to Nero's aunt, being the well-wishing comrade of the Emperor's debaucheries, escaped.[3] One of Nero's freedmen, Polyclitus, was actually employed as an arbitrator between a senator and a knight; for when Suetonius Paullinus, the legate of Britain, had disputes with his procurator, Polyclitus was sent to settle their differences. He proceeded to the island with the gorgeous train of an Oriental potentate, but the barbarians failed to comprehend why their conqueror, whose energy and courage their rugged chivalry had begun to admire, should bow the knee to a slave.[4] When Nero went on his theatrical tour to Greece

[1] Suet. *Claud.* 29: 'His (libertis) ut dixi uxoribusque addictus, non principem sed ministrum egit, compendio cuiusque horum vel etiam studio aut libidine honores exercitus impunitates supplicia largitus est, et quidem insciens plerumque et ignarus.'

[2] Tac. *Ann.* xii. 1–7.

[3] Tac. *Ann.* xiii. 21, 22: 'De Atimeto supplicium sumptum, validiore apud libidines principis Paride quam ut poena adficeretur.'

[4] Tac. *Ann.* xiv. 39.

he left the freedman, Helius, in charge of Rome. Twelve years before this menial had been employed by Nero to murder Silanus;[1] he was now absolute master of the imperial city—apparently there was no senatorial *praefectus urbis* at the time—with unrestrained power of life and death. 'The Roman Empire was enslaved to two tyrants, and I cannot say which was the worse.' Such was the judgement of Dio.[2] Along with Polyclitus, his second in command, Helius played the brigand with striking success. Everything lay open to his pilfering hands, for no reference to Nero was necessary before even a confiscation or execution. He sought to increase his favour with his master by executing Sulpicius Camerinus because the *agnomen* 'Pythicus' which his family bore seemed to rival the recent victories of Nero at the Pythian games.[3]

Freedmen were almost as notorious in the three short reigns which followed, except that Galba and Otho executed some of the most infamous favourites who had served their predecessors, and that Vitellius strove to exclude freedmen from the highest court offices.[4] Helius, Polyclitus and Patrobius all paid the extreme penalty under Galba;[5] but Halotus, one of the most abandoned of all Nero's creatures, who possibly was the poisoner of Claudius, was not only spared, but presented with a high procuratorship.[6] Galba's own freedman, Icelus, gained a notorious ascendancy over his master, and some of the worst excesses of Nero's reign were repeated by his career of political brigandage.[7] Otho had him executed amid public rejoicings,[8] but did not scruple to put Moschus, his own freedman, in charge of the whole fleet or to impose upon him the duty of spying on the conduct of the upper

[1] Tac. *Ann.* xiii. 1.

[2] Dio, lxiii. 12: *Οὕτω μὲν δὴ τότε ἡ τῶν Ῥωμαίων ἀρχὴ δύο αὐτοκράτορσιν ἅμα ἐδούλευσε, Νέρωνι καὶ Ἡλίῳ· οὐδ' ἔχω εἰπεῖν ὁπότερος χείρων ἦν.*

[3] Dio, lxiii. 18.

[4] Tac. *Hist.* i. 58.

[5] Dio, lxiv. 3; Plut. *Galba*, 17.

[6] Tac. *Ann.* xii. 66; Suet. *Claud.* 44; *Galba*, 15.

[7] Suet. *Galba*, 14.

[8] Tac. *Hist.* i. 46.

classes.[1] Vitellius did not carry out the spirit of his reform in the secretariate. Even in his short reign he allowed his freedman Asiaticus to rival Polyclitus and Patrobius in crime.[2]

The close of the civil wars heralded an emperor who kept freedmen in check better than any before, with the possible exceptions of Augustus and Tiberius. Neither under Vespasian nor under Titus do we hear of any scandalous oppression or peculation on the part of freedmen. They held the great court offices, it is true; the reform in 69 was not lasting; but their crimes are now a thing of the past. Suetonius records a story that Vespasian appointed the most rapacious of his freedmen to procuratorships in the provinces, so that he could execute them and confiscate their augmented properties.[3] If there is any truth in this, it is that the Emperor was more than a match for his servants. Yet even over this wary prince the worthless Hormus seems to have exercised some influence.[4]

Under Domitian freedmen regained something of their old power. The chamberlain's office began to be a lucrative one. Martial and Statius were not ashamed to write flattering odes to the Emperor's ex-slaves.[5]

The reigns of Nerva and Trajan ushered in a new era as far as freedmen were concerned. While the age of the 'Five Good Emperors' was one of humanitarian progress in legislation affecting slavery, it was also one in which insolence and corruption among the great freedmen were repressed with an iron hand. Pliny bestows eloquent praises upon Trajan for the new order of things. 'The majority of emperors, though the despotic masters of citizens, were the slaves of their freedmen. . . . You entertain the highest respect for your freedmen, but always

[1] *Ib.* i. 87: 'curam navium Moschus libertus retinebat ad observandam honestiorum fidem.'

[2] Tac. *Hist.* ii. 57, 95.

[3] Suet. *Vesp.* 16.

[4] Tac. *Hist.* iii. 12, 28; iv. 39.

[5] Martial to Parthenius, iv. 45, v. 6, viii. 28; to Sextus, v. 5; Statius to Abascantus, v. 1.

such respect as befits their station. Your belief is that the reputation of honesty and good service is a liberal and sufficient reward'.[1] When one of his freedmen, Eurythmus, was accused of forgery, the prosecutors feared to press the charge. The Emperor reassured them with the magnanimous words, 'He is no Polyclitus and I no Nero'.[2] Yet even this prince was believed to be swayed occasionally by his freedmen. Hadrian is said to have stooped to bribe Trajan's freedmen in order to make sure of his accession.[3]

But, if this is true, all hopes that Trajan's servants may have cherished of influencing his successor vanished at the outset of his reign. The new emperor proved himself the most implacable foe of libertine power that the Empire had yet seen. 'He desired his freedmen neither to be known in public affairs nor yet to possess influence with himself; in his own words he attributed the vices of freedmen to all his predecessors on the throne; he punished all his own freedmen who made any boast about him.'[4] The sweeping changes which he made in the civil service have already been shown. Yet such was the charm of the Oriental servant that even Hadrian showed marked favour to his freedman Antinous. The latter became so prominent that for a short time almost every fresh piece of sculpture was an Antinous in some form or another.

After Hadrian, Antoninus Pius was a stern repressor of peculation on the part of his procurators. He allowed his freedmen to take no liberties, and neither his courtiers nor his servants made profit by disseminating rumours of his

[1] *Paneg.* 88: 'plerique principes, cum essent civium domini, libertorum erant servi . . . tu libertis tuis summum quidem honorem sed tamquam libertis habes, abundeque sufficere eis credis si probi et frugi existimentur.'

[2] Plin. *Ep.* vi. 31, § 9.

[3] *Hist. Aug., Hadr.* 4: 'corrupisse eum Traiani libertos . . . per ea tempora quibus in aula familiarior fuit, opinio multa firmavit.'

[4] *Hist. Aug., Hadr.* 21, § 2: 'libertos suos nec sciri voluit in publico nec aliquid apud se posse, dicto suo omnibus superioribus principibus vitia imputans libertorum, damnatis omnibus libertis suis quicumque se de eo iactaverant.'

mood.[1] Under the gentle Marcus Aurelius freedmen regained some of their ancient power, chiefly because Verus was indulgent to them. Geminus and Agaclytus were notorious for their influence.[2] Then the accession of Commodus soon brought a revival of the times of Claudius and Nero, and freedmen enjoyed a regular carnival under that weak-willed prince.[3] Chief among them was the chamberlain Cleander, who was able to sell the highest offices of state as he wished.[4]

The riches that freedmen amassed by fair means or foul were generally spent in the most extravagant luxury and ostentation. In their mansions were some of the wonders of furniture which are mentioned in Pliny's *Natural History*. Nomius, a freedman of Tiberius, had a costly citron-wood table;[5] Callistus in the time of Claudius possessed a most pretentious dining-room with thirty pillars of oriental alabaster.[6] Four such ornaments from the East had sufficed for a whole theatre two generations before. Martial describes how Entellus, a freedman of Domitian, laid out magnificent gardens in which he sought to rival Alcinous.[7] Similarly imperial freedmen were always ready to display their wealth and win popularity by means of gladiatorial shows.[8]

Yet they could occasionally sink their love of self in a genuine desire to promote the interests of their fellow-citizens. Posides, a freedman of Claudius, developed a hot well near Baiae and constructed baths for the people of the neighbourhood.[9] So another imperial freedman restored baths at Anagnia;[10] a temple at Neapolis was the gift of another.[11] Of course ostentation may have been the

[1] *Hist. Aug.*, *Anton. P.* 11: 'quia et ipsi numquam de eo cum libertis per fumum aliquid vendiderunt.'

[2] *Hist. Aug.*, *M. Aurel.* 15.

[3] Dio, lxxii. 10.

[4] Dio, lxxii. 12.

[5] Plin. *N. H.* xiii. 94.

[6] Plin. *N. H.* xxxvi. 60.

[7] Mart. viii. 68.

[8] e. g. Plin. *N. H.* xxxv. 52; Tac. *Hist.* i. 76.

[9] Pliny, *N. H.* xxxi. 5.

[10] *I. L. S.* 1909: 'Quod thermas longa incuria neglectas sua pecunia restituerit.'

[11] *Inscriptiones Graecae*, xiv. 714.

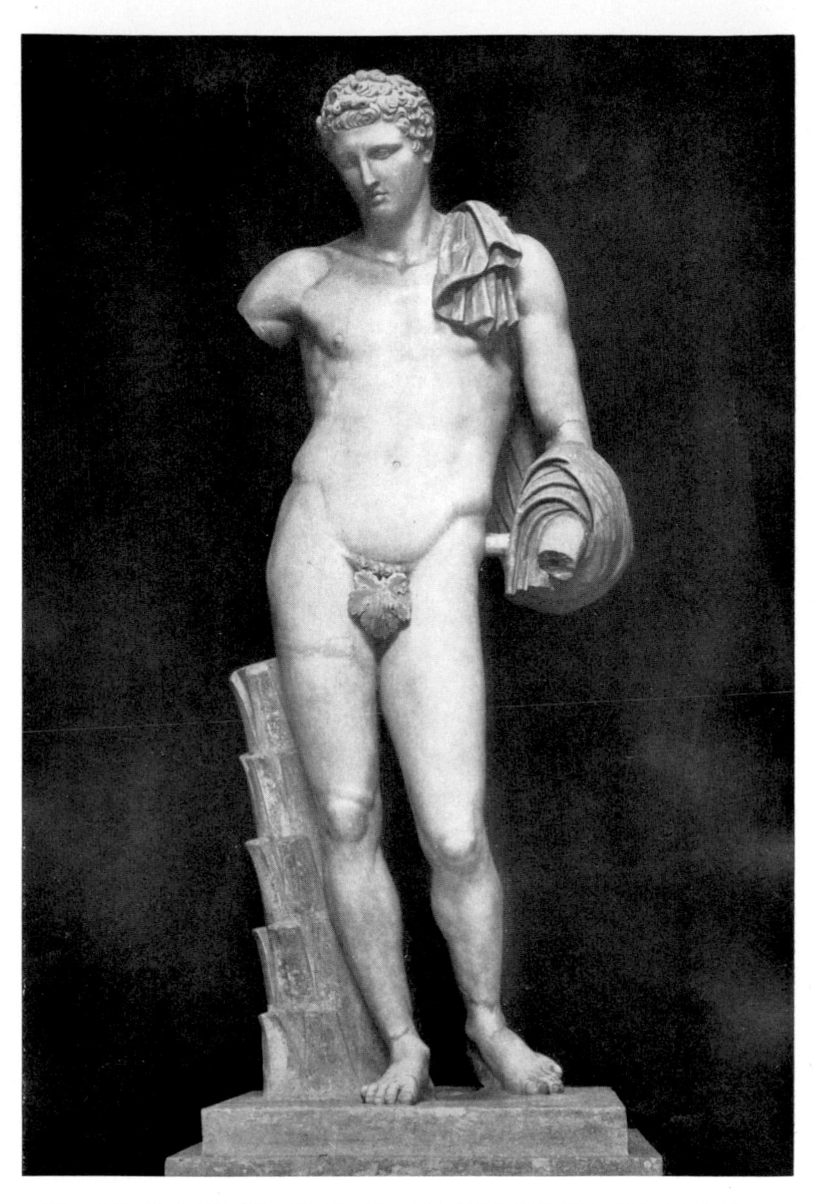

XI. ANTINOUS, FREEDMAN AND FAVOURITE OF HADRIAN
Vatican, Rome

motive here also, but it is at least equally likely that public spirit prompted beneficence.

Naturally eminence was often accompanied by extreme peril. A freedman in the Emperor's confidence not infrequently was entrusted with some dangerous enterprise. Helius was ordered to murder Silanus;[1] Anicetus was charged with the removal of the far more formidable Agrippina.[2] Having emerged unscathed from one perilous venture, a man might soon be plunged into another. Anicetus was a second time approached by Nero on the subject of ruining Octavia.[3]

From his very master the freedman favourite had much to fear. Consummate tact was needed with capricious princes like Caligula and Nero, especially when there were hosts of rivals who were ready to place a false construction on every word. Moreover, the riches of imperial freedmen often excited the Emperor's avarice. It was believed, and probably correctly, that both Pallas and Doryphorus owed their death to their own ill-gotten gains. With a treasury almost emptied by extravagance, Nero poisoned two of those with whom he had shared the results of his earlier confiscations.[4]

But the most stormy crisis through which an influential freedman had to steer his craft was a change of rulers. The death of the reigning Emperor might remove the sole stay of a favourite's power. Forthwith would ensue a tempestuous interval while the new monarch's favour was still in doubt. Many a freedman failed to weather the storm. Narcissus ruined Messallina, but in the question of the Emperor's next consort he was unfortunate enough to support the wrong candidate. He incurred the hostility of Agrippina, for whose ascendancy his execution of the previous empress had nevertheless paved the way. When Claudius died, Agrippina lost no time in hunting her opponent to death.[5] Similarly, as we have seen, some of Nero's creatures soon followed their master out of this life,

[1] Tac. *Ann.* xiii. 1. [2] *Ib.* xiv. 3 ff. [3] *Ib.* xiv. 62.
[4] *Ib.* xiv. 65. [5] *Ib.* xiii. 1.

and the ascendancy of Icelus lasted no longer than that of the sovereign he served. Vespasian was quick to crucify Asiaticus, the most notorious of Vitellius' favourites.[1]

High office, however, even under Gaius, Nero or Domitian, if discharged with integrity, did not necessarily involve the final doom that overtook so many imperial freedmen. If they were honest in the fulfilment of their duties, secretaries of state neither amassed those fortunes which excited their master's cupidity, nor occasioned the cries for vengeance with which populace and aristocracy invoked succeeding sovereigns. At the same time, their salaries were such as to enable them to live in comfort and moderate luxury. The best example of the freedman who combined greatness with safety is the father of Claudius Etruscus, whose career Statius commemorated in the third poem of the third book of his *Silvae*. Entering the imperial household in the reign of Tiberius, he was freed either by him or by Claudius; he came into personal contact with Caligula and under Claudius rose to prominence. The death of that monarch did not affect his fortune; he lived unscathed through the terrors of Nero's reign and the bloody revolutions which followed; through the comparative calm of the first two Flavian reigns he enjoyed one of the highest offices of state, the financial secretariate. He fell into disgrace under Domitian, but his old age saved him from a heavy penalty. A short period of relegation to the Campanian coast was soon succeeded by a restoration to favour. Finally he died at a ripe old age, mourned by at least one duteous son and surrounded by splendid but probably not inordinate wealth. He had served ten sovereigns, of whom six had perished by violent death. Well might Statius say, 'Thou unscathed hast duly borne the yoke of princes that have changed so oft; on every main thy craft has sailed secure!'[2] Such was the

[1] Tac. *Hist.* iv. 11.

[2] Stat. *Silv.* III. iii, lines 83–4:

> 'Tu totiens mutata ducum iuga rite tulisti
> Integer, inque omni felix tua cumba profundo.'

brilliant life of this happiest of the great freedmen. The success which attended his life through stormy years is the best testimony to his general honesty.

Very probably there were many like him. Much is related of the peculation, extortion and crime of Pallas and Icelus. There is no doubt that Helius and Asiaticus were among the greatest blackguards in history. But it is the iniquities of these scoundrels that Tacitus, Suetonius and Dio thought worth recording. No one ever troubled to give the careers of the more honourable; they were not exciting enough. Yet the general prosperity and good government which prevailed in the first two centuries of the Roman Empire was of a standard the like of which not many other imperial powers can boast. Whereas extortion and corruption were the rule under the Republic, they became the exception under the Empire. The world as a whole was well administered, though the courts of Claudius and Nero were dominated by infamous freedmen. Even the dissolute and pleasure-loving Commodus sided with the *coloni* against the unjust *procurator* and *conductores*.[1] When the Empire was established, Tacitus says, the provinces welcomed the change. He does not say they repented afterwards, Republican though he was in his sympathies.[2]

If imperial government reached such a high level, to whom is the praise due? Much has to be accorded to the genius of Augustus, who organized such a system of checks and counter-checks among the various officials in charge that provincial misgovernment was well-nigh sure to be reported. Another share of the credit has to be ascribed to the governors and the lower officers, knights and freedmen, who bore authority in the provinces. But on the home department also depended something. Even to Narcissus and Epaphroditus belongs some portion of the praise. Orientals were the superiors of the Romans in business ability. Many a freedman exercised this ability

[1] *I. L. S.* 6870.

[2] Tac. *Ann.* i. 2: 'Neque provinciae illum rerum statum abnuebant.'

honestly and energetically, be it in the home department or in the provinces and imperial domains. Perhaps he feared the punishment that threatened slackness and corruption; but just as possibly he was attached by gratitude to the master who had set him free, or by public spirit to the people whom he governed or whose needs he supplied, especially if, as was not unlikely, that people was of the race from which he himself was sprung.

IX

GOVERNMENTAL POLICY TOWARDS FREEDMEN AND THEIR INFLUENCE ON SOCIETY

I. Government policy towards freedmen a blend of conservatism, utilitarianism, and humanitarianism — conservative elements — utilitarian elements — humanitarian elements.

II. Parts of the world where freedmen abounded most — foreign extraction of most of Rome's citizens — the decline in the native stock — freedmen's influence on administration — on the common mode of life — on luxury — on literature — on art, science, and philosophy — on religion — intermixture of race an important cause of Rome's decline — summary of the effects of manumission — what manumission might have accomplished.

IN the last chapter it was seen how at certain times a freedman rule was established in the Empire. The reins of government, according to the policy which individual emperors followed towards their own servants, were either held fast by the *Princeps* or given to imperial freedmen. We have now to examine the government's policy towards freedmen as a whole. It is no longer a question of Pallas and Narcissus and their comrades, but of the general class of *libertini*. The licence or suppression of imperial freedmen depended on the character of the ruler, and, as has been noticed, their fortunes were subject to momentous changes. But the personal relation of an emperor to his servants did not enter into the question of how to treat the freedmen of ordinary citizens. Accordingly while Claudius was pampering his own freedmen and while Antoninus was keeping them sternly in check, we must be prepared to find a totally different attitude adopted towards the general mass of those who had issued from slavery.

I. The discussion which follows will contain a great deal of recapitulation. Throughout the earlier chapters several stray suggestions have been made as to the policy of the legislature. These suggestions will now be welded into proper arrangement; from them it may be possible to learn valuable lessons as to the state-craft of the first two centuries of the Empire.

Conservatism is often accused of being utterly unprogressive and of refusing to recognize the needs of the moment. Yet the imperial government in its policy towards freedmen mingled the healthy conservatism of its founder Augustus with practical provision for needs that arose and with a progressive humanitarianism of which any Christian nation could be proud. This sphere of the statesmanship of imperial Rome is a clear example of how respect for great traditions did not prevent her from remedying material evils or from advancing on the path of progress.

Accordingly her policy ran on three distinct lines, the conservative, the utilitarian, and the progressive or humanitarian. At first, as was natural after emerging from the whirlpool of revolution, the government laid especial stress on the conservative element. Augustus strove to uphold the rights of the patron, to preserve the Italian character of the citizen population, and at all costs to save that of the aristocracy. At the beginning of the Empire the dangers against which Augustus struggled were very real. The old relations between patron and freedman, regulated by custom rather than by law, were falling into decay owing to the increasing frequency of manumission and the constant strain of civil war. At the same time the *plebs urbana* was a cosmopolitan mass, swollen by the influx of Oriental freedmen, and even the aristocracy was not untainted by foreign blood. It could be said in the Senate under Nero that a large proportion of the senatorial and equestrian nobility was of servile extraction.[1] Unlimited manumission of slaves and frequent intermarriage with freedmen had done their work. It was, then, the task of Augustus to repair, as well as might be, the fatal consequences of *laissez-faire* under the Republic.

[1] Tac. *Ann.* xiii. 27: 'Quippe late fusum id corpus (*sc.* libertinorum), hinc plerumque tribus decurias ministeria magistratibus et sacerdotibus cohortes etiam in urbe conscriptas; et plurimis equitum plerisque senatoribus non aliunde originem trahi.'

To preserve the rights of the patron, the *obsequium* and *officium* were legally recognized. If a freedman wronged his patron, his offence was the more heinous because it was against his legal father. Even Claudius, the slave of his own freedmen, was especially severe against those who plotted against their patrons. In the second century, while humanitarian legislation was gradually recognizing the rights of the slave, Hadrian and Antoninus were staunch conservatives in their treatment of ungrateful freedmen. Apart from the measures which followed from the recognition of the *obsequium*, there were miscellaneous enactments which strengthened or at least preserved the rights of the patron. In Claudius' reign, when women over twenty years of age were exempted from the *tutela*, freedwomen were excluded. His successor ruled that, when a master had been murdered by his slaves, even those slaves who were to be manumitted by will should be included in the death-penalty. In the case of a Latin obtaining citizenship by imperial grant, the consent of the patron was made necessary by Trajan.

More stringent were the regulations to repress the rapid Orientalization of Rome and Italy. Augustus, as we have seen, put severe restrictions on imprudent manumission. In the *Lex Iunia* he legalized informal manumission and by so doing discouraged it. In the *Lex Fufia Caninia* he limited the proportion of a *familia* which could be freed by testament. In the *Lex Aelia Sentia*, among other things, he forbade all manumission by masters under twenty years of age, unless special authorization were secured.

Similarly efforts were made to prevent the immediate passage of slaves into citizenship by means of manumission. The words of Persius—

> momento turbinis exit
> Marcus Dama.[1]

gave a satiric touch which many an aristocratic Roman

[1] Pers. *Sat.* v. 78, 79.

heartily endorsed. Augustus, therefore, created two new classes. The *Lex Iunia* called into being the *Latini Iuniani*; the *Lex Aelia Sentia*, the *dediticii*. In the latter class were placed those whose criminal propensities made them permanently unfit for citizenship. The former comprised the recipients of informal manumission, and after 4 A. D. all *liberti* freed at an age below thirty; these last were debarred from full citizenship and made Latins by the *Lex Aelia Sentia*. But, as we have seen, Augustus checked any attempt of the master to take sordid advantage of this system. He opened an avenue by which the slave freed under thirty years of age could obtain citizenship one year after becoming a father; and, if any masters still informally freed slaves solely in order to possess their whole estates when they died, Vespasian finally stopped the practice by allowing such freedmen the same opportunities of enfranchisement as the other *Latini Iuniani*.

Intermarriage between *ingenui* and *libertini* had gone too far to be checked under the Empire. The free-born were already so much tainted with servile blood that it would have been impolitic to legislate generally in the matter. Yet Augustus felt that some particular restriction could be made without endangering his throne. He forbade alliances between freedmen and members of senatorial families. The Senate could not oppose such a measure without implying that they wished to degrade their order. Similarly the government was anxious to preserve the caste division between freedmen and free-born. As already stated, freedmen were excluded from various military, religious and administrative offices, and both they and their sons from the ranks of senators and knights. With very few exceptions these exclusions were maintained throughout the early Empire.

Parallel with these efforts to uphold all that was best in ancient traditions went the recognition of certain needs. The government realized that in supplying these needs freedmen could prove themselves worthy citizens of Rome. They were, therefore, given the utmost encouragement to engage in social service. The inducements offered, such as liberation from the *operae* or the privilege of full citizenship, generally deprived patrons of some of their rights; but this arbitrary procedure nevertheless fitted in well with the policy of restricting manumission. Masters who curtailed the gift of freedom by imposing heavy obligations in the form of *operae*, or by manumitting in such a way that their slaves became Latins, were now warned that these half-measures might be of no avail. An avenue was opened through which the freedman could by public service be excused the *operae*; many more were opened by which the Latin could become a Roman and thereby gain the right of making his own will. It was, therefore, made almost impossible to give freedom with one hand and take away a great part of it with the other. Masters had to regard manumission, even if covered by promises of *operae* or with reservations of citizenship, as a leap in the dark. They could not be certain that it would not deprive them of all the economic advantages of ownership and leave them merely with the more sentimental rights of *obsequium* and *officium*. Consequently greater forethought was exercised before taking a step which was now an irrevocable alienation of possession, and manumissions therefore tended to be less frequent.

One of the most serious evils with which the imperial government was called upon to contend was the decline in the population. Not only had the Italian stock almost disappeared from the towns, but the descendants of freedmen had not been born in sufficient numbers to take its place. Accordingly, while the *Lex Papia Poppaea* offered privileges to free-born citizens for the possession of three children, it used the whole question of the inheritances of freedmen and freedwomen for the encouragement of procreation. Two sides had claims on the estate of a dead freedman—his heirs and the patron or the patron's descendants. On the side of the freedman, the children's rights tend to increase as they are more in number; on the patron's side, the claimants have a better chance if they have children. For instance, while his patron or a male descendant of his patron is alive, a freedman can obtain control over an estate of above 100,000 sesterces if he has three children. In the case of a freedwoman the patron or his male descendant has rights over the whole estate unless she has four children. At the same time procreation is encouraged on the other side. It was only by the possession of three children that a patroness could be admitted to the same rights as a patron, or the female descendants of a patron to the rights of male descendants.[1]

Reasons have already been stated for holding that the grant of Roman citizenship to the Latin father of one child is to be referred rather to the conservative policy of restricting manumission than to the utilitarian object of raising the birth-rate; and, on the same grounds *mutatis mutandis*, the liberation of the father of two sons from the *operae* is to be ascribed more to the former than the latter, though probably in this case both reasons prompted the legislator.

Marriage also, as the first condition of legitimate procreation, received the attention of the reformer. All unnecessary bars to marriage were swept away. Thus, in the case of freedmen, the oath of celibacy that masters sometimes exacted at manumission was declared by the *Lex Aelia Sentia* to be not binding; and it was enacted that a freedwoman when once married should be freed from the *operae*, provided the patron had consented to her marriage. Yet, although the promotion of marriage seems to be the main object, it may fairly be questioned whether the legislator was not in both these measures influenced by mixed motives. The latter enactment may be partly due to the recognition that a married woman had sufficient duties in that capacity, without being burdened further by obligations towards her patron. The former provision was probably prompted by two sub-

[1] Gaius, iii. 39–53; Ulpian, xxix. See Abdy and Walker, *Gaius and Ulpian*, 3rd edition, appendix M.

sidiary motives. Firstly, the oath of celibacy was regarded as an unjust extortion; and, secondly, so long as such an oath was valid, masters could prevent slaves whom they had freed before the age of thirty from obtaining full citizenship by means of one child. But undoubtedly the primary purpose of these laws was to encourage marriage and thereby the production of children.

The other needs of a material nature which the government tried to supply are quickly enumerated. Firstly, Latins were encouraged to join the fire-brigade. After six years' service they could obtain citizenship. Secondly, the co-operation of freedmen was invited in supplying Rome with her daily bread. Those who built at their own expense a ship to hold 10,000 *modii*, and continued in the corn-trade for six years, were granted certain privileges by Claudius; a citizen was freed from any disabilities that the *Lex Papia Poppaea* might impose upon him; a woman was granted the *ius quattuor liberorum*; and a Latin obtained the full franchise. Thus a freedman gained the whole control over his inheritance; a freedwoman was liberated from the *operae* and her patron had only an equal share with each of her children in a legacy; a semi-privileged freedman became a Roman citizen. With the same object of providing food, Trajan gave Roman citizenship to any Latin who set up a large bake-house in the capital. Thirdly, when the fire of Rome made housing an acute problem, the help of the Latin was again invited. He was given immediate citizenship if he spent half a fortune of at least 200,000 sesterces in the construction of houses. Fourthly, utilitarian considerations directed the institution of the *seviri Augustales*. Rich freedmen were employed to give games in honour of the Emperor. Loyalty was thus fostered both among the great men who were proud to serve the sovereign and among the proletariat who came as spectators. But there was a stronger motive behind the institution. The capital of the wealthy freedman class was in this way applied to the all-important task of keeping the populace amused.

The humanitarian element in the imperial policy was slow in evolving itself. In antiquity the slave was legally regarded as a piece of property towards which there could be no obligations. For a long period of her history Rome was a conspicuous example of this rule. Augustus, as we have seen, was prejudiced against slaves by the turmoil of the civil wars. He made strenuous efforts to restrict manumission. Yet even his political programme contained some humanitarian elements. The establishment of the Council of Manumission under the *Lex Aelia Sentia* of 4 A. D. came from a recognition that certain classes of slaves, in virtue of faithful service, deserved both liberty and citizenship, even though they themselves might be under thirty years of age or their masters under twenty. Moreover this council gave facilities to a freedman under twenty years of age to redeem his relatives from servitude. By the same law masters were forbidden to exact at manumission the promise of an impossibly large sum of money, simply in order to render their freedmen debtors for life.[1] Similarly, their duty of supporting their freedmen, if they fell in need, was confirmed. Of course, all cases where the claims of freedmen were recognized, or patrons' rights were limited, may have been part of the policy of restricting manumission. The confirmation of patrons' burdens necessarily tended to make manumission less popular among the selfish. But there can be little doubt that at least a prominent motive was consideration for the welfare of the freedman.

One clear and undoubted example of humanitarian legislation was the edict of Claudius that a sick slave exposed or abandoned by his master should be free. A generation later Vespasian directed that in certain circumstances a slave prostituted by her master should be given her liberty.

Then comes a pause in the history of slavery reform. During this pause, however, the philosophy of the Stoics was acquiring a greater and greater ascendancy over the

[1] 'Onerandae libertatis causa,' *Dig.* XXXVIII. i. 32 and XLIV. v. 1, §5.

minds of the nobility. The more puritanical elements of this system were gradually modified, and in the latter half of the first century Seneca and Epictetus made Stoicism a living force in the upper classes of Roman society. For our present purpose we need only mention two of the great Stoical doctrines—the brotherhood of mankind and its corollary, the duty towards slaves. Stoics adopted as their watchword the line of Terence derived from Menander, 'I am a man; nothing human do I deem foreign to myself.'[1] Seneca announces clearly 'Man is a sacred thing to man'.[2] Applying these principles to slavery, he is careful to warn masters that the essential dignity of manhood is unchanged by the accident of condition; that the slave may be free by virtue while the master may be slave by vice; and that not only cruelty but even contempt towards his slaves should be avoided by the good man.[3]

As these ideas had permeated the aristocracy by the end of the first century, it was necessary that sooner or later they should affect the legislature. Thus Hadrian and his two successors, under the influence of the Stoics, began an energetic campaign for the amelioration of slavery. Masters who killed their slaves were made guilty of murder. The practice of selling unsatisfactory slaves to gladiatorial companies was suppressed. The *ergastula* or rural slave-prisons were destroyed. When a slave murdered his master, only the slaves within hearing at the time of the act could be tortured or in any way held responsible. Officers were appointed to hear the complaints of slaves, and, if excessive severity was proved, the master was compelled to sell the slave he had maltreated.[4] It was inevitable that such a triumph of humanity should be manifested also in the sphere of manumission. Hadrian

[1] 'Homo sum : humani nil a me alienum puto', Ter. *Heauton Timorumenos*, I. i. 25, cf. Sen. *Ep.* xcv. 53.

[2] 'Homo sacra res homini', Seneca, *Ep.* xcv. 33.

[3] Seneca, *De Benef.* iii. 18–28; *De Vita Beata*, 24; *De Clem.* i. 18; *Ep.* 47.

[4] Wallon, *Histoire de l'esclavage dans l'antiquité*, vol. III, chap. ii.

put an end to the anomaly that provincial towns were not, like the state, allowed to free their slaves; in the reign of Marcus Aurelius the right of manumission was granted to *collegia*. But one of the most striking evidences of the humanitarian movement is the history of fideicommissary manumission which evolved itself into legal form between Trajan and Marcus Aurelius. About twenty *senatus-consulta* and imperial *constitutiones* are known to us with reference to *fideicommissa*. Some are of great importance, such as the first recognition that a *fideicommissum* was legally as well as morally binding on the heir. Others are merely answers to exceptional questions which probably did not arise more than once in a generation. Still, they all serve to illustrate the attitude of the Antonine government. Of those twenty rescripts and decisions all are in favour of the slave. If it was quite clear that the testator wanted a certain slave to be freed, then he had to be freed, and no legal forms or theories could prevent it. If a slave had earned the gratitude of a citizen so much that the latter wanted him to be free, then the heir, if he accepted the legacy, was formally bound to carry out the deceased man's wishes. When the process of legal clarification is finished, the man who agrees to be heir may in certain conceivable circumstances be compelled to free one of his own slaves or even buy the slave of another in order to free him.

It may be asked whether Christianity had anything to do with the progress of the humanitarian movement. In legislation, it had no influence; to the most enlightened government of the second century Christians were still an obstinate and traitorous sect that clung to a ridiculous Eastern superstition. Their teaching was not noticed at all; if any conceptions were formed of the Gospel in official circles, they would be that it inculcated cannibalism and immoral rites. Nor can any influence on imperial policy be traced through Stoicism to a Christian source. The debt of second-century Stoicism to Christianity is negligible. Seneca never mentions the new religion.

Epictetus and Marcus Aurelius content themselves with a scornful reference to the obstinacy of martyrs. The alleged correspondence between Seneca and St. Paul is a manifest forgery. The truth is that Stoicism and Christianity were parallel and independent revelations. The latter, founded upon the belief in a personal God and a personal manifestation of His love, was *a priori* assured of its triumph. But the former, though immeasurably inferior, must nevertheless be accorded the full credit for the benevolent legislation of the second century.

Yet it must not be denied that Christianity helped to promote manumission. It did not guide the rulers in their policy, but as its influence grew in society it undoubtedly made its converts feel that their slaves were 'brothers in Christ', and that the charity which their religion enjoined was best displayed in manumission. Stoicism had never made an effective appeal to the masses, but Christianity fulfilled the task in which its great predecessor had failed. The religion of Jesus, carrying the doctrine of the brotherhood of mankind into the life of the lower classes and more slowly superseding other religions and philosophies among the aristocracy, gradually became one of the most potent causes of manumission.

II. Such was the policy of the government towards Roman freedmen: before we can say whether it succeeded or not, we must estimate the influence the freedman exercised on the social and economic history. In the first place it may be asked what was the proportion of freedmen to the whole population. Unfortunately, sufficient evidence has not yet come to hand even for an approximate estimate. So many questions on which there are little or insecure data have first to be answered that to determine the freedman population is impossible under present conditions. One cannot tell, for instance, what proportion of his life a freedman ordinarily enjoyed in liberty. This would involve deciding what was the average age at which manumission was performed, and what was the average duration of life among freedmen and among citizens.

Obviously, if one finds a hundred inscriptions in a town of which fifty refer to freedmen and fifty to free-born, one cannot therefore say that in the population of the city the two classes are equally balanced. The freedman has only been free a certain period of his life; the free-born citizen has been a citizen from birth.

One may, however, be allowed to record where especially inscriptions of freedmen are to be found. Some typical towns and districts of the Roman Empire have been examined in the *Corpus Inscriptionum Latinarum*, and below is given the percentage of freedmen among the persons mentioned. In all cases honorary inscriptions and epitaphs of magistrates, priests, and soldiers are omitted.

Italy.	
Mediolanum	22 per cent.
Ostia	14½ ,,
Capua	48 ,,
Potentia, Grumentum and Tegianum (Lucania)	15 ,,
Ager Amiterninus (Sabini)	43 ,,
Picenum	31 ,,
Gaul.	
Narbo	37 ,,
Arelate	12½ ,,
Spain.	
Tarraco	10 ,,
Emerita	14 ,,
Corduba	35 ,,
Hispalis	12 ,,

These results are not altogether satisfactory. It is difficult to see why Narbo differed so fundamentally from Arelate. Both were important harbours of Southern Gaul, and we should have expected the percentages of freedmen in each to be similar. Corduba and Hispalis, too, were towns whose economic features must have been very much alike. Yet the proportion of freedmen in the former is three times that in the latter. But the number of inscriptions available from these Spanish cities is very small, and therefore percentages must not be too confidently relied upon.

Ostia has a surprisingly small proportion. She was one of the greatest ports in imperial times and we should have expected to find a large number of freedmen playing their busy rôle in the trade of Rome's harbour. Perhaps some portion of the explanation may lie in the hypothesis that the town was full of imperial freedmen who were buried with other servants of Caesar at Rome and therefore do not figure among the Ostian inscriptions.

The most valuable information which these figures yield concerns the country districts. Some rural parts, it will have been noticed, were almost as full of freedmen as Capua was. Inscriptions from the Ager Amiterninus, whose principal industry was probably olive-growing, mention 190 persons of whom 89 are freedmen. Picenum, the home of tillage, gives 31 freedmen out of every 100 persons. The percentage is noticeably less in the small towns of South Italy where pastoral farming was the order of the day. But the high proportions met with in Picenum and among the Sabini are surprising. Probably freedmen captured the retail trade of the rural districts as much as they did that of the large towns. Moreover, it was a frequent custom for landed proprietors to give their freedmen small farms on their estates.[1] In view of the statistics from corn and olive regions, it is likely that this custom was followed far more extensively than has been hitherto supposed.

With this somewhat bare statement of figures, which are only relative in value, we must leave the question of the freedman population. But, although it cannot be said with any certainty what proportion the number of freedmen bore to that of the whole citizen body, an estimate has been made of the extent to which men of servile descent dominated Rome. Prof. Tenney Frank,[2] after an

[1] e. g. *Dig.* XXXII. xxxviii. 5.

[2] *Am. Hist. Rev.* 1916. Prof. Frank's article assumes all Greek names to indicate Hellenistic blood. As we have seen (pp. 5, 6), the assumption

examination of some 13,000 urban inscriptions, has conjectured that, among the ordinary citizens of Rome, little over ten per cent. were able to boast pure Italian descent. Of the remainder very few, he thinks, were free *peregrini* or their descendants; an overwhelming proportion therefore—about five-sixths—of Rome's citizens were freedmen and their posterity. This conjecture based on the evidence of 13,000 inscriptions cannot be far wrong; but in other parts of Italy the ratio must have varied, and it is hardly likely that it anywhere exceeded the high percentage in the capital. It may be asked in this connexion what became of the Latin and Italian stock. Reasons may be given for the coming of the foreigner, but at the same time some explanation may be demanded for the disappearance of the native. In the first place there was a marked decline in the birth-rate among the aristocratic classes. These latter were the chief sufferers from the proscriptions of the Republic and the capricious tyranny of early emperors. But it was the increase of luxury that was most effective in deleting old Roman families from the records. As society grew more and more pleasure-loving, as convention raised artificially the standard of living, the voluntary choice of celibacy and childlessness became a common feature among the upper classes. Of forty-five patrician families in Caesar's day, all save one were extinct by the reign of Hadrian. Augustus and Claudius found it necessary to reinforce the patrician order with twenty-five plebeian houses. Of these only six survived till Nerva's reign.[1]

But what of the lower-class Romans of the old stock? They were practically untouched by revolution and tyranny, and the growth of luxury cannot have affected them

requires modification. But the proved examples of Westerners bearing Greek names are either slaves or Germanic guardsmen and therefore do not invalidate Prof. Frank's general conclusion as to the decline of the Italian stock. On that decline, cf. Rostovtzeff, *Social and Economic History of the Roman Empire*, Oxford, 1926, chap. III, note 31.

[1] Tenney Frank, *A. H. R.* 1916.

to the same extent as it did the nobility. Yet even here the native stock declined. The decay of agriculture, brought about by the establishment of *latifundia* and intensified by confiscations and veteran settlements, drove numbers of farmers into the towns, where, unwilling to engage in trade, they sank into unemployment and poverty, and where, in their endeavours to maintain a high standard of living, they were not able to support the cost of rearing children. At the same time many were tempted to emigrate to the colonies across the sea which Julius Caesar and Augustus founded. Many went away to Romanize the provinces, while society was becoming Orientalized at home. Of course freedmen must have shared in those colonies also; we know they participated very freely in the restoration of Corinth;[1] and they probably did so in many other colonies of the Dictator;[2] but, often past the prime of life at manumission, frequently held by obligations towards their patrons, and more often than not comfortably settled in employment, for the most part they could not or would not leave the land of their slavery. Thus it was the free-born Italian, anxious for land to till and live upon, who displayed the keenest colonizing activity.

Among all the causes of the change of race (apart from manumission) war was the most important. The armies of the late Republic and civil wars had consisted largely of Italians, who, if they were not killed off, were at least deprived of domestic life during their prime. Meanwhile the freedmen, usually excluded from the army, and the freedman's descendant, never a keen solder, were

[1] Strabo, VIII. vi. 23 (Tozer, No. 42): *ἡ Κόρινθος ἀνελήφθη πάλιν ὑπὸ Καίσαρος τοῦ θεοῦ διὰ τὴν εὐφυΐαν, ἐποίκους πέμψαντος τοῦ ἀπελευθερικοῦ γένους πλείστους.*

[2] The liberal share of freedmen in Julius Caesar's colonies represents a far-sighted policy which apparently was not sufficiently followed during the Empire. Julius encouraged freedmen to emigrate and thus for the first time assailed that Orientalization of the *plebs urbana* which Augustus was to attack by other means such as restrictions on manumission. Cf. p. 66, note 3.

allowed an uninterrupted family life and produced offspring with greater freedom. Moreover, after his twenty years' service, it was frequently the case that the legionary never returned home, but joined with his fellow-veterans to found a colony in the province where he had served.[1]

The Roman thus gave way to the Easterner in Italy, while he made a place for himself in the provinces. Meanwhile what was the influence of the Oriental, and especially the freedman, on history?

The imperial freedman in administration has already been treated. Many offices of the utmost imperial importance were nevertheless attached too closely to Caesar's person to be given to senators and knights, who, though anxious to serve the state, would not show the same keenness to serve the *Princeps*. Accordingly, unless he openly declared 'L'état c'est moi', Augustus could not offer the great secretariates to these two orders. Freedmen solved the difficulty for the early emperors; they bridged the theoretical gap between the republic and the monarchy. As the freedmen's offices by degrees went to the knights, so the principate gradually came to be recognized as a despotism.

So the freedman satisfied the logical minds of the first emperors. We have seen his actual record in government, and it is only necessary to reiterate our conclusion, that, though under the Empire his official career was stained with greater corruption than that of senator and knight, yet his business ability and the many unknown cases of honest lives force us to accord him a large share in the credit for the sound administration of the Empire.

Under the Republic those freedmen who had not been born in slavery, but had come into the market through capture, brought the habits and ideas of their native land into Italy. For instance, freedmen probably helped to revolutionize Italian horticulture. They showed their masters how to grow the fruit-trees which they had

[1] Tac. *Ann.* xiv. 27: 'Dilapsis pluribus in provincias in quibus stipendia expleverant.'

tended in their youth and in their freedom. Lucullus may have first introduced the cherry into Italy.[1] It was his Asiatic captives who made it an Italian fruit.

But some of the innovations which freedmen effected were not so harmless as the cherry. Oriental luxury destroyed the sterling simplicity of the early Roman. Freedmen of course were not the only avenue by which luxury gained access to the Roman Republic. The pretentious ideas of the wealthy East no doubt were to some extent adopted by Romans themselves when they went thither to fight or to govern. They saw the gorgeous city palaces, the magnificent country mansions, the collections of gold and silver plate. They tasted gastronomic wonders yet unknown to Italy. Still, slaves and freedmen helped greatly to introduce these ideas into the land of their slavery. They must have directed their masters' minds to luxuries which Roman simplicity had never dreamed of. Then, too, when freed, they must have introduced into a wider society than that of the house such of the less expensive refinements as their means could afford.

New luxuries created new trades. When Romans and Italians found their wants vastly multiplied, and when they intensified their prejudice against banausic crafts, freedmen and their descendants stepped into the breach, supplying all the labour and much of the capital to industry. They made a bold bid to develop Italy into a manufacturing country and to save her from becoming wholly dependent on foreign lands for her needs and luxuries.

If slaves and freedmen developed Roman industry, they were largely instrumental in the very start of Roman literature. They brought the Greek influence which awoke the native talent of the Romans and inspired them to emulate their Hellenic predecessors. Further, freedmen are among the significant names of literature. Under

[1] Friedländer, *op. cit.* ii, p. 306; Eng. Trans. ii, p. 167. Cf. Plin. *N. H.* xiv. 48–51, where certain freedmen introduce new methods of viticulture; and xviii. 41, where a freedman raises better crops than his neighbours and draws upon himself the suspicion of sorcery.

the Republic we have Livius Andronicus, the first Latin poet known; Caecilius Statius, a dramatist of no mean ability; Terence, whose name stands second only to that of Plautus in Roman comedy; and Publilius Syrus, a distinguished writer of mimes. To represent the imperial age may be mentioned Phaedrus, the greatest Roman fabulist, and Epictetus who was perhaps the ablest post-Christian Stoic and whose Greek teaching has been handed down by Arrian. Moreover many a freedman whose works are now lost must have figured prominently in his day. For instance, every imperial freedman who held the office *a studiis* was probably a man of some literary attainments. C. Iulius Hyginus, who occupied a literary post under Augustus, wrote commentaries on Cinna and Virgil, treatises on theology, agriculture, bees, and eminent personages in Roman history, as well as a topographical work entitled *De Situ Urbium Italicarum*.[1] Polybius, the literary adviser of Claudius, had translated Homer and Virgil, apparently into prose.[2] Sextus was probably responsible for Domitian's poem on the revolutions of 69, on which Martial bestows such flattery.[3]

In art, science and philosophy freedmen played their rôle. Though the greatest names in the imperial period are those of Greek *peregrini*, yet slaves and freedmen must have in countless cases inspired their masters with a taste for art, and, after manumission, brought the same influence to bear upon the society in which they mingled. It was slaves and freedmen pre-eminently who spread the principles of Greek scientists around the Roman hearth, and who disseminated the thought of Academy and Stoa.

The same holds good in religion. Soldiers learnt of alien religions in the East, but they would never have introduced them permanently into Italy if it had not been for the Eastern slaves who brought them into their masters'

[1] Teuffel, *History of Roman Literature*, § 262; Cichorius believes (*Römische Studien*, Leipzig, pp. 293–4, 1922) that the inscription *C. I. L.* vi. 10395, line 18, refers to him.

[2] Sen. *Ad Polyb.* 8, § 2; 11, § 5.

[3] Mart. v. 5.

homes, and, after obtaining freedom, impressed them upon society in general. Finding Romans dissatisfied with their own beliefs, they preached religions which seemed to offer a wider and more certain promise, or which made a more living appeal through the character of their ceremonies. Some of these cults were low and degrading and were celebrated by means of the most immoral rites. As early as 186 B.C. the profligacy of Bacchanalian orgies was unmasked, and it was found that some thousands of citizens were involved.[1] Under the late Republic the religion of Isis was several times suppressed because of suspicions cast upon its ceremonial,[2] but such was the power it exercised over society that in the early years of the Empire the government was forced to surrender, and Isis was recognized as a Roman deity.[3] The prejudice against Christianity was largely due to the general opinion held of obscure Eastern religions.

Yet by no means all the religious innovations which freedmen effected were for the worse. Freedmen may have been among the first in Italy to listen to Christian missionaries and to carry the glad tidings throughout society. Quite a number of those unknown men with Greek names whom St. Paul mentions in the last chapter of his Epistle to the Romans may have been freedmen; Judaism in all probability owed its introduction primarily to Hebrew and proselyte slaves. Mithraism, the worthiest of Christianity's rivals, must perhaps ascribe its popularity not so much to slaves and freedmen as to the soldiers on the Eastern frontier.

The cumulative effect of these Oriental religions helped to break the old Roman character. Another more powerful solvent was also inherited from slavery and manumission. The profuse intermixture of race, continuing without

[1] Livy, xxxix. 8 ff.

[2] 58 B.C., Tertull. *Apol.* 6; 56 B.C., Dio, xl. 47; 50 B.C., Val. Max. I. iii. 3; 48 B.C., Dio, xlii. 26.

[3] A temple was erected to Isis at Rome in 43 B.C., Dio, xlvii. 15. In 69 A.D. she had a shrine on the Capitol. Suet. *Dom.* 1.

interruption from 200 B.C. far into the history of the Empire, produced a type utterly different from that which characterized the heroes of the early Republic. Instead of the hardy and patriotic Roman with his proud indifference to pecuniary gain, we find too often under the Empire an idle pleasure-loving cosmopolitan whose patriotism goes no further than applying for the dole and swelling the crowds in the amphitheatre. The question whether foreign blood benefits a nation or not cannot yet be answered dogmatically. The Anglo-Saxon race has not suffered from its Celtic, Danish and Norman elements, to say nothing of Flemish and Huguenot immigrants. On the other hand race-mixture hastened the decline of the Persian Empire, and American statesmen to-day are justifiably alarmed by alien immigration. Now as a class the freedmen had sharp wits and abundant enterprise. Many were honest, industrious folk who had earned their freedom by loyal service or by legitimate additions to their *peculium*. Others, however, during their slavery had been thieves on every opportunity, and doubtless were prepared to continue this career after they had purchased manumission with their ill-gotten gains. Others again were men who had for a long time past left all their arduous duties to *vicarii*, or who had spent several years performing specialized functions which occupied about half an hour *per diem*; these on passing into society were not likely to be its most energetic members. Such were the men whom indiscriminate manumission kept thrusting into the citizen body. Good points many of them had; but at best they were a motley throng. Moreover, one is tempted to believe that the Italian and Eastern characters were so diverse that satisfactory amalgamation was impossible. The virtues of each disappeared and the vices predominated. The cross-bred descendant of a Hellenistic freedman and a Roman citizen often lacked the enterprise and intellect of the one and the simplicity and hardihood of the other, while the defects of both stocks remained unabated.

This race-degeneration which manumission had set afoot was accelerated in the third century by another factor. Constant warfare, whether between claimants to the throne or against barbarians, killed off the hardiest and ablest of the citizens and left the poorest stocks to reproduce themselves. The fact that the Romans who resisted Hannibal and those who succumbed to the Goths were totally different peoples is one of the main explanations of the great decline and fall. Laughing to scorn the simplicity of the early Italians, the citizens of the Empire exported most of their capital beyond the frontiers to pay for their luxuries. Protected by a standing army, they lost energy and enterprise and the power of defending themselves. Of course it would be absurd to say that racial decay was the sole cause of Rome's deterioration. Other factors operated simultaneously. The less fertile provinces whose tribute did not repay the expense of their administration made for heavy taxation which effectively obliterated the few vestiges that remained of a middle class. Mechanical progress was barred by the benumbing influence of slavery. No strong unifying religion inspired the exhausted Empire. The general decay had gone too far when Christianity triumphed, and even the conversion of Constantine did not imply at once a universal religion. But these features in the situation would not have wrought such havoc among the Decii, Fabii, Cornelii, and the other great houses of Republican Rome. It was because the giants of the past had given place to a bastard brood that the final catastrophe came.

It seems, then, that freedmen and their descendants in a great measure ruined Rome. The progressive and the utilitarian elements in the government's policy succeeded only too well in promoting slaves to Roman citizenship, while, as far as restrictions on manumission are concerned, the conservative element failed to achieve its object. In modification of this view one word must be said. Even in Augustus' day the process of Orientalization had gone too far. The great emperor saw the clouds, but he did not know they had actually burst. His legislation would have been prudent and not a whit excessive a century earlier; but in his time Rome was a cosmopolitan city, and the doom of the Empire was already sealed.

Must it then be concluded that manumission bore nothing but evil fruit? Certainly in its developments at Rome it had fatal consequences. The grant of liberty to a slave, so full of charity in the abstract, was in practice the ruin of an empire. Yet it had its good points. In the first place, it benefited the individual slave. During slavery it offered him a hope and an ambition which alleviated his lot. After a slave had obtained freedom, it gave him opportunity of developing his capabilities which servitude had naturally cramped. It opened to the foreign captive and the home-born slave a new and a higher civilization to which he might adapt himself. Yet in some cases one slave freed meant another needed. Thus the slave-trade was indirectly encouraged by manumission. But, as we have pointed out, manumission often made no difference to a slave's employment, and, whether bond or free, he remained in his master's service. Any objection, therefore, that the slave trade varied exactly with manumission would have to be seriously modified.

At the same time, manumission, if performed through benevolence or gratitude, was a moral benefit to the individual master. Similarly the charity which may produce dire results in society never fails, if actuated by the correct motive, to benefit the character of the giver. Manumission enabled the master to perform a good act; it enabled him to set on his feet a man in whom he took a charitable interest. Perhaps it was bad for the slave; perhaps it was bad for the state; but it broadened the master's sympathies and it quickened a right spirit within him.

Finally, manumission, if it had been directed aright, need not have worked with such deplorable effects upon the population. If Cato the Censor had been the author of Augustus' reforms, there would not have been such an influx of foreigners into society. If the Romans had conquered their lamentable tendency towards celibacy and childlessness, their stock would have held its own. If masters had not indulged their vanity to such an extent, fewer and worthier slaves would have passed into the citizen body. Nay, if state legislation and private prudence had guided manumission in the right path, it would assuredly have benefited not merely slave and master but also the whole population. If, instead of indulging their vanity and lavishing promiscuous manumission, slave owners had exercised a wise and just discrimination, they could have effected that only the better type of slave should enter the citizen body. How different would Roman society have appeared if masters had only given freedom in gratitude for good service and only sold it to those who had increased their *peculium* by honest means! The influx of Oriental blood would not have been so overwhelming, and further, the slaves freed in such circumstances would on the whole have been men of good character, who had loyally served their masters and who might be expected to prove good citizens. No jest could then have been made by the satirist about Tiber and Orontes. The vast throngs of idle and worthless freedmen that left their curse upon Rome would never have issued from the bonds of servitude. The indigenous stock would not have been ousted from its predominance; at the same time a small body of conscientious Orientals, probably marrying among themselves rather than with Italians, would have contributed art, science and industry to Republic and Empire, without destroying the native character. Something of the brilliance and versatility of Periclean Athens might have existed alongside of the simple dignity and steadfast patriotism of Republican Rome.

APPENDIX I

DATE OF THE *LEX IUNIA*

SCHOLARS and historians are not yet agreed upon the date of the measure which created the class of *Latini Iuniani*; suggested dates range from 83 B.C. to 19 A.D.[1] The view taken in this treatise is that the *Lex Iunia* belonged to the reign of Augustus, was passed before the *Lex Aelia Sentia*, and should probably be assigned to the year 17 B.C.

Solutions of the problem must not be based on the name sometimes applied to this law—*Lex Iunia Norbana*. If this were the correct title of the measure, then the presumption would be strong in favour of 19 A.D., when M. Iunius Silanus and L. Norbanus Balbus were consuls. But in our authorities the double designation *Iunia Norbana* is found only once, in the Institutes of Justinian,[2] and there the text is doubtful. The law as Gaius and Ulpian know it is always the *Lex Iunia*; Justinian's Code and the *Novellae* likewise only speak of *Lex Iunia*. The name *Norbana* (if this reading be accepted) is an arbitrary addition by one of Justinian's jurists who wanted to distinguish this act from others of the name *Iunia*.[3] Either he took 25 B.C. as the date of the law and added *Norbana* to its title from the consul of 24, C. Norbanus Flaccus;[4] or else taking 19 A.D. found Iunius and Norbanus consuls for that year. In either

[1] Mommsen (Bekker, *Jahrbücher des gemeinen Rechts*, ii. (1858), 335–41 = Momm. *Gesammelte Schriften*, III. iv.) and Girard (*Manuel de droit romain*, 1918, p. 128) ascribe the law to the last years of the Republic between 43 and 31. Schneider (*Zeitschrift der Savigny-Stiftung für Rechtsgeschichte*, v. 225 ff., vi. 186 ff., vii. 31 ff.) argues for 25 B.C. Buckland (*Roman Law of Slavery*, 534 ff.), waiving the question of the actual year, believes the *Lex Iunia* to be prior to the *Lex Aelia Sentia*. Cuq (*Institutions juridiques des Romains*, ii. 148); Karlowa (*Römische Rechtsgeschichte*, i. 621 ff.); Hölder (*Zeitschr. d. Sav.-Stift.* vi. 205 ff.), and Steinwenter (Pauly-Wissowa *s. v. Latini Iuniani*) place it in 19 A.D.

[2] Just. *Inst.* I. v. 3.

[3] e.g. *Lex Iunia Velleia*, Gaius, ii. 134; Ulp. xxii. 19.

[4] The consuls of 25 were Augustus and M. Iunius Silanus, and those of 24 Augustus and C. Norbanus Flaccus. It is quite conceivable that a jurist, five and a half centuries later, might erroneously adopt for the law the names of the two non-imperial consuls. Romanet du Caillaud (*Date de la loi Junia Norbana* in *Comptes rendus de l'Acad. des Inscr.* 1882) argues from the collocation of consuls in 25 and 24 that two separate enactments took place, one being a confirmation or modification of the other. But nomenclature of a law from such causes has no parallel, and surely a more general occurrence of the double designation *Iunia Norbana* would have followed from such a unique set of circumstances.

case the jurist's opinion is not of much weight coming after such a long period and after the chaos of the fifth century. We are not justified then in seeking help from the name *Norbana*.

Another consideration might erroneously be made an indication of date. The *Lex Iunia* recognized *manumissio minus iusta* as a legal grant of liberty. Hence, it will be said, it favoured the acquisition of freedom, whereas the legislation of Augustus restricted manumission. This argument, if sound, would militate against an Augustan date. But it has been shown in Chapter V how the *Lex Iunia* is to be regarded as a check on the giving of liberty. The content of the law therefore is not incompatible with its ascription to the reign of Augustus.

Now any date before 43 B.C. is impossible. Cicero in the *Topics* says definitely no freedom is valid unless obtained by the Rod, Census or Will.[1] The *Lex Iunia*, therefore,—legalizing *manumissio minus iusta*—is still a law of the future in 43 B.C.

A date between 43 and 31 is extremely improbable. The main argument in favour of such a date, the alleged inconsistency between the tendency of the *Lex Iunia* and that of the freedman legislation of Augustus, has already been answered. Other considerations put a date between these years out of the question. Firstly, no year in this period saw a consul named Iunius; this is not conclusive, since the *Lex Iunia* is not necessarily a consular law. Secondly, the troubled times gave the authorities no leisure to regulate the status of the informally freed. Thirdly, Ulpian attributes to the *Lex Iunia* a measure which Gaius gives to the *Lex Aelia Sentia* of 4 A.D. One of them, therefore, is confusing the two laws.[2] It is inconceivable that an eminent jurist should confuse a Republican law with one passed when the Empire was more than a generation old. The *Lex Iunia*, therefore, must belong to the Empire, and, if it is to be confused with the *Lex Aelia Sentia*, to the early Empire.[3]

Thus all dates before 31 are well-nigh impossible; 19 A.D. is the latest suggested date, and no subsequent year is at all likely. The question therefore lies between the reign of Augustus and the early part of that of Tiberius. As we have seen, the name *Iunia Norbana* which would suggest 19 A.D. has too slight authority to be admitted as a serious argument. One or two juristic texts are urged as

[1] Cic. *Top.* 2: 'Si neque censu nec vindicta nec testamento liber factus est non est liber.'

[2] Gaius, i. 29, 31; Ulp. iii. 3.

[3] The expression 'per legem Aeliam Sentiam et Iuniam' (Gaius, i. 80) shows that the laws were not separated by a great interval of time.

evidence that the *Lex Iunia* was later than the *Lex Aelia Sentia*. Gaius[1] uses the expression 'per legem Aeliam Sentiam et Iuniam', apparently treating the *Lex Iunia* as the later; but it is quite possible he begins with the law which was nearer in time to his own age, and then proceeds to the more remote. Ulpian's words in two passages,[2] if taken together, suggest that the *Lex Aelia Sentia* refused legal freedom to persons manumitted under the age of thirty without reference to the Manumission Council, and assimilated their status to that of the informally freed, while the *Lex Iunia*, coming after, granted *Latinitas Iuniana* to both classes and allowed those freed before the age of thirty to acquire the full franchise by *anniculi probatio*. Serious difficulties beset this argument. It is nowhere stated that the *Lex Iunia* changed *libertas domini voluntate* into *Latinitas Iuniana* in favour of any but *manumissi inter amicos*; and no other text besides this passage in Ulpian says that any but the informally freed were ever *in libertate domini voluntate*. Moreover not only several passages in Gaius but also one in Ulpian himself ascribe not to the Junian but to the Aelian-Sentian law the measure granting Roman citizenship to persons freed below the age of 30 for the possession of one child.[3] Apart from the fact that Gaius repeats consistently the ascription to the *Lex Aelia Sentia*, while Ulpian is self-contradictory, other considerations compel the belief that Gaius is right. Firstly, he is a superior authority; he lived two generations before Ulpian and his works have been handed down more faithfully. Secondly (to recur to an argument already used against the period 43 to 31), if Gaius is wrong and the *Lex Iunia* is placed in 19 A.D.,

[1] Gaius, i. 80.

[2] Ulp. i. 12: 'Eadem lege (*sc.* Aelia Sentia) cautum est ut minor triginta annorum servus vindicta manumissus civis Romanus non fiat, nisi apud consilium causa probata fuerit. Proinde sine consilio manumissum †Caesaris† servum manere putat; testamento vero manumissum perinde haberi iubet, atque si domini voluntate in libertate esset, ideoque Latinus fit.' *Caesaris* is obviously corrupt; *eius aetatis*, *Cassius*, *Lex Aelia Sentia* are suggested in its place. According to the opinion of the subject of *putat*, the *manumissus vindicta* under 30 is legally a slave (but probably is under praetorian protection like the *manumissus inter amicos*) while the *manumissus testamento* under 30 definitely has the same status as the informally freed, with the advantage that his master is dead. *Ideoque Latinus fit* describes what takes place in Ulpian's own day and is not necessarily what the *Lex Aelia Sentia* directed.

The other passage is Ulp. iii. 3: 'Libertus ius Quiritium consequitur Latinus qui minor triginta annorum manumissionis tempore fuit: nam lege Iunia cautum est, ut si . . . uxorem duxerit . . . postea filio filiave nato natave et anniculo facto possit . . . causam probare et fieri civis Romanus.'

[3] Gaius, i. 29, 31, 66; Ulp. vii. 4.

then he has confused two laws, one belonging to the reign of Augustus and the other to that of Tiberius; surely it is more likely that Ulpian confused two laws both belonging to the same reign. Thirdly, the provision in question fits in with the content of the *Lex Aelia Sentia* more naturally than with that of the *Lex Iunia*; the former was mainly concerned with *dediticii*, owners under twenty, and slaves freed before the age of thirty; the latter's scope was confined to *manumissio minus iusta*; consequently a clause giving citizenship for *anniculi probatio* to persons freed under thirty years of age is *a priori* more likely to belong to the *Lex Aelia Sentia*. Ulpian therefore is almost certainly wrong when he ascribes the regulation regarding *anniculi probatio* to the *Lex Iunia*.

Now the texts in Gaius[1] which destroy the argument from Ulpian i 12 and iii 3 constitute in themselves a strong reason for the priority of the *Lex Iunia*. According to Gaius the *Lex Aelia Sentia* gave citizenship in some circumstances to certain freedmen with Latin rights; the *Lex Iunia* created the status of Latinity for freedmen;[2] thus the *Lex Aelia Sentia* presupposes the *Lex Iunia*. It may be objected that *et Latini facti* refers to a time later than the *Lex Aelia Sentia* and that that law knew these persons only as slaves *in libertate domini voluntate* or as *peregrini*. But this is not the natural interpretation of the passage, and it is unlikely that access to citizenship by such a simple process as *anniculi probatio* was ever granted to any but Latins, especially since some Latins were until 75 denied the privilege.

Further evidence comes from Ulpian's account of *dediticii*. He says that slaves of proved desperate character become *dediticii* after manumission, *quoquo modo manumissi sunt*; this he adds was enacted by the *Lex Aelia Sentia*. The words quoted must refer to formal and informal manumission. Now, if the *Lex Iunia* were still a law of the future, a person freed *inter amicos* would be a slave if honest, but a free *dediticius* if criminal.

Juristic authority may thus be said to argue the priority of the Junian to the Aelian-Sentian law. *A priori* considerations lend support. Augustus, the restorer of order and regulator of freedmen's status,

[1] i. 29: 'Ex lege Aelia Sentia cautum est ut minores triginta annorum manumissi et Latini facti . . .'; i. 31: 'Hoc tamen ius adipiscendae civitatis Romanae etiamsi soli minores triginta annorum manumissi et Latini facti ex lege Aelia Sentia habuerunt . . .'

[2] *Frag. Dos.* 12: 'Lex Iunia quae Latinorum genus introduxit.' The name *Latinus Iunianus* is additional proof.

[3] Ulp. i. 11.

was not likely in his long reign to leave untouched a state of things whereby *manumissio minus iusta* was continually filling society with persons who were *de iure* bond and *de facto* free; his attack on imprudent emancipation has much more force if it is preceded by the *Lex Iunia*; for in that attack he could not have touched informal manumission unless he had first legalized it and brought it under the cognizance of the law.

The *Lex Iunia* therefore falls between 31 B.C. and 4 A.D. Two years stand out as more likely than others, 25 and 17 B.C. Both saw consuls of the name of Iunius. 19 A.D. being out of the question, the name *Norbana* is slightly in favour of 25, in view of the collocation of consuls in 25 and 24; but the opinion of a sixth-century jurist, who has already made a mistake in calling the law *Norbana*, does not carry much weight. On the whole 17 B.C. is the more probable. It brings the *Lex Iunia* nearer to the rest of the freedman legislation of Augustus. It was a year of comparative quiet. Augustus was in Rome and able to give his attention to legislative measures. In 25, on the other hand, he was absent in Spain, and the subjugation of Galicia was occupying most of his thoughts.

APPENDIX II

THE *IUS ANULI AUREI*

IT has been assumed in the text that throughout the imperial age the *ius anuli aurei* carried with it no more than a fictitious *ingenuitas*. Further discussion is necessary here.

The most recent account of the *ius anuli aurei* is that of Prof. Arthur Stein (*Der Römische Ritterstand*, Munich, 1927). While he quotes or alludes to practically all the available evidence, he nevertheless leaves unsolved some difficulties raised by that evidence.

(1) The first problem is the inconsistency between the *Senatusconsultum* of 23 A.D. (Plin. *N. H.* xxxiii. 32) and the *Lex Visellia* of the very next year (*Cod. Iust.* ix. 21). The former forbids the grant of the *ius anuli aurei* to freedmen; the latter implies that numbers of freedmen did obtain the grant in order to proceed to offices reserved for the free-born.

(2) The persons recorded to have obtained the gold ring by grant and the persons who assumed it illegally were always freedmen. If the *ius anuli aurei* meant the *equus publicus* (as is the general view), then we should have expected to find it granted to and assumed by *ingenui* also.

(3) It is generally agreed that from the time of Hadrian the *ius anuli aurei* only conferred *ingenuitas*. This has never been reconciled with the evidence of Herodian (iii. 8) to the effect that it was only in 197 that legionaries were granted permission to wear the gold ring.

The following account claims to solve these difficulties.

The *anulus aureus* started as a privilege confined to a portion of the Senate (Plin. *N. H.* xxxiii. 11, 18, 21). In the later Republic and under Julius Caesar senators and knights wore it (Dio, xlviii. 45, § 8) and there was no idea of using it as a mark of fictitious *ingenuitas*. (This is evident from Cic. *Ad Fam.* X. xxxii. 2; Suet. *Iul.* 39; Macrob. *Saturn.* II. iii. 10; where free-born persons receive the ring.) On the other hand, from Hadrian onward the *ius anuli aurei* is recognized as merely granting to freedmen the right of being deemed free-born. (*Dig.* XL. x. 6; a rescript of Hadrian treats the *ius anuli aurei* as a mark of fictitious *ingenuitas*. Cf. *I. L. S.* 1899, where a mere *apparitor magistratuum* obtains the ring from Commodus; it is inconceivable that such a nonentity should by special dispensation become a knight; a fictitious ingenuity is therefore all that is implied. Cf. also Dio, xlviii. 45, § 9; speaking apparently of his own time he says of freedmen who received the gold ring: *ὥς καὶ βελτίοσιν ἢ κατ᾽ ἀπελευθερίαν ἱππεύειν τε δυναμένοις*—i.e. the bar of servile origin is swept away and they are eligible to become knights by a separate grant. *N.B.* He does not say *ἱππεῦσι* but *ἱππεύειν δυναμένοις*.)

The question now is: In the period from Augustus to Hadrian did the ring signify anything more than *ingenuitas*?

Until the time of Martial it seems to have betokened the equestrian census; no grant was made to persons of a capital less than 400,000 sesterces; and when a man's fortune fell below that sum he forfeited the right to wear the gold ring (Hor. *Sat.* II. vii. 53, *anulus equester*; Mart. viii. 5; xiv. 122). This meaning was subsequently lost, probably quite soon. Certainly by the end of the second century, when the whole army received the gold ring, the property qualification had completely disappeared.

Now Mommsen (*St. R.* iii. 517–9) and subsequent scholars and most recently Prof. Stein (*op. cit.* 30–47 and 54–7) have held that the *ius anuli aurei* between Augustus and Hadrian carried with it the *equus publicus*, i.e. full equestrian status. The arguments in favour of this view are as follows:

(1) In most instances where the *ius anuli aurei* is granted in the

first century, equestrian status seems to be granted also, e.g. Menas in 38 B.C. (Dio, xlviii. 45, § 7); Icelus (Suet. *Galba*, 14; Tac. *Hist.* i. 13); Asiaticus (Suet. *Vit.* 12; Tac. *Hist.* ii. 57); the father of Claudius Etruscus (Stat. *Silvae*, III. iii. 143–5); and a passage in Pliny (*N. H.* xxxiii. 33), 'Passimque ad ornamenta ea etiam servitute liberati transiliant . . . ita dum separatur ordo ab ingenuis, communicatus est cum servitiis', i.e. ex-slaves have entered the *ordo equester* by possession of the *ius anuli aurei*.

Of these the strongest are the passages from Pliny and from Suetonius, *Vitellius*. The rest are quite inconclusive. They show, it is true, the *ius anuli aurei* to be an indispensable preliminary to equestrian rank, but they do not show that a separate grant was not required to elevate the possessor of the gold ring to the position of *eques equo publico*.

The passage in Pliny must be taken in connexion with the rest of his excursus on the gold ring. In xxxiii. 29–30 he says '. . . Quod antea militares equi nomen dederant, hoc nunc pecuniae indices tribuunt. Nec pridem id factum. Divo Augusto decurias ordinante maior pars iudicum in ferreo anulo fuit, iique non equites sed iudices vocabantur. Equitum nomen subsistebat in turmis equorum publicorum.' Despite the prevailing view that all *equites* were *equites equo publico*, these words must mean that while in Augustus' time the *ordo equester* only comprised the *equites equo publico*, in Pliny's day it included all *ingenui* of equestrian census. Accordingly, when Pliny wrote, all free-born possessors of 400,000 sesterces must have called themselves knights, although the only *equites* who obtained posts in the equestrian civil service were the *equites equo publico*. Now Pliny's remarks in xxxiii. 33 obviously refer to the *ordo equester* in the wide sense. His words prove therefore not that freedmen on obtaining the gold ring obtained *ex facto* the *equus publicus* also, but that they merely called themselves *equites*, like any other owners of the equestrian census.

It is probable that the passage in Suet. *Vitellius* is to be explained in the same way. The words are 'Primo imperii die aureis donavit anulis super cenam, cum mane rogantibus pro eo cunctis detestatus esset severissime talem equestris ordinis maculam'. All that this sentence necessarily proves is that Asiaticus on receiving the gold ring became entitled to consider himself an ingenuous owner of the equestrian census, an *eques* though not an *eques equo publico*.

(2) First-century evidence of the *anulus aureus* generally shows imperial freedmen of high rank obtaining the honour; while the

second-century evidence (*I. L. S.* 1899, 5631) shows quite ordinary freedmen gaining it.

But the evidence is not so one-sided. *Cod. Iust.* ix. 21 (*Lex Visellia* 24 A.D.) and Pliny *N. H.* xxxiii. 32–33 imply that quite insignificant freedmen obtained the gold ring in the first century. The absence of pre-Commodan inscriptions showing freedmen in possession of the *anulus aureus* may easily be explained. To mention an imperial grant of the gold ring was to imply one's servile origin. Persons possessed of a fictitious *ingenuitas* were not anxious to parade the fact that it was fictitious.

(3) A *senatusconsultum* was passed in 23 A.D. knowing nothing of a legal grant of *ingenuitas* through the gold ring. The measure is recorded in Pliny *N. H.* xxxiii. 32: 'Constitutum ne cui ius id esset nisi qui ingenuus ipse ingenuo patre avo paterno HS. CCCC. census fuisset et lege Iulia theatrali in quattuordecim ordinibus sedisset.' According to Pliny, then, the *senatusconsultum* of 23 A.D. confined the gold ring to senators and knights who could show the *ingenuitas* of their forbears for two generations back. While the decree was in force the *ius anuli aurei* cannot have been used as a means of conferring fictitious *ingenuitas*.

Now the *senatusconsultum* was a dead letter almost as soon as it was passed. Pliny actually dates the vulgarization of the gold ring from shortly after this measure which was supposed to prevent such a vulgarization; and the *Lex Visellia* of the year immediately after its passing implies that the *ius anuli aurei* was the recognized means for freedmen to pass out of their libertine status.

The evidence for the view of Mommsen and Stein is therefore inconclusive. On the other hand there are at least four indications that the *ius anuli aurei* conferred only *ingenuitas* and not the *equus publicus*.

(1) The fiction of the *restitutio natalium* was not legally established as a means of making a *libertinus* into an *ingenuus* till the time of M. Aurelius. In the absence of that fiction it would be strange if the early emperors had not established some method of conferring *ingenuitas* without at the same time conferring the *equus publicus*. This suggests that the gold ring may have been used for this purpose.

(2) It is recorded in Pliny (*N. H.* xxxiii. 33) that during Claudius' censorship 400 freedmen were prosecuted for illicit assumption of the gold ring. What was the object of such an assumption? If the gold ring was the sign of the *equus publicus*, they would gain

nothing by the illicit assumption thereof; for the advantages of possessing the *equus publicus* (posts in the equestrian civil service) were only to be got by imperial grant, and mere assumption of the gold ring would not deceive the Emperor. If, on the other hand, the *ius anuli aurei* meant *ingenuitas*, a much better reason is forthcoming. Municipal magistracies and priesthoods were the prizes, and the persons or bodies of persons who bestowed them could be much more easily deceived than the Emperor.

Yet Suetonius' account of this affair during Claudius' censorship is 'Libertinos qui se pro equitibus Romanis agerent publicavit' (Suet. *Claud.* 25). *Equites Romani* is here used in the wide sense of all ingenuous citizens possessed of the equestrian census. Otherwise it is difficult to see why only freedmen and not *ingenui* also assumed falsely the equestrian status.

(3) Except in the army (for which see *infra*) there is no instance throughout the imperial period of the gold ring being granted to *ingenui*. This suggests that in civil life the grant was only made to freedmen. Indeed Dio (liii. 30: *καὶ τὸ χρυσοῖς δακτυλίοις—ἀπελεύθερος γὰρ ἦν—χρῆσθαι . . . ἔλαβεν*) explains a grant of the gold ring by saying that the recipient was a freedman. If the *ius* gave the *equus publicus*, why was it never bestowed on *ingenui*? If it merely gave *ingenuitas*, its confinement to freedmen is perfectly logical.

(4) *Cod. Iust.* ix. 21 says of the *Lex Visellia* of 24 A.D.: 'Lex Visellia libertinae condicionis homines persequitur, si ea quae ingenuorum sunt circa honores et dignitates ausi fuerint attemptare vel decurionatum adripere, nisi iure aureorum anulorum impetrato a principe sustentantur.' The honours reserved for *ingenui* (not those reserved for knights) are what the *Lex Visellia* thought were thrown open by the *ius anuli aurei*.

The *ius anuli aurei* did not, then, in itself give the *equus publicus*. It merely took away the social disqualifications remaining from servitude. Freedmen possessed of the gold ring had not the full privileges of knighthood, unless they obtained the *equus publicus* by a further imperial grant.

In one sphere, however, the *anulus aureus* retained for a long time its old significance of knighthood. In the army a strict division was marked between officers on the one hand and centurions and men on the other, and the gold ring could be worn by the former but not by the latter.

Three pieces of evidence concern the gold ring in the army. The earliest is a Gallic inscription of the reign of Augustus (*I.L.S.* 2531):

'C. Iulio Agedil[li f. Fabi]a Macro Sant(oni) duplicario alae Atectorigiana(e) stipendis emeritis xxxii aere incisso . . . clup(eo) coronis aenulis aureis donato a commilitonib(us).' Ramsay (*J. R. S.* xvi. 1926, p. 208) attempts to translate *aenulis aureis* 'brass pots gilded'; but *auratis*, not *aureis*, would in that case be expected. It seems more likely that *aenulis* is an error for *anulis*. Now the gift is recorded as coming from the veteran's fellow-soldiers; it is highly improbable that a portion of the army could bestow the *ius anuli aurei*. The truth must be not that the right of wearing the ring was conferred, but that a material present of rings was given. Possibly in addition the soldiers subscribed a sum which raised the retiring warrior's fortune to 400,000 sesterces. Be that as it may, the veteran on his discharge was free from any military law forbidding him to wear the ring; and, if he possessed the requisite census, he could assume it without any application for permission.

The other two items of evidence prove more conclusively that the gold ring continued to distinguish officers from men until 197 A.D. Suetonius (*Galba* 10) says 'Delegit et equestris ordinis iuvenes, qui manente anulorum aureorum usu evocati appellarentur excubiasque circa cubiculum suum vice militum agerent.' By undertaking duties which usually fell to private soldiers (cf. *vice militum*) these knights were in danger of having to forfeit the gold ring. It was only Galba's express mention of *manente anulorum aureorum usu* that reassured them. We may therefore infer that according to time-honoured practice private soldiers were not allowed to wear the gold ring.

In 197 A.D. a change was made. The evidence is Herodian, iii. 8: *ἄλλα τε πολλὰ συνεχώρησεν ἃ μὴ πρότερον εἶχον· καὶ γὰρ τὸ σιτηρέσιον πρῶτος ηὔξησεν αὐτοῖς καὶ δακτυλίοις χρυσοῖς χρήσασθαι ἐπέτρεψε*..., i.e. Septimius Severus abolished the old rule that ordinary soldiers might not wear the gold ring. It was at last felt that the *anulus aureus* could no longer do the double duty of marking both a civil and a military distinction. The legionary could no longer be excluded from a privilege which in civil life meant no more than free birth. Until Severus' reign the anomaly had not been obvious. It was not till the second century that the lapse of the property qualification vulgarized the right completely. Moreover, armies had usually been near the frontiers; freedmen who obtained the gold ring for the most part resided in Italy and the more peaceable provinces like Narbonensis, Baetica, and Africa. The excluded soldier and the fortunate ex-slave had not had the opportunity of comparing their positions. The years 193–7, however, witnessed a struggle for the throne. Armies traversed populous regions of Italy and Gaul. Legionaries beheld freedmen vaunting the ring of gold which they themselves were forbidden to wear. Accordingly a demand was made that the ring should no longer be the mark of distinction between officers and men, and Septimius Severus, anxious to conciliate the soldiery, granted the demand.

For the sake of lucidity our conclusions may be summarized. While preserving the gold ring as a distinguishing mark in the army between officers and men, Augustus found in the *ius anuli aurei* a convenient fiction for making rich freedmen ingenuous and letting them play a more prominent part in the municipal life. In 23 A.D. a reactionary measure attempted to end such fiction; in 24 A.D. it was realized that the act of 23 A.D. was not practicable, and freedmen were again permitted to win the *ius anuli aurei* from the *Princeps* and so proceed to the honours of the free-born. Throughout the first century the gold ring probably was confined to men of equestrian census, though later (certainly before 197 A.D.) a departure was made from this practice. In 197 the distinction between a military and a civil usage was abolished; and the whole army, men as well as officers, were permitted by Septimius Severus to wear the gold ring.

APPENDIX III

THE IMPERIAL CIVIL SERVICE

BELOW is given a rough view of the imperial civil service, especially those parts of it where freedmen and knights competed with each other. I treat the various offices in a somewhat different order from that which I have followed in the text, because it was necessary there to discuss the three great secretariates together, whereas here it is more convenient to divide the civil service into two main departments, Revenue and Administration. The dates given are inevitably only approximate. In the freedmen's columns they err, if at all, on the early side. For instance, M. Ulpius Cadmus is referred to the reign of Trajan. Doubtless he was freed by Trajan, but he may have held some office long after the death of that emperor. Lastly, it must not be presumed that the table given below is exhaustive or even nearly so. It merely gives examples to support some of the statements in the text.

LIST OF ABBREVIATIONS USED

Afr.	Africae.	l. or lib.	libertus.
Aug.	Augusti.	p.	publicorum.
Aurel.	Marcus Aurelius.	Pann.	Pannoniorum.
Calig.	Caligula.	praef.	praefectus.
citer.	citeriorem.	proc.	procurator.
Claud.	Claudius.	prov.	provinciae.
Comm.	Commodus.	prox.	proximus.
Delmat.	Delmatiorum.	rat.	rationis.
d. n.	domini nostri.	reg.	regionis.
Dom. or Domit.	Domitian.	Sept. Sev.	Septimius Severus.
epist.	epistulis.	Sev. Alex.	Severus Alexander.
fam.	familias.	super.	superioris.
Flav.	Flavian age (69–96).	Traj.	Trajan.
Gall.	Galliarum.	Vitell.	Vitellius.
glad.	gladiatorias.		
Hadr.	Hadrian.	iiii p.	quattuor publicorum.
hered.	hereditatum.		
Hisp.	Hispaniam.	xx.	vicesimae.
imp.	imperatoris.	xxxx.	quadragesimae.

PART I.

I. The senatorial treasury was the *aerarium Saturni*, with which neither freedmen nor knights had any concern.

II. The treasury for pensions for discharged soldiers was the *aerarium militare*, with which neither freedmen nor knights had any concern.

FREEDMEN.

	C.I.L.	I.L.S.	Date.	Title.
III. *Procuratores patrimoni.*	VI. 8501	1487	Claud.	proc. Aug. a patrimonio.
	VI. 8499	1489	Nero	proc. patrimoni et hered.
IV. *a rationibus.*	VI. 8411	1473	Claud.	Aug. l. a rationibus.
	XIV. 2104	1475	Pius	proc. Aug. a rationibus.
	III. 348	1477	Aurel.	proximus rationum.

The Revenues of the Empire were as follows:

A. *Direct taxes* (viz: *tributum capitis* and *tributum soli*). In imperial provinces the *procuratores provinciarum* were responsible; in senatorial provinces at first the quaestors and later the *procuratores provinciarum*. The direct taxes of imperial provinces went to the *fiscus*, those of senatorial at first to the *aerarium Saturni* and later to the *fiscus*.

B. *Indirect Taxes.*

i. *Centesima rerum venalium.* Duty on auction sales. Went to the *aerarium militare*. Abolished by Caligula in Italy.

ii. *Vicesima quinta venalium mancipiorum.* Duty on sale of slaves. Went, certainly at first, to the *aerarium Saturni*.

iii. *Vicesima hereditatum.* Duty on legacies. Went to the *aerarium militare.*

iv. *Vicesima libertatis.* Duty on manumissions. Went to the *fiscus*.

v. *Portoria* or *Vectigalia.* Customs duty varying according to the district. Went

FREEDMEN.

		C.I.L.	I.L.S.	Date.	Title.
A. Procuratores provinciarum.		XIV. 176	1484	Hadr.	proc. prov. Pannoniae super.
		VI. 8450	1521	Pius	proc. prov. Belgicae.
		III. 348	1477	Aurel.	proc. prov. Britanniae.
B. Indirect taxes.	iii.	VI. 8443	1546	Claud.	proc. xx hered. prov. Achaiae.
		VI. 5554	1547	Pius	proc. xx hered.
	iv.	III. 249	1396	After Traj.	praepositus xx libertatis Bithyniae Ponti Paphlagoniae.
	v.	X. 6668	1549	?	proc. iiii p. Afr. et xxxx Gall.

REVENUE

III. Caesar's private property was called the *patrimonium*, administered by a *procurator patrimoni*.

IV. State moneys entrusted to Caesar formed the *fiscus*, controlled by the official *a rationibus*.

KNIGHTS.

C.I.L.	*I.L.S.*	*Date.*	*Title.*
XI. 5028	1447	Vitell.	proc. imp. a patrimonio et hered.
VI. 798	1448	Domit.	proc. a patrimonio.
XIV. 2922	1420	c. 180	proc. patrimoni.
VI. 1625	1340	Traj. or after	proc. a rationibus Aug.
V. 867	1339	Pius	proc. a rationibus Aug.

to the *fiscus*.

Possibly at first the *aerarium Saturni* took iv and v in senatorial provinces.

In connexion with at least the last three of these taxes there were general bureaux in addition to departmental offices for particular districts.

C. *Profits from imperial domains*. The greater part belonged to the *fiscus*, though the *patrimonium* claimed some. Caesarian officers (under the *procuratores provinciarum*) were: either (i) in charge of estates or groups of estates; (ii) in charge of revenue from estates of a particular character, e.g. mines.

D. *Miscellaneous*.

i. *Bona caduca*. Property to which there was no legally qualified heir. Belonged to the *fiscus*.
ii. *Bona damnatorum*. Property of those who were condemned on a capital charge. Destination varied.
iii. *Hereditates*. Estates left to the Emperor. Belonged to the *patrimonium*.

KNIGHTS.

C.I.L.	*I.L.S.*	*Date.*	*Title.*
V. 875	1374	Domit.	proc. prov. Asiae.
IX. 4753	1350	Traj.	proc. prov. Lusitaniae.
V. 867	1339	Pius	proc. prov. Lugdunensis et Aquitanicae.
VI. 3720	1418	Traj.	proc. Aug. xx hered.
XIII. 1808	1454	Pius	proc. xx hered. Romae.
V. 8659	1412	Aurel.	proc. Aug. xx hered. per Hisp. citer.
VIII. 10500	1409	?	proc. Aug. xxxx Galliarum.
III. 249	1396	After Traj.	proc. vectigaliorum quae sunt intra Padum.

FREEDMEN (*contd.*)

		C.I.L.	*I.L.S.*	*Date.*	*Title.*
C. Domains.	i.	VI. 8608	1485	After Traj.	proc. tractus Carthaginiensis.
		XIV. 176	1484	Hadr.	proc. Africae reg. Thevestinae.
		III. 536	1575	Sev. Alex.	proc. ad praedia Galliana.
					proc. saltus Domitiani.
	ii.	III. 1312	1593	Traj.	proc. aurariarum.
		III. 348	1477	Aurel.	proc. marmorum.
		III. 536	1575	Sev. Alex.	proc. rationis purpurarum prov. Achaiae et Epiri et Thessaliae.
D. Miscellaneous.	i.	III. 1622	1532	Aurel.	proc. a caducis.
	ii.				
	iii.	VI. 8439	1527	Flav.	ab auctoritate rat. hered.
		VI. 8433	1520	Flav.	proc. hered.
		Eph. Epig. VII. 1263	1518	Traj.	proc. hered.

PART II.

I. All *military* commands were denied to freedmen. Legions were led by senators or, exceptionally, knights; young men of senatorial or equestrian birth became *praefecti alarum*, *praefecti cohortium* and *tribuni militum*. The *praefectus vigilum* was always a knight, and the *praefectus praetorio* on occasions a senator but usually a knight.

II. *Provinces*. A. *Senatorial*. The proconsul and his attendant quaestor were always senators.

B. *Imperial*. The governor (*legatus Augusti pro praetore*) was always a senator. His subordinate procurator was generally a knight, sometimes a freedman. See above (Revenue A).

COURT OFFICERS—FREEDMEN.

	C.I.L.	*I.L.S.*	*Date.*	*Title.*
A.	VI. 8614	–	Flav.	Aug. lib. a libellis.
	VI. 8615	–	Aurel.	a libellis adiutor.
B.	VI. 8603	1670	Claud.	ab epistulis.
	VI. 8604	1519	Flav.	ab epistulis.
	VI. 8606	1668	Aurel.	ab epistulis Graecis.
	XIV. 2815	1669	Aurel.	prox. ab epist. Latinis.

KNIGHTS (*contd.*)

C.I.L.	*I.L.S.*	*Date.*	*Title.*
III. 726	1419	Traj.	proc. Aug. regionis Chersonesiacae.
VIII. 5351	1435	Hadr.	proc. Aug. praediorum saltum Hipponiensis et Thevestini.
Eph. Epig. v. 699.	1436	Aurel.	proc. tractus Karthaginiensis.
III. 7127	1421	After Traj.	proc. argentariarum Pannoniarum et Dalmatiarum.
III. 8361	1443	?	proc. metallorum Pann. et Delmat.
VI. 1634	1423	After 136.	proc. ad bona damnatorum.
XI. 5028	1447	Vitell.	proc. imp. ab hereditatibus.
III. 431	1449	Hadr.	proc. hereditatum.

ADMINISTRATION

II. *Provinces.* C. *Third Class.* Here the governor was called *praeses*, *praefectus* or *procurator*. Posts of this sort were held by knights.

D. *Egypt.* Here the governor was a *praefectus*. This post was reserved for knights.

III. *Court Offices.* A. *a libellis.*

B. *ab epistulis.*

C. *a studiis.*

D. *a cognitionibus.*

COURT OFFICERS—KNIGHTS.

C.I.L.	*I.L.S.*	*Date.*	*Title.*
XI. 5028	1447	Vitell.	proc. imp. a libellis.
XI. 5213	1338	Hadr.	a libellis Aug.
XIII. 1808	1454	Pius	a libellis.
VI. 798	1448	Domit.	proc. ab epistulis.
VIII. 1174	1451	Pius	ab epist. divi Antonini.
III. 431	1449	Hadr.	ab epistulis Graecis.
VI. 1564	1452	Pius	ab epistulis Latinis adiutor.

FREEDMEN (*contd.*)

	C.I.L.	*I.L.S.*	*Date.*	*Title.*
C.	vi. 8636	1682	Claud.	a studiis.
.	vi. 8637	1683	?	prox. a studiis.
D.	vi 8628	1679	Flav.	a cognitionibus.
	vi. 8635	1681	Aurel.	adiutor a cognitionibus.

IV. *Departments of General Utility.*

A. Senatorial Departments.—The *praefectus urbis*, *curator aquarum*, *curator operum publicorum*, and the *curatores ripae et alvei Tiberis* were always senators. The *curator viarum* also was a

FREEDMEN.

	C.I.L.	*I.L.S.*	*Date*	*Title.*
B (i) Subordinate officers in central bureau.	vi. 8470	1535	Claud.	adiutor praefecti annonae.
Departmental Officers.	xiv. 163	1533	Claud.	proc. portus Ostiensis.
	xiv. 2045	1534	Hadr.	proc. annonae Ostiensis.
B (ii) (cf. chap. viii. pp. 168–170.)	xi. 3612	1567	Domit.	proc. aquarum.
B (iii).	vi. 8461	1637	Aug. or Calig.	superpositus auri monetae nummulariorum.
	vi. 8464	1638	Hadr.	adiutor praepositi scalptorum sacrae monetae.
B (iv).	vi. 8542	–	Traj.	ab vehiculis.
B (v).	x. 1739	1587	Claud.	proc. bybliothecarum.
B (vi).	xiv. 2045	1534	Hadr.	proc. pugillationis et ad naves vagas.
	iii. 348	1477	Aurel.	proc. summi choragi.
B (vii).	vi. 8694	1687	?	ab actis.
	iii. 536	1575	Sev. Alex.	proc. ab ephemeride.
	vi. 8695	1688	Flav.	adiutor ab actis.

These various departments were well staffed with clerks and accountants, who

KNIGHTS (*contd.*)

C.I.L.	*I.L.S.*	*Date.*	*Title.*
v. 8972	1459	late second century.	a studiis et a consiliis Augustorum.
II. 1085	1406	Sept. Sev.	a cognitionibus d.n. imp. L.Septimi Severi Pertinacis Aug.

senator, though knights might become *curatores* or *subcuratores* of some particular road.

B. Non-Senatorial Departments.—(i) Corn; (ii) Palace water-supply; (iii) Mint; (iv) Post; (v) Libraries; (vi) Shows; (vii) Journal.

KNIGHTS.

C.I.L.	*I.L.S.*	*Date.*	*Title.*
x. 7584	1359	Aurel.	subpraefectus annonae.
VI. 1633	1426	After Traj.	proc. ad annonam Ostiae.
x. 6569	–	third cent.	proc. aquarum.
VI. 1607	1450	c. 138.	proc. monetae Augusti.
VIII. 822	1347	Hadr. or after	proc. sacrae monetae.
x. 6976	1434	bef. 162	praef. vehiculorum.
x. 6662	1455	Comm.	praef. vehiculorum.
x. 7580	1358	?	proc. bybliothecarum Laurentium Lavinatium.
XIV. 2922	1420	Aurel.	proc. ludi magni.
v. 8659	1412	Aurel.	proc. ad fam. glad. Transpadanas.
VIII. 7039	1437	?	proc. Aug. ludi matutini.
II. 1085	1406	Sept. Sev.	subproc. ludi magni.
VIII. 11813	1410	c. 180	proc. Aug. ab actis urbis.

were always slaves or freedmen of Caesar. The following are examples of freedmen in such positions (see next page).

Part I. REVENUE

Reference to Department.	*C.I.L.*	*I.L.S.*	*Date.*	*Title.*
III	XI. 3885	1643	Claud.	tabularius rationis patrimoni.
IV.	VI. 8450	1521	Pius	tabularius a rationibus.
A.	II. 485	1493	Hadr.	tabularius prov. Lusitaniae.
	II. 6085	1560	Aurel.	a commentariis prov. Baeticae.
B iii.	VI. 8449	1552	Flav.	adiutor tabulariorum xx hered.
	VI. 8446	1551	Traj.	princeps tabularius in statione xx hered.
	VI. 4184	1556	?	a commentariis xx hered. Hispaniae citerioris.
iv.	VI. 8451	–	?	tabularius Caesaris xx libertatis.
v.	II. 6085	1560	Aurel.	commentariensis xxxx Galliarum.
	III. 4063	–	?	ex tabulario vectigalis Illyrici.
C. i.	VI. 8580	–	Flav.	tabularius reg. Picenensis.
ii.	VI. 8184	1599	Flav.	tabularius marmorum Lunensium.
	III. 1297	1594	after Traj.	tabularius aurariarum Dacicarum.
D. iii.	VI. 8933	1689	Claud.	a commentariis rationis hereditatum.

Part II. ADMINISTRATION

Reference to Department.	*C.I.L.*	*I.L.S.*	*Date.*	*Title.*
III. A.	VI. 8617	1675	Claud.	scriniarius a libellis.
III. B.	X. 527	1671	Claud.	scriniarius ab epistulis.
IV. A.	II. 6085	1560	Aurel.	a commentariis alvei Tiberis.
	XI. 3860	1603	Traj.	a commentariis operum publicorum.
	VI. 8466	1606	Traj.	tabularius viae Appiae.
IV. B. i.	VI. 8474	1541	Flav.	a libellis fisci frumentari.
	VI. 8477	1543	?	tabularius fisci frumentari.
IV. B. iii.	VI. 8463	–	Traj.	nummularius officii monetae.
IV. B. iv.	VI. 8543	–	Flav.	tabularius a vehiculis.
IV. B. vi.	VI. 10086	1769	Traj.	tabularius summi choragi.

APPENDIX IV

BIBLIOGRAPHY OF ANCIENT SOURCES AND MODERN AUTHORITIES.

A. ANCIENT SOURCES

I. Historians.

Author.	*Date.*	*Title of Work.*	*Remarks.*
Dionysius Halicarnassensis	ob. 7 B.C.	Ῥωμαϊκὴ Ἀρχαιολογία	History of Rome in 22 books. First 9 complete, x and xi almost so. The rest fragmentary. One important chapter on manumission—iv. 24.
C. Velleius Paterculus	19 B.C.–31 A.D.	*Historiae Romanae*	Universal and especially Roman history to 30 A.D.
Flavius Iosephus	37–100	Ἰουδαϊκὴ Ἀρχαιολογία	In 20 books. Contains a few notes on imperial freedmen such as Callistus and Felix.
C. (?P.) Cornelius Tacitus	54–120	*Historiae* *Ab Excessu Divi Augusti Annalium Libri*	The extant books of the Histories (i–iv) deal with the years 68–69. The surviving portions of the Annals (i–iv, vi, xii–xv, parts of v, xi, xvi) cover most of the reign of Tiberius (14–37) and the whole of the period 48–66. Tacitus has strong republican sympathies, and is prejudiced against imperial freedmen.
C. Suetonius Tranquillus	75–160	*De Vita Caesarum*	Lives of Julius Caesar and the Emperors to Domitian. Biased against imperial freedmen.
		De Grammaticis Illustribus	Lives of famous grammarians (ranging from *cir.* 120 B.C. to the reign of Nero) many of whom were freedmen.
Cassius Dio	155–230	Ῥωμαϊκὴ Ἱστορία	History of Rome in 80 books to 229. Fragmentary to xxxv. Mainly complete xxxvi–lx (68 B.C. to 54 A.D.). Except for some fragments, the last twenty books only survive in an epitome.
'Aelius Spartianus'	fl. 300 (?)	*Vita Hadriani*	Part of the *Historia Augusta*.
'Iulius Capitolinus'	fl. 300 (?)	*Vitae Antonini L. Veri, M. Aurelii*	Part of the *Historia Augusta*.

II. Other Prose Authors (including Menippean Satire).

Author.	*Date.*	*Title of Work.*	*Remarks.*
C. Petronius	ob. A.D. 66	*Satyricon*	Contains the *Cena Trimalchionis*, an exquisite picture of the freedman *nouveau riche*.
L. Annaeus Seneca	5 B.C.– 65 A.D.	*Consolatio ad Polybium*	Letter to a *libertus a libellis*, showing incidentally the duties of this official.
		De Beneficiis *De Vita Beata* *De Clementia* *Epistulae Morales*	Contain comments on contemporary manners and applications of Stoicism to slavery.
C. Plinius Secundus (the Elder)	23–79	*Historia Naturalis*	Encyclopaedic details of contemporary history; e.g. prices of slaves, the *anulus aureus*, freedmen's wealth and luxury, games given by freedmen, agricultural innovations made by freedmen.
C. Plinius Secundus (the Younger)	61–113	*Epistulae*	Reveal a Roman humanitarian, whose humanity is exemplified conspicuously in his relations with his slaves and freedmen.
		Panegyricus	Addressed to Trajan in 100 A.D. Relations of emperors with their freedmen are noticed.

III. Poets.

Author.	*Date.*	*Title of Work.*	*Remarks.*
P. Papinius Statius	40–96	*Silvae*	Two of the *Silvae* show in a poetical way the duties assigned to the freedmen *ab epistulis* and *a rationibus*.
A. Persius Flaccus	34–62	*Satyrae*	Vivid pictures of contemporary life. The Roman client system and the freedman upstart are two prominent features. Naturally this evidence is not impartial. In the main, only the black side of the picture is shown.
M. Valerius Martialis	40–104	*Epigrammata*	
D. Iunius Iuvenalis	60–130	*Satyrae*	

IV. Jurists.

Author.	*Date.*	*Title of Work.*	*Remarks.*
Gaius	fl. 160	*Institutiones*	
Iulius Paulus	fl. 210	*Sententiae*	
Domitius Ulpianus	fl. 215	*Regulae*	
(*Fragmentum Dositheanum*)	–	*Disputatio forensis maxime de manumissionibus*	Contained among the *Interpretamenta* of Pseudo-Dositheus. Belongs to second or third century. Gaius, Scaevola, Paul and Ulpian have each been suggested as the author.

IV. Jurists (*contd.*).

Author.	*Date.*	*Title of Work.*	*Remarks.*
	438	*Codex Theodosianus*	
	533.	*Digesta*	
	534.	*Codex Iustinianeus*	
	534.	*Institutiones Iustinianeae*	
	535–565.	*Novellae Constitutiones*	Supplementary *constitutiones* issued by Justinian after 535

V. Inscriptions.

Corpus Inscriptionum Latinarum (Berlin, 1863–).
Ephemeris Epigraphica (*Corporis Inscr. Lat. supplementum*) (Berlin, 1872–).
H. Dessau, *Inscriptiones Latinae Selectae* (Berlin, 1892–1916).

B. MODERN AUTHORITIES

W. W. Buckland, *The Roman Law of Slavery.* (Cambridge, 1908.)
R. Cagnat, *Étude historique sur les impôts indirects chez les Romains.* (Paris, 1882.)
Daremberg-Saglio, *Dictionnaire des antiquités grecques et romaines.* (Paris, 1887–1919.)
W. S. Davis, *The Influence of Wealth in Imperial Rome.* (New York, 1910.)
S. Dill, *Roman Society from Nero to Marcus Aurelius.* (London, 1905.)
J. Wight Duff, *A Literary History of Rome in the Silver Age.* (London, 1927.)
Tenney Frank, *Race Mixture in the Roman Empire.* (Article in the *American Historical Review*, 1916, p. 689 ff.).
—— *An Economic History of Rome.* (Second ed., London, 1927.)
L. Friedländer—G. Wissowa, *Darstellungen aus der Sittengeschichte Roms.* (Ninth-tenth ed., Leipzig, 1919–21.)
P. F. Girard, *Manuel élémentaire de droit romain.* (Paris, 1918.)
—— *Textes de droit romain.* (Paris, 1923.)
Mary L. Gordon, *The Nationality of Slaves under the Early Roman Empire.* (*J.R.S.* xiv—1924—pp. 38 ff.)
W. E. Heitland, *Agricola.* (Cambridge, 1921.)
O. Hirschfeld, *Die kaiserlichen Verwaltungsbeamten bis auf Diocletian.* (Berlin, 1905.)
G. Kühn, *De Opificum Romanorum Condicione Privata Quaestiones.* (Halle, 1910.)
R. H. Lacey, *The Equestrian Officials of Trajan and Hadrian: Their Careers, with some notes on Hadrian's Reforms.* (Princeton, 1917.)
R. Lanciani, *I comentarii di Frontino intorno le acque e gli acquedotti.* (*Atti dei Lincei, Ser. III, vol. iv*, 1879–1880.)
W. E. H. Lecky, *History of European Morals from Augustus to Charlemagne.* (London, 1882.)
H. Lemonnier, *Étude historique sur la condition privée des affranchis aux trois premiers siècles de l'empire romain.* (Paris, 1887.)
J. Marquardt, *Privatleben der Römer.* (Leipzig, 1886.)
C. Merivale, *History of the Romans under the Empire.* (London, 1890.)
T. Mommsen, *De Collegiis et Sodaliciis Romanorum.* (Kiel, 1843.)

T. Mommsen, *Das römische Staatsrecht.* (Leipzig, 1893.)

R. G. Nisbet, *The Festuca and Alapa of Manumission.* (*Journal of Roman Studies*, vol. viii, 1918.)

Pauly-Wissowa, *Real-Encyclopädie der classischen Altertumswissenschaft.* (Stuttgart, 1894– .)

H. F. Pelham, *The Domestic Policy of Augustus*; *The Imperial Domains and the Colonate*; *Pascua*; (contained in *Essays on Roman History.* Oxford, 1911).

Seymour de Ricci, *A Latin Deed of a Manumission of a Slave.* (*Proceedings of the Society of Biblical Archaeology*, vol. xxvi—1904—pp. 145–163.)

M. Rostovtzeff, *The Social and Economic History of the Roman Empire.* (Oxford, 1926.)

G. Salvioli, *Le capitalisme dans le monde antique.* (Paris, 1906.)

J. E. Sandys, *Companion to Latin Studies.* (Cambridge, 1921.)

R. Sohm, *Institutes of Roman Law.* (English translation by J. C. Ledlie, Oxford, 1901.)

A. Stein, *Der römische Ritterstand.* (Munich, 1927.)

L. R. Taylor, *The Augustales, Seviri Augustales and Seviri.* (*Trans. Amer. Philol. Assoc.* xlv—1914—pp. 231 ff.).

—— *Seviri Equitum Romanorum and the Municipal Seviri.* (*J. R. S.*, xiv—1924—pp. 158 ff.)

H. Wallon, *Histoire de l'esclavage dans l'antiquité.* (Paris, 1879.)

APPENDIX V

FREEDMEN IN THE GNOMON OF THE IDIOS LOGOS.[1]

IN the famous Berlin papyrus which contains an abridgement of the central sections of the *γνώμων τοῦ ἰδίου λόγου*—the set of regulations evolved out of arrangements due to Augustus, which guided the Treasurer of the Special Account in Egypt—a number of rulings throw light on the position of freedmen.

The Special Account seems to have received irregular revenue such as *bona vacantia* and *bona caduca*.[2] Its *γνώμων*, in the abridged and fragmentary form in which we have it, starts with rules of inheritance (§§ 1–36) and of personal status (§§ 37–57). A section follows on the registration of property (§§ 58–63) and the passport system (§§ 64–9). By the next paragraph officials were debarred from bidding for government property. Paragraphs 71–97 define in certain aspects the relations between the Roman government and the Egyptian church, while the remainder of the papyrus gives a number of miscellaneous regulations for whose contravention penalties (generally fines) are specified. The most prominent feature in the *γνώμων* is the rapacity of the *fiscus*. Again and again the rightful heirs to an estate are cheated for irrelevant reasons. The peculiar province of Egypt was treated by imperial authorities as a realm specially designed to supply the needs of the treasury.

The paragraphs relating to freedmen are conveniently classified under four heads: (*a*) freedmen's estates; (*b*) their competence to inherit; (*c*) intermarriage; (*d*) belated marriage and celibacy.

A. Freedmen's Estates.

The division of the Egyptian inhabitants into *τάξεις* or classes was in this sphere rigorously applied, in order to prevent for the sake of fiscal convenience the transference of property from class

[1] Cf. W. Schubart, *Berliner Griechische Urkunden*, v. 1 (text and German translation; juristic and historical commentaries by E. Seckel and W. Schubart respectively still to follow); Th. Reinach, *Nouvelle revue historique de droit français et étranger*, 1919 (text and French translation) and 1920 (commentary); H. Stuart Jones, *Fresh Light on Roman Bureaucracy*, Oxford, 1920; P. M. Meyer, *Juristische Papyri*, Berlin, 1920, no. 93 (text); O. Lenel and J. Partsch, *Sitzungsberichte der Heidelberger Akademie der Wissenschaften*, 1920, no. 1 (juristic discussion).

[2] Strabo, xvii. i. 12.

to class. The two highest classes were Romans and Alexandrians; then followed various Greek and Egyptian categories; one of these, *ἀστοί* or 'burghers,' is perhaps identical with the Alexandrian class. A freedman was prevented from leaving a legacy to any person outside his own *τάξις*, and any property bequeathed in contravention of this rule was confiscated.[1]

Paragraph 9 states that, when a 'burgher's' freedman died intestate and without descendants, his property went to his patron or the male descendants of his patron.[2] In default of these the *fiscus* took the estate, daughters and other relatives of the patron having no claim. Little information is given here, and some problems suggest themselves. The rules applying in classes other than that of *ἀστοί* are not mentioned; nor is there any hint of what was decided when the freedman did not die intestate; probably Roman law was followed here,[3] subject of course to the clause forbidding inter-class legacies. Moreover, nothing is said of the provision in Roman law by which the daughter of a patron was allowed to rank as a son if she had three children. In some other connexions the *γνώμων* takes account of the privileges for children, and it is difficult to believe they were not recognized here also.

Estates of *Latini Iuniani* went generally to the patron, as in Roman law;[4] still, an ingenious method of cheating the patron in certain cases was discovered by the fiscal officers in Egypt. If the Latin left no will, the property went to the patron or the patron's heirs; but, if a will was left, it was declared invalid and the property covered by it went not to the patron but to the *fiscus*.[5] Instead of arguing the Latin's non-possession of the *ius testamenti factionis* from the patron's right to the property, the authorities took the Latin's incompetence to make a will as the primary fact and confiscated any property he tried to bequeath. In actual practice the law had the effect of enabling the Latin to choose between his patron (or his heirs) and the *fiscus* as his successor.

Among the *ἀστοί* women were not allowed to make wills, and therefore freedwomen of 'burghers' (and possibly freedwomen in other *τάξεις*) were compelled to remain intestate.[6] In Roman law

[1] § 10. Possibly this rule only applied to the 'burghers', if one treats the paragraph as a closely linked continuation of § 9.

[2] i. e. male themselves and descending through males.

[3] See pp. 43–4.

[4] In the matter of succession all slaves freed under 30 or *inter amicos* were reckoned as Latin, even if the condition of their patrons debarred them from Latin status in other respects.

[5] § 22.

[6] § 15.

a freedwoman was competent to make a will, only if she had four children. Presumably the property of 'burgher' freedwomen was disposed of in accordance with the usual rules applicable to persons dying intestate.

B. The Competence of Freedmen to inherit.

Certain limitations attended the competence of freedmen to inherit estates. As in Roman law, Latins and deditícians were debarred from receiving legacies.[1] Moreover, in the 'burgher' class, and quite possibly in some other τάξεις also, freedmen were not allowed to receive in a single legacy a capital sum of more than 500 drachmae or an annuity of more than 60.[2] No woman, either free-born or freed, could inherit if she was over 50 years of age; under that age ingenuous women could inherit if they had three children, and freedwomen if they had four.[3]

A special case is treated by § 16. A legacy is made to a Roman freedman on condition that it shall pass to his children at his death. If it is proved that the said children were still unborn when the will was made, the *fiscus* takes the legacy at the freedman's death. This is an application of the Roman law that legacies to *incertae personae* are null and void;[4] but, whereas in Rome in such a case the legacy passed to the rightful heirs (determined either by circumstances or by the freedman's will), in Egypt on the contrary it was seized by the *fiscus*.

C. Intermarriage.

Intermarriage between the bond and free was forbidden as in Roman law. Imperial slaves seem to have been able to disregard this law not only in Egypt but elsewhere also.[5] However, a paragraph in the γνώμων forbids at least the *vicarii* among the Emperor's slaves to marry freedwomen; presumably they could not marry *ingenuae* either.[6]

Intermarriage between the τάξεις was discouraged; the *fiscus* often made a union of this sort an occasion for extortion at the death of either party. If 'burghers' were Alexandrians, freedmen were sometimes treated more rigorously than the free-born. An

[1] §§ 19, 20. Like the governors of other provinces, the prefect could, no doubt after *causae probatio apud consilium*, allow a freedman under 30 to have full Roman liberty (though not Roman citizenship unless his patron was a Roman citizen). § 21.
[2] § 14.
[3] § 28.
[4] Gaius, ii. 238; Ulp. xxiv. 18.
[5] *I.L.S.* 1605.
[6] § 110.

ingenuous 'burgher' was allowed to marry an Egyptian, though the *fiscus* intervened rapaciously at his death.[1] Freedmen, however, of the Alexandrian class were categorically forbidden to marry Egyptian wives.[2] Unions between 'burgher' freedwomen and Egyptian husbands were lawful; precedents varied as to the fate of their property, and the *γνώμων* gives no hint as to which precedent it preferred.[3]

D. Belated Marriage and Celibacy.

Roman law confiscated, after the death of the wife, the dowry brought by a woman over 50 to a man under 60.[4] Such a union not only was doomed to sterility but meant that a man still capable of producing healthy children was tied to a barren wife. In Egypt the fiscal authorities went further and confiscated the dowry brought by a woman under 50 to a man over 60, if they were Roman citizens;[5] apparently not even in the event of issue was the dowry saved. The *ἴδιος λόγος* left untouched a dowry brought by a wife over 50 to a husband over 60, because, though no issue could be expected, the union did not withdraw from the circle of possible husbands and wives any person whom the law desired to partake in the procreation of children; an exception was made, however, if the wife was a *Latina Iuniana*; Latinity was used as a pretext for an act of extortion, and the dowry was confiscated.[6]

While they remained unmarried, Roman women in Egypt paid an annual capital levy of one per cent., provided their fortune amounted to 20,000 sesterces. The *γνώμων* states that here the rules were the same for freedwomen and for *ingenuae*.[7]

[1] § 45. [2] § 49. [3] § 50. [4] Ulp. xvi. 4. [5] § 25. [6] § 26. [7] § 29.

INDEX

PRINTED IN ENGLAND AT THE UNIVERSITY PRESS OXFORD
BY JOHN JOHNSON PRINTER TO THE UNIVERSITY